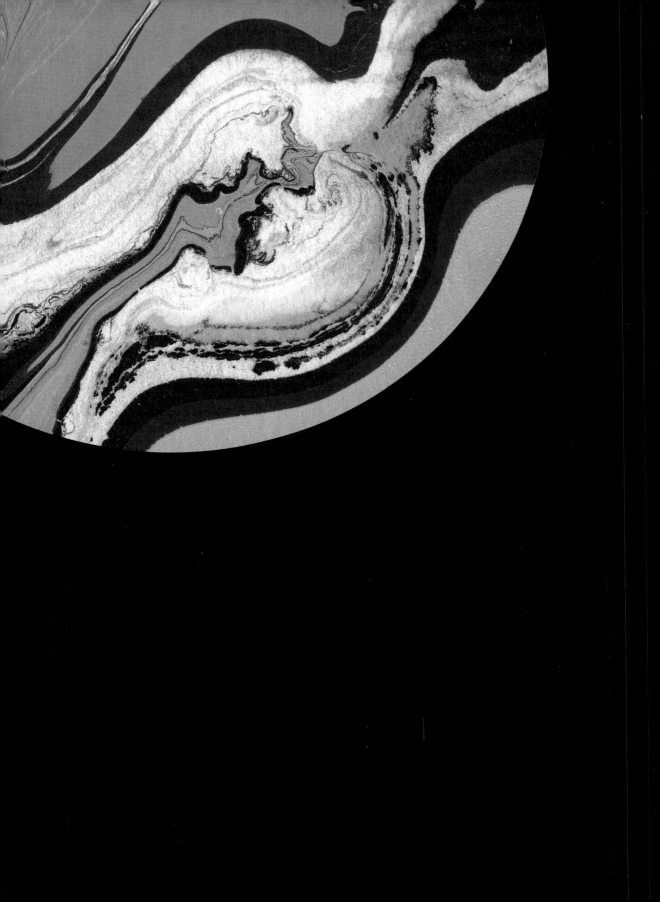

LIVING
ASTROLOGY

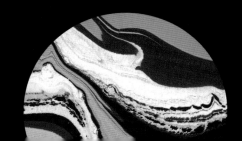

LIVING ASTROLOGY

How to Weave the Wisdom
of All 12 Signs into Your Everyday Life

BRITTEN LARUE

ARTWORK BY ANGELA GEORGE

Gibbs Smith

First Edition
28 27 26 25 24   5 4 3 2 1

Published by
Gibbs Smith
P.O. Box 667
Layton, Utah 84041

1.800.835.4993 orders
www.gibbs-smith.com

Designer: Angela George
Art director: Ryan Thomann
Editor: Juree Sondker
Production editor: Renee Bond
Manufactured in Guangdong, China, in October 2023 by RR Donnelley
Gibbs Smith books are printed on either recycled, 100% postconsumer waste, FSC-certified papers, or on paper produced from sustainable PEFC-certified forest/controlled wood source. Learn more at www.pefc.org.

Library of Congress Control Number: 2023940757
ISBN: 978-1-4236-6504-5

Dedicated to

My younger self,
who longed for this book, and
made of her life a path
to find her way to it.
She is my inspiration.

And to

My future self,
who always already knows
what to do.
She is my mentor.

CONTENTS

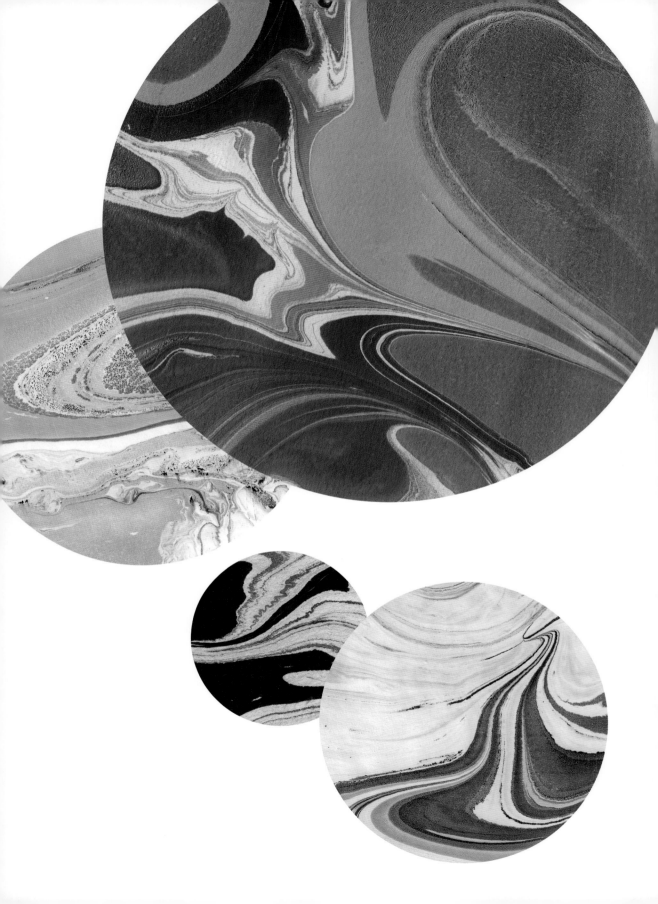

It all had to go somewhere

If I could go back to your wilderness
Years I would try to find the words to
Thank her. I would say something like

Thank you for all you didn't know
For gathering your deepest lusts for
Following that unknowing for trusting

In its maddening perfume. Did you know
That you would invent courage from salt
And from silence? Did you know that you

Would become a serpent? A great beast
To carry your wildness into the folds of
Your darkest selves? Did you know that

All along the offerings on your alter and
The candles you would light you were
Lighting for her? Maybe you did.

And maybe you guessed even then what
She would become. The stars' own poem.
A verse connecting sky and ground.

Holding so much for so many. Teaching
Us to build homes in that wilderness.
Gifting yourself such true mourning.

Which she taught you was another
Word for love. All that love
It all had to go somewhere.

Thank you. For planting it where you did.

—MATT BULL

Prelude

It was the Moon that claimed me first.

It was 2017, and I was thirty-nine years old. I looked up on a warm summer night to see a deliciously swollen full Moon, and it was as if I were seeing it for the first time. The Moon wanted my attention. It was trying to talk to me.

You have to understand that this was fairly preposterous for me at the time. I wasn't in the habit of monitoring the lunar phases. I didn't know anything about astrology, or magic, or mysticism, nor did I associate with anyone who openly talked about these topics. I had spent the last two decades in academia and was nearing the end of my PhD studies. I was married and raising two kids in conservative Dallas, Texas.

But I was also in a period of dissolution, loosening and untying the strands of who I thought I was. My long-upheld identities were no longer that compelling to me. I had always strived to be "good" and do whatever I needed to do to accomplish the safety of goodness. For the most part, that meant setting aside my fairly radical opinions and dreams in order to stay protected by the perceived respectability of institutions like marriage, academia, and privilege. But I was looking at my daughters, then eight and ten, and realizing I was performing an identity I didn't want them to aspire to. I yearned to walk a life of possibility, disruption, and liberation.

I was also starting to see how I had made all kinds of life choices in order to avoid feeling difficult emotions like grief, anger, and shame. My dad went to work one day when I was sixteen and never came home. He died of a heart attack. Two years later, I learned that the man I'd been dating and giving all of myself to for four years had been openly cheating on me. I was publicly humiliated and betrayed. Between the abandonment and shock of both events, my trauma response was to dissociate, and in college I discovered that alcohol can be a reliably comforting friend. Numbing is intelligent when you don't want to feel anything.

After so many years of not listening to an authentic internal "yes" or "no," I realized how little I trusted myself. The consequence of not listening for my truth was that I regularly participated in my own disempowerment by ceding authority to other people. I saw that because of my patterns of overworking and taking on other people's needs, I was often too depleted to access my inherently joyful self. In my bones, I craved to remember her.

In the cracks that opened up with all this new consciousness, the Moon started talking. The Moon called to me, saying, *Come home.* The Moon's first lesson was an invitation to slow down and tune in to my inner voice, something I'd been terrified to do. Why? Because some part of me knew that if I heard myself name what I wanted and didn't want, my world would have to change. I wanted to be out of my marriage. I wanted the space to hear myself from a place of truth. Beyond that, I didn't know what would come next. I just knew that the contract I had made and was currently living in was forged from my trauma, from not fully participating in my life.

That No opened a doorway to synchronicities.

This change would be confusing to people. This change would mean being judged by people. And this change would even hurt people, people I loved very much.

I looked at that Moon on that summer night, and it was as if I saw my own reflection for the first time. It was both loving and firm: *It's time.*

Like ice melting in the sunlight, I let myself surrender to a state of change that was initiated by this huge No I was ready to notice and name. The No to my marriage also included a No to social conformity. It was certainly a No to financial security and a comfortable lifestyle. It was a No to many friendship ties. And it was a No to a lot of old goals and strivings that were never really mine, but which I had taken on in the partnership.

That No was a spell.

In the liminal space of my separation period, new pathways and possibilities emerged that I'd never considered before. A lot of magical and mysterious things started to happen. While receiving a massage, I had a vision of a circle with crescent shapes on either side, and I knew that this symbol was being shown to me as a tattoo to put on the left side of my torso. Later, I learned that the symbol is called the Triple Moon, representing the phases of the lunar cycle. Next, I followed an instinct to learn about the Moon from specific teachers who ended up being pivotal to my path as a mystic. And I rented an apartment from a woman who gifted me the tree stump I still use as my altar today. Simply put, that No opened a doorway to synchronicities in ways I couldn't ignore.

The first person to introduce me to astrology was my brother (a double Aquarius), who knew I was looking for spiritual tools. He sent me my chart and the links to some astrologers he admired. At the time, I didn't even know that birth charts existed! My chart felt miraculous to me. I looked at it and instinctively knew that I would be able to understand it—and myself—if someone would teach me the codes.

My obsession was initiated. I became absolutely consumed with teaching myself this language, and every waking moment when I didn't have my kids or work to do, I was reading about and meditating with astrology.

I came to astrology with a specific set of questions:

- Is it possible for me to experience new ways of being in my body, on this planet, in this moment?
- Is it possible for me to transform old patterns into unforeseen pathways that feel creative, empowering, and fun?
- Is it possible for me to enliven my life with stories that feel more expansive, open, generous, and buoyant?

And astrology responded with a loving Yes, and it might:

- be uncomfortable;
- take time;
- mean letting people have their reactions to you;
- mean receiving love in unfamiliar ways;
- mean no more excuses;
- feel very cyclical and nonlinear;
- be bigger than you have the capacity to imagine right now, and that's okay too.

Since the Moon claimed me, my life has become anything but automated. It is wildly alive. Six months into my relationship with astrology, I first said out loud, "I want to be a professional astrologer, and I want to help people understand how astrology can help them rebirth through change."

At the time, the people around me thought this was ridiculous. My mom was terrified that I would be socially ostracized and financially ruined. My professors were disappointed that I wanted to abandon my research on the politico-aesthetics of mid-century popular science. My friends were mostly too weirded out to even bring it up with me.

I just kept listening to and living astrology. Within a couple of years, I was prolifically teaching, writing, and reading astrology. I became financially stable, a huge success given I had zero business experience and had never even paid a bill before I said No to my marriage.

Astrology has given me more than I allowed myself to imagine back before I dared to look up at that magical Full Moon. I am the Future Self that my Younger Self couldn't even dream of. My middle age is sexy, creative, and mystical af. My work simply dazzles me. And my partnerships are rich, honest, aligned, and deeply present.

This doesn't mean life is comfortable all the time. What I've learned while healing with astrology is that there is no getting around feeling. If I want to feel more love, I will need to expand my capacity to feel everything. This means feeling unprocessed grief, anger, and shame. Feeling more means feeling more—of all that life offers.

I wonder if parts of my story resonate with you. Is the Moon calling to you too? Maybe you're at a crossroads in your life and longing to trust that voice inside and follow it. Maybe you're in the midst of huge shifts—whether you initiated them or they've been thrust upon you—and the destabilization has you looking for a new kind of strength to lean on. Perhaps you've had an ongoing interest in astrology but sense that there is more to learn than the basics of your birth chart and are intimidated to dive in.

No matter why you're here or how you found this book, welcome. Like moonlight on a forest path, may the words you find here illuminate your own knowing. May my voice be a bridge back home to your own.

One of the most powerful aspects of astrology is how it encourages us to reframe experience in magical language, which is the core of what we'll be doing together throughout this book. The way I discuss astrology may feel different to you. I may challenge your prevailing assumptions about what astrology can be and how it can help you in your day-to-day life.

This book does not have answers.

This book is a question:

What does it mean for you to live astrology?

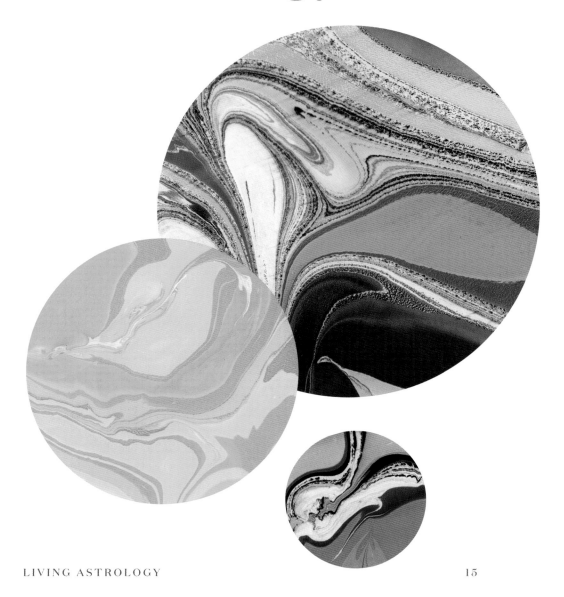

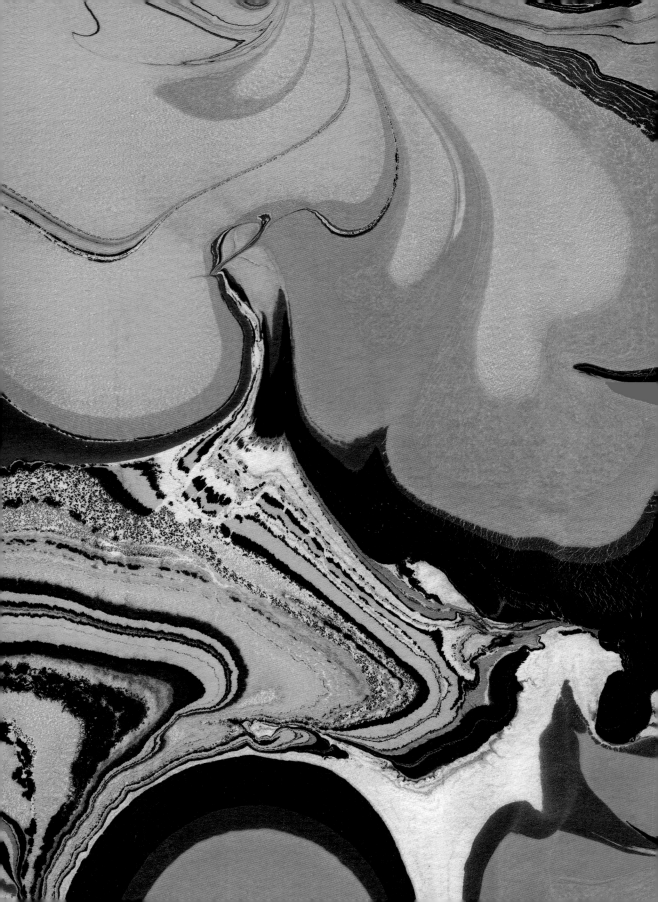

PART ONE

The Living Astrology Approach

Imagination is never reached by knowing where one is going; one knows one is in the right place only after one has arrived.

—Linda Sussman, *The Speech of the Grail: A Journey Toward Speaking That Heals and Transforms*

Welcome to Living Astrology

Astrology isn't something that happens to you. It's something you live.

Since unfathomably ancient times, human beings of all cultures have wondered if what goes on above us in the sky might help us contextualize what goes on here on planet Earth. Astrology as a system has guided our species in tracking how the patterns and relationships of the celestial bodies correlate to patterns and principles of human experience.

The snapshot of any celestial pattern is known as a chart. Charts show us which signs of the zodiac the planetary bodies are located in at a given moment in time, as well as information about the planets' relationships to one another in that moment. So regardless of whether we're looking at a chart from the past, present, or future, astrology always relates to time.

Astrologers across history have taken it to be true that the quality and nature of a chart of the moment something is initiated will indicate the quality and nature of the pathway of that which was initiated, whether we're looking at a business contract being signed or someone's life. The most common chart is a birth chart (or natal chart)—the snapshot of the moment of a person's birth. Astrologers ask questions and

explore possibilities about the experiences of their client by studying their birth chart.

Today, those of us living in the West have inherited an astrology of many lineages. As a wisdom tradition, astrology suffers from the shame of delegitimization from both Christianity and the scientific community since the Enlightenment. This is baggage that must be acknowledged by anyone who seeks to learn here. Astrology is taboo. But this wasn't always so. If you are interested in more information about the history and different lineages of astrology, there are many great books that can guide you.

In the face of so much invalidation, the astrology I discovered back in 2017 was, and in many ways remains, one made to perform its validity as an entertaining personality test and future predictor. While that brand of astrology has certainly solidified its place in our zeitgeist, that's not what I'm interested in. I participate in an emergent discourse in the astrological community that seeks language for a more holistic approach. Let me explain.

I understand astrology as a living, responsive system. My approach is an animist's one, which sees astrology as part of the interconnectedness of all beings. In my learning community, I refer to the cosmos as the *Cosmic Body*. If the cosmos has a body, then it's a living being that includes Earth and everything and everyone on it. The cosmos isn't a separate thing "up there." It's right here.

As you live astrology, it becomes part of you at the cellular level, indivisible from the rest of you, and as you make a home for astrology inside yourself, you become the sky. While some part of you might think I'm just being poetic, another part of you—both ancient and childlike—has been yearning for an astrology that helps you trust this.

Most people come to astrology with an ache. You may not even know how to articulate what it is. There's just something guiding you to it. It's unlanguageable and mysterious. Looking back on my hard-and-fast love affair with the cosmos, I see now that what I ached for was to build a home inside myself where it would be safe to emerge.

Emerge to rest.
To listen.
To desire.
To savor.
To fuck up.
To be shiny.
To get into myself.

Where it would be safe to emerge as enraged.
To not apologize for my boundaries.
To be messy.
To not know.
To say no.
To grieve.
To do things queerly.
To change my mind.

Astrology didn't just help me *build* a home. Astrology *is* the home.

I built a home inside myself where it's safe to receive the gushing love from my delicious partner, the adoration of my daughters, and the appreciation of my community. I built a home inside myself where I feel worthy to receive wealth and attention. I built a home inside myself where I can trust it's okay to be a soccer mom, a nerdy academic, and a provocative witch all at once. I built a home inside myself so I could share myself with *you* because I want everyone to experience the wonder, abundance, and liberation of this language. In sharing myself, I share astrology. Astrology wants to be lived through our stories.

Through the course of working with astrology for myself and my community, I developed my own approach to this ancient wisdom tradition, one that I call Emergence Astrology. Emergence Astrology is interested in helping us participate in the present moment—the only place where we can create, where we can love, and where we can show up.

This is no small task because the present moment is triggering. All astrology is a time practice. It's the study of both time and cycle, something that continues moving no matter what we think or try or feel. Both time (every day being in a body) and Time (the whole of it we try to fathom) are triggering because we can't control them. We can't know for certain we'll be "okay."

> Astrology wants to be lived through our stories.

Emergence Astrology wants us to hold ourselves in the present so that no matter what happens, we feel "okay"—whatever that means in the moment. Emergence Astrology wonders: What does it even mean to be okay? Can it be okay to be messy? Can it be okay to be alone? Can it be okay to be confused? Can it be okay to not know?

Emergence Astrology wants you to call yourself out of the past. Emergence Astrology wants you to come back from the future. Emergence Astrology invites you to be here, in the present moment, listening inside to let the cosmos talk to you about what wants to emerge. Emergence Astrology says there is no future potential. There is only *that which emerges in present time.*

Because, as I began with, astrology isn't something that happens to you. It's something that you live.

Hence the title of this book.

Throughout this book, astrology will support you in reframing your stories in its magical language. For, in addition to being a practice, it is a wisdom tradition and it is also a language. Like other languages, astrology takes patience, practice, and immersion to grow fluency. Unlike other languages, astrology doesn't care about right and wrong so much as it wants to empower you to feel into your own intuitive relationship to it. In an astrological reading, as in this book, there are three players: the astrologer (me), the querent (you), and the magic of astrology. Together, we are collaborating with this moment in time to conjure the most resonant language to inspire you to hear your own knowing.

For astrology to be spoken the way you've been longing for, you need to feel yourself inside of astrology, and you need to feel astrology inside of you. And for this to unfold, you have to surrender any hope that astrology is an outside authority with answers or predictions. Answers are within you. I will show you how to find them.

What Living Astrology Is (and Isn't)

Astrology is a vast wisdom tradition, and it's literally impossible to know everything about it. You can spend your whole life studying it and never get bored. You can have hundreds of readings and still learn something new about your chart. Astrology itself is less of a discipline and more of a body of ideas, dreams, symbols, questions, invitations, and codes to enchant, guide, heal, and infuriate you.

The astrology I share with you here is a broken lineage that is messy and fascinating. I didn't realize when I dove in that there are many astrologies: Vedic, Chinese, Hellenistic, modern, archetypal, Evolutionary, medical, and so on. Whether ancient or fairly new, each astrology has its own reasons for existing with precepts, techniques, and rules that relate to its specific histories.

For my part, I acknowledge on the one hand that all astrologies are inseparable from their histories and were written by human beings with unique positionalities, biases, and motivations for needing the service of the stars. On the other hand, I also hold that astrology is bigger and beyond any specific historical way of considering the planets and how they engage with us. Astrology to me is a language for speaking the divine and naming what feels mysterious, numinous, and otherwise unlanguageable; it unites us and helps us know we're all connected to a Cosmic Body greater than our species, planet, or universe.

From this perspective, all voices are valid—even and especially those new to the tradition. I invite you to trust in the channels you dial into as you allow astrology to talk to you. It's my take that anyone engaging with astrology is an astrologer. There is no governing body decreeing who gets to be anointed with the authority to share their astrological wisdom. This disruption of our concept of "expertise" is one of the most liberating aspects of playing with astrology.

The way to connect with my kind of astrology is through practices of listening and asking questions, rather than through techniques and delineation. The point here is not to get things "right" about astrology as much as to attune to what feels "true." I share with you what resonates in my body, mind, and heart as relevant, interesting, and helpful.

Those three adjectives have been what I look for since I stood in front of my first students in 2001, teaching seventh-grade humanities. If something doesn't seem *relevant* to the lives we're living, if the topic doesn't zing as inherently *interesting* to me, and if I can't connect how a story or skill might be *helpful* to being human, I don't want to spend time thinking about it.

Through that subjective lens, living astrology is a framework that grew out of my own quirky, personal self-care practice. As I said in the beginning, I came to astrology when I was at a crossroads. I wanted to reorient to myself before I made another move because I had lost myself along the way. I wanted to find rooms in the house of myself that I didn't know were there. I wanted to know my own reflection without seeing other people's version of it.

To that end, I chose not to enter into a learning container with a teacher or community, instead following the hermit's path of the autodidact. When I began creating this process for myself, I began with the lunar cycle. The New Moon was in the sign of Libra.

I opened a portal inside myself called *Libra* and went exploring. I asked myself Libra things, contemplating deeply what it means to be a relational being; noticing my attachment patterns and being honest about my struggles to be fair to myself in the face of someone else's needs; and being real about the consequences of my lack of honesty with past partners that was spurred by fear. Libra helped me open doors to myself that I'd been afraid to open for a long, long time.

The next month I did it again with the New Moon in Scorpio. I walked through a portal called *Scorpio*, and it was an entirely different experience of self-traveling. And so, I continued the practice, through the whole year across the twelve signs.

The idea of the signs as portals is rooted in my experience of holding deep trauma from the sudden death of my father when I was sixteen. To survive my grief, I developed numerous coping patterns, including a very understandable desire to numb regularly through drinking and overworking. Across decades, what began as a trauma response hardened into what felt like flaws in my character. Shame and self-mistrust were woven into every area of my life.

When I decided I had the courage to heal, astrology found its way to me. For every part of me that I wanted to heal and reprogram, there was a sign to help. So I began to see the signs as portals for transformation. Each sign has its own suggested guidelines for the death process we crave in order to rebirth. Caution: when you approach the signs as portals this way, your world will have to change.

The practice of learning about and holding my truth month to month with each sign is the basis of what I will be sharing with you in this book. We will move together from sign to sign every thirty days with the movement of the Sun. As the Sun moves into each sign, you may notice, both in yourself and in those around you, more expression of the traits and feelings of that sign. Both the wondrous and less delightful expressions of each sign may intensify. In Scorpio season, for example, you may feel you have an increased capacity to speak your truth with more courage, and you also may notice patterns around any unprocessed trauma you carry. One of the central ideas of my work, and of this book, is that if we're aware of these shifts before they happen, we can meet them gratefully and lovingly.

Build a home where you're safe to emerge as you are.

Living astrology offers you a monthly guide to practice the numinous. We need structure and dependable rhythm to hold so much expansiveness and mysticism. Month to month, season to season, living astrology is a practice of aligning with the present and clearing out the past. It's a practice of showing up to participate in your life with vigor and bravado. It's a practice of listening to your dream field and willing things to happen that feel beautiful, resonant, and right for you and your ecosystem. It's a practice for healing and reprogramming.

And because it's all practice—not prediction—the only way to fuck it up is to not show up. Whether you're feeling raw, prickly, hungover, hangry, or anything else, just show up and the practice will guide you through. The signs are portals to different types of remedies and nourishment. Emergence Astrology is about accessing the deeper wisdom of the language, which counsels us in seeking medicine where we hurt. Tell me where you ache, and I'll tell you which portal to enter for balm. As you show up, sign by sign, to learn and to listen to yourself, you bring the sky into your body. You build a home where you're safe to emerge as you are, where you have the space to recognize the exquisite, multitudinous beauty of your own truth. When you live astrology, it starts to feel like it came to us as an outreach program from the cosmos to help us cute, limited humans speak the divine.

Charts and Chartlessness

As I began exploring each of the astrological seasons, I didn't need my birth chart to self-witness through the lens of the sign's invitations. And in this way, we can think of living astrology as a "chartless" approach (a term I made up). Being with astrology "chartlessly" means relating to it without worrying about your specific chart's invitations.

Let me be clear, I am obsessed with charts. I actively teach students and guide clients in reading their birth charts. Birth charts are endlessly helpful, magical tools. But in order to accurately interpret what the chart is telling us, we must first unlearn the misconception that the chart is an ATM for our life's purpose. When we come to the chart with pressure to unlock a purpose or potential, it can become a fraught site for projection. If you come to the chart looking for proof that you're fucked up, you will figure out how to find the evidence. It's difficult to love your chart if you don't love yourself! And astrology wants you to love yourself. Without a deep connection to the planets and the expansiveness of astrology's language in a chartless way, we are limited in how supported we can be by our charts.

Living astrology chartlessly helped me see the signs not as a map of the future but of my own heart. For me, living astrology is a daily practice of checking in with myself to sense what's going on mentally, emotionally, spiritually, and physically. Month to month, we will do it solely through the lens of the sign that the Sun is in. You don't need your chart at all here.

While at first that idea may seem like I'm sending you out into the dark with no lantern, I have instead found this to be true: you don't need your chart to access the most profound and personal depths of the language of astrology. I see this again and again with my students. Even in my courses designed specifically for learning chart reading, I encourage everyone to take time away from their chart and let the language talk to them from a broader place.

In the past decade, our culture has become accustomed to what I call Sun-Moon-Rising Astrology. This is a perspective that encourages you to get to know astrology through the "Big Three" signs of your chart. The idea is that between these three (or two or one if you have the same sign for any of these three placements), you can understand more about your core motivation and direction (Rising), the light of your creative spirit (Sun), and your emotional needs for safety and security (Moon).

I love Sun-Moon-Rising Astrology. I fell in love with this language through Sun-Moon-Rising astrologers like the brilliant Chani Nicholas! In my own chart, I am a Pisces Sun, Capricorn Moon, and Aries Rising. Learning about the quests and struggles for each of these three was absolutely life changing when I needed astrology to help me see myself. There's no question that when you are dominant in a sign in some way—whether because that sign is one of your Big Three or because you have multiple placements in that sign—it's crucial to spend time building a relationship to that sign if you want astrology to help you with the experience of being human.

While all of this is true, I still think we're losing the bigger experience available to us when we rely solely on the chart for astrological authority. You are deeply nurtured by spending time with signs where you have no placements. Those may even end up being your favorite parts of this book.

So I propose we draw down the whole of the zodiac and live all twelve signs equally. I want you to temporarily release your identifications with certain signs and explore the truth that *you are all twelve signs*.

What happens when you think you're only one specific sign is that you surrender all of the personal exploration, self-actualization, and skills-building that every other sign represents. Maybe you think it would be inauthentic to act like someone you're not. The pushback I often initially get around this idea has to do with identity: *Who am I if I don't stick to a consistent identity?* But identity isn't a constant; it changes and evolves as we grow and learn. Think about how your interests and skills have adapted and changed across your life thus far. I'm proposing that any sign you're not acknowledging in yourself and building a relationship with is just a part of you that is unseen. You have it in you—you're just ignoring it.

What if authenticity isn't about fine-tuning a set identity but about cultivating a repertoire of responses to the world such that you can trust you have the skill to play whatever role is most exciting and appropriate in the moment? What if authenticity is self-creation, moment to moment? The twelve signs provide you the creative skills to become any image in your imagination.

Have the audacity to claim all signs for yourself. Let yourself be the whole sky.

I am not suggesting you throw out chart reading altogether, but it is not something you will find in this book. If you want, you can pair living astrology with learning to read your chart. This is a beautiful strategy for deepening your astrological fluency quickly. As long as you invite yourself now and then to step back from your chart to just be with where you are, you can be nourished by this approach. I especially encourage you to do this whenever you feel overwhelmed or frustrated with your chart and the process of trying to read it.

Learn by Practice, Live in Wonder

I have found that astrology is meant to be learned and lived holistically: intellectually, emotionally, somatically, and spiritually. This is why each chapter of part two offers not just information for you to think about but also a set of invitations for you to engage with in your daily life. This is also why I don't provide a long introduction to astrology before you dive in. You will learn by showing up. You will learn through practice.

The word *practice* can have a connotation that feels boring. "Ugh, I have to practice the piano!" We get this idea that practice isn't the thing we want to do but rather the thing we "have to do" until we get to the "real" thing: the show, the game, the final test.

In this book, I'm referring to practice as a rhythmic way of showing up in devotion to what you care about. You might talk about your meditation practice, your journaling practice, your running practice. When you invoke practice this way, you feel affection for all that the showing up brings to your life to help you feel more grounded, in touch with yourself, and present to your experience.

Living astrology means to actively apply astrological, esoteric, symbolic, mythological, and imaginative ideas toward a discipline of showing up for yourself in your daily life.

Every day is a new practice. You get to begin anew. Each day you show up as you can, as you are, based on your current resources (tools, capacity, and circumstances). And that means that showing up will be different every day, every season of the year, every cycle of your life. In this framework, there is no "bad" practice. There is only "what is here now" for practice.

You already know the signs intimately simply because you're a human being. There is no need to memorize information about the signs if you're a beginner. Let what you're learning land inside the parts of you that already know expressions of each sign from simply being here.

Astrology doesn't want to be tracked and filed in your head. Learning astrology is a process that can't be hurried or managed. Take some space to unlearn the programmed fear that if you don't process things quickly, you're behind or there's a problem. When you move through the signs slowly, month to month, the language will drop in to places where you can't forget it because it becomes a part of you. And you can't be wrong about what feels true for you. That is something only *you* can determine. Let living astrology unfold on its own time as you engage with it across the year.

I am asking you to remember as we go that anything you're learning about astrology already exists inside of you. I encourage you to return to this idea regularly, especially if you feel a conditioned frustration that you aren't "getting it." Bring the terms back to yourself. Ask, for example: *Where am I inside Aries? How does Water live in and through me? Where is Venus fruiting in my world?*

The practice of astrology is a vow of love for yourself. When you decide to show up for astrology, what you're doing is deciding to show up for your life. It's a commitment to live here and participate. It's a choice to give yourself permission to matter. As you grow fluent with astrology, you will notice that the signs and planets start hanging around your field of awareness, wanting to be in relationship with you in a regular way. When you nurture these relationships, you will expand your tools for being human.

What happens next is pretty miraculous. The more you love yourself through the practice of astrology, the more you find that you have compassion for others: from your loved ones to people you'll never meet. In the humility of radical self-acceptance, you find the humility to accept other people in their own messy wholeness.

Astrology is a love practice. Astrology is a healing practice. Astrology is a wonder practice.

So what does it mean to *live* astrology?

Everyone who engages with any aspect of astrology must grapple with one very important truth: how astrology works so brilliantly is, in large part, a mystery. The fact that astrology is impossible isn't the astrologer's fault. To enjoy the experience of astrology, there's a required surrender to the ridiculous wildness of it, the implausible weirdness. This isn't easy. It can be profoundly uncomfortable. But some part of us knows that letting go of logic is important. Some part of us knows that surrendering certainty is nourishing. And after submitting to this important, nourishing nonsense, what's left is wonder.

Emergence Astrology invites you into a daily microdose of the preposterous, to dream a new world into being. Showing up is a gift to yourself, one that requires radical openness. Openness to love and to pain and to the improbability of astrology's wonder. *To live astrology means to live in wonder.*

Healing Your Relationship to Time

I want you to trust that the wonder you seek is inevitable. It's giggling in its hiding place, sensing how close you are, excited to see the delight on your face.

I want you to remember how wonder already lives in every moment you let yourself be enchanted by the strange and startling beauty in all things everywhere.

I want you to notice how wonder animates your world when you approach anything like it's the first time—and like it might be the last.

In this way, wonder might be your most powerful tool for living in a world governed by the poignant truth that change is the only sure thing. The tricky thing is that we sweet humans are designed to fear change because we fear time. We fear time as the devourer of all things we love. We fear we're not "using" time the ways we "should." We fear "unproductive" time will be "wasted" time. But with this book, you're going to be invited to radically shift and heal how you relate to the experience of time.

Modern humans have an especially complicated relationship with time because of the urgencies of capitalism and the instantaneity of technologies for communication. And this has had consequences. If a state of wonder in the present moment is hard for you to access, it's not your fault. You've been conditioned to dissociate from soft and slow experience as if your life was at stake. Of course wonder feels destabilizing if your body has been conditioned to constantly chase a future. You can have compassion for how difficult it is to trust wonder if you're always running out of time. Urgency is what scarcity feels like in the body.

A wonder-based position is not bypassing real pain, real violence, and real grief. For it is numbness that bypasses these traumatic realities, and wonder is not numbness. Wonder is destabilizing *because* it doesn't bypass. Astrology helps us increase our capacity to hold so much high sensation. In this way, increasing capacity for wonder will actually increase your capacity to feel anger, grief, and pain.

Astrology wants you to re-wild to time. For thousands of years, astrology has been helping humans as a timing technology. In order to receive its medicine, you need to become approachable to it. I want you to take responsibility for becoming approachable, and all you need to do is listen.

Make no mistake: astrology is about path*making*, not path*finding*. Pathfinding requires the belief that our path is out there somewhere, and if we were better at adulting, we'd figure out where it was and take it. When you approach astrology for a path to follow, you presume that there is a path at all. Emergence Astrology proposes that there is no path stretching out in front of you. There is only pathmaking—the path emerging exactly where you are in this moment. And over time, as you live emergently, you know in your bones that you're not trying to get to a future. Rather, the future is trying to get to you.

Earlier I said that this book does not have answers. This book is a question. Do not presume to have answers until you go within to let them emerge as your counsel. The magic is the appearance of your own voice, seducing you again and again, Moon to Moon, from a place inside. As you start to trust that voice, you'll follow it, your path emerging in the dark as you walk it. The more confi-

> Emergence Astrology proposes that there is no path stretching out in front of you.

dent you become in your own pathmaking, the more you realize that you feel safe to trust life, which is to say, to trust change.

In that sense, astrology is very much a technology for laying down the tracks for the timeline you dream of walking. I speak often of the younger self, the present self, and the future self. It is my philosophy that you always have access to the wisdom of all of your ages. The future self I discuss throughout the book already exists inside you now and is someone you can turn to for counsel.

Overculture—the dominant culture whose constructs are followed by most people—tries to sell us on a different version of our future self. Its version is all about maximizing potential, but it is never attainable. Overculture's future self dangles keys to your potential just out of reach, like a bully laughing at you for your inability to grab them. The future self of overculture is distinct from the one I refer to.

Here's the hot truth: *There is no such thing as potential.* There is only emergence. Potential is the same performance-oriented, results-based urgency that separates you from the present moment. Potential is a fantasy that shames you. Potential feeds on attachments and expectations, which bring you disappointment and grief. Astrology wants to stop you from engaging so unkindly with yourself. The planets embolden you to love yourself, as you are now. The cosmos reassures you that you are right on time to learn this.

This book offers a cyclical approach to time, one where time unfolds and unfurls rather than plods on. We will work with the cycles of the two luminaries, the Sun and the Moon, and their cyclical wisdom will support you in repairing linearity and urgency. Listening to yourself as you conspire with astrology through its cycles, you begin to notice that you belong to the moment you're in. You belong because you are participating in the emergence of your life. Astrology creates a home for belonging to the present.

It's a common feeling to regret that the empowering change you're currently experiencing didn't come for you earlier. But in living astrology you see that there is an inherent intelligence behind all the reasons your younger self did not have the capacity to grow the tools you are magnetizing today. And in this way, everything unfolds precisely on time.

What if you could trust that everything you're experiencing couldn't have happened any earlier or later on your timeline?

What if it was always meant to be right now that you have the realization, the revelation, the transformation that's here for you today?

What if the planets have all along been conspiring to bring the shifts of the cycle you're in?

What if you're right on time?

Astrology creates the conditions for you to notice what you truly want as well as what you're not showing up for anymore. Astrology helps you trust that you know the way. This is the gift of showing up to the cyclical practices. You notice the conditions for empowering change because you've been listening.

These conditions feel like cracks: The rupture that appears when an illusion is shattered and you trust you have the bravery to stand what you see. The gap created when paradox is welcome and you let yourself be exquisitely complicated and undefinable. The fissure that breaks up your shame so you soften into compassion. Cracks are magical because they create a doorway to receive what you're ready for. These are openings you might not otherwise notice when you experience time in an automated, linear way that urgently demands consistency.

There's a portal appearing for you right now as you read this. It's the universe flirting with you in response to your curiosity. Let me be clear: this courtship with astrology is utterly dangerous. Because it has consequences. Your world will change. And in changing your world, so you will change mine.

How to Navigate This Book

After these introductory chapters in part one, this book becomes a choose-your-own-adventure—a playground for you to explore depending on what works best for you and what season you are currently living in.

Before you dive in, it will be important to get yourself a journal. Whether you have a journaling practice or not, I recommend having a separate journal for your living astrology practice. It will be a companion on this journey, a self-therapy tool to track your progress, remind you of breakthroughs, and help you see patterns. Whether a sumptuous, leather-bound beauty or a classic spiral notebook—it doesn't matter as long as it's something you're not afraid to pour everything into, from practice with tarot spreads to stream-of-consciousness downloads.

Part two has twelve chapters, one for each sign season. There are many ways to study the signs and feel them inside yourself. Across each sign's chapter, the different sections offer ways to practice, experiment, and play. In the following pages, we're going to take a look at the sections included in each chapter so I can offer some background information. For now, don't worry about memorizing if any of this is new. Just let this information incubate somewhere in your unconscious. You can always refer back to this section if you need a refresher.

I suggest reading through each chapter at the beginning of the new sign season so you can begin weaving the sign into your life. But these are just suggestions, places to start. Let listening to how you feel like showing up guide how you show up. Let your preferences, needs, desires, and motivations edit the practice to make it yours. Month to month, season to season, you will begin to create practices all your own, though this book is always here to support you whenever you want to anchor back in.

Remember to always think about each chapter as a suggested curriculum that you can add to, amend, and delete to your taste. Do what excites you, engage with what resonates, and ignore the rest. It's just as valuable to recognize what's not for you as it is to identify what is.

The Zodiac

I have found that the most basic building blocks of the astrological language are the most profound. Advanced techniques are no match for the richness of the foundational. The more you contemplate and come back to the beginner's tools, the more you will be gifted with insight you can't even imagine at the start.

For living astrology, we begin with the twelve signs of the zodiac, which correspond to constellations that have been studied since ancient times. As Earth orbits around the Sun, our view of the sky shifts, and the Sun aligns with each of the constellations in turn. Each constellation occupies about thirty degrees on a circular path that the Sun takes through the sky each year, which is called the *ecliptic*. Together, the signs create a wheel of the year:

ARIES (March 20–April 19)
TAURUS (April 19–May 20)
GEMINI (May 20–June 20)

CANCER (June 20–July 22)
LEO (July 22–August 22)
VIRGO (August 22–September 22)
LIBRA (September 22–October 22)
SCORPIO (October 22–November 21)
SAGITTARIUS (November 21–December 21)
CAPRICORN (December 21–January 20)
AQUARIUS (January 20–February 19)
PISCES (February 19–March 20)

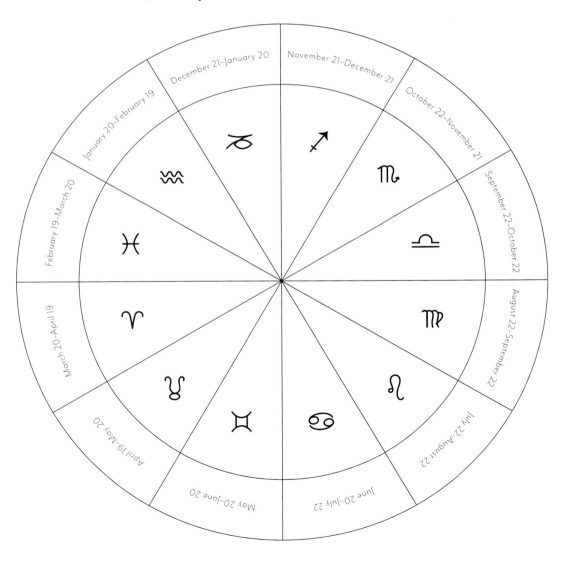

The way I talk about the location of the Sun in the sky in relation to the signs is rooted in the Western approach to astrology I follow known as the *tropical zodiac*, based on where the sun was stationed on each calendar day some 2,000 years ago. The sky isn't fixed, however, and you may hear about the *sidereal zodiac*, which calculates where the Sun is based on the current observable sky. Both systems are considered accurate because they have their own built-in systemic integrity. I recommend learning astrology with just one system at a time, keeping in your back pocket the awareness that the other exists.

No matter which system you follow, the zodiac always goes in the same order. Aries is the first sign because Aries initiates the spring season and the renewal of the yearly cycle of Life-Death-Life. Taurus always follows Aries, and so on until Pisces, which is the twelfth sign. There is nothing arbitrary about the zodiac. Its design is exquisitely wise. I invite you to trust in the order as well as the pattern the signs make with one another. Each sign has a meaningful and important relationship to the ones before and after it, as well as to the signs it sits across from at various angles. The more you attune to the relationality of the zodiac, the less you will need to memorize any of it.

This book is organized around the cyclical rotation of the zodiac. Each chapter in part two is an invitation to get to know the part of you that is each sign in real time with the movement of the Sun. The book starts with Aries, but there is no need to wait until Aries season to start this book. Start with whichever sign is "in season," and wherever you begin, you can then just follow along chronologically. The idea is that the content in this book is evergreen, here for you year after year, so there's no pressure to do it all at once in a linear way.

The exact start and end of each sign shifts every year.

To help you, the dates for each season are indicated on the contents page as well as each chapter opening page. However, note that the exact start and end of each sign shifts every year and is also different depending on your time zone. I recommend using an astrology app to determine the exact day the signs progress forward. I personally use TimePassages to track daily astrology. (CHANI and The Pattern are the best of the horoscope apps.)

Everything about the design of the zodiac is purposeful. This underlines a central theme in living astrology: Everything is connected, and all connections are significant. Astrology wants you to listen to and participate in your life from this understanding.

The signs are portals to different wells of wisdom, each like a doorway to understanding yourself. Between the twelve, you have the entire range of the human experience. There is no part of yourself that doesn't fit inside the whole of the sky. You were surrounded by all of the signs when you were born, and they all live within you in every moment.

Questions to Live Into

Action begins with listening.

With every turn of the zodiacal wheel, you will greet an entirely different part of yourself. As such, each chapter begins with three questions related to that sign's unique offering. If, at the start, you only have capacity for one practice each month, focus on leaning into these questions for thirty days and see what happens.

Every day ask yourself the three questions to live into and notice what feelings, physical sensations, thoughts, and stirrings arise as you sit with them. What matters most is not the answer to the question but *what comes up inside you when you ask the question*. This becomes data you collect as part of your practice of living astrology.

For example, let's start with the first question of Aries: *What bold actions can I take today to serve what I want to see happen in my life?* When you ask this to yourself, you might notice an immediate intrusive thought, something like, *I never do anything boldly*, or even, *I hurt people when I'm bold*. Or maybe you constrict at your solar plexus when you think about being bold and there's a tightening you notice. Or maybe you feel swollen with sadness, and it feels like the surrender of *nothing ever happens in my life*.

These are ways in which what instinctively comes up with the question is much more valuable than an actual answer to the question. To honor what comes up is to honor what is true in a moment. And recognizing your own truth is intuition. Most of us learned to mistrust our intuition, so this practice is a loving commitment to repair. So the process for the questions to live into becomes: Notice. Name. Record. (This is where your journal comes in.)

You will do this as you move through the rest of each chapter as well—a practice I call Field Research for Yourself, which I teach my astrology students. Field researchers collect data, and the work of data collection is to simply note what you observe. This is not a time for judgment, and it's certainly not a time for conclusions. Researchers lose their credibility if they make claims about meaning before the data is in.

Living astrology is an invitation to simply collect data and be a field researcher for your emotional, physical, mental, and spiritual life. At the end of each month, you can study the data and begin to lovingly make any claims about what the data has to teach you. How you record that data is totally up to you and will be emergent with your practice.

Until the end of the month, I want you to simply notice, name, and record, and then get on with your day. There is nothing to manage or fix. Trust that the data is cohering, and that your future self will know what to do with it once it does.

And when it does, allow the data to

- Make suggestions about ways to support yourself
- Help you remember how to love yourself
- Invite you to dream new ways of being into your world

How can it do all of this? Most of the time, we fear the data of our lives because we project all kinds of things onto it. We don't want to see how it's stacking up because we think we'll have to start problem-solving. We fear the data will feel like feedback to shame us. We fear the data will be proof that our life is shitty.

If you have a narrative that the present is shitty, you will perpetuate that belief onto the future, and the abundant resources the universe knows you inherently possess for empowering change will not flow in. The goal of data collection is *to practice creating a present that is protected from your fear of it*. You are learning how to let go of controlling the future so that you can create from the present.

Make no mistake, data collection may sound tedious, but the kinds of data you will be asked to collect in this book will reanimate your life. When

I ask you to sit with each of the twelve parts of yourself, you will experience feelings, memories, thoughts, ideas, sensations, and insights that were previously unconscious to you. These will bubble up and spill out in ways that you cannot ignore. Each sign will have their own brilliant, loving, and honest ways of nudging you to release and let go of limiting self-beliefs, fears, blocks, and old stories that just aren't relevant to the path that's emerging for you.

Each chapter thus walks you through a month of death and rebirth. It is for good reason that my logo has an ouroboros, a snake eating its own tail. The ouroboros is an ancient symbol for regeneration. And as you compost old material, you make space for new ways of being to live through you. This happens from one turn of the zodiacal wheel to the next.

Altar

Astrology takes it as a point of exploration that what happens above us in the heavens relates to what happens here on Earth. There's a saying from the early medieval Arabic text known as the *Emerald Tablet* that has been paraphrased in more modern times as "As above, so below." The idea is that the macrocosm—the Cosmic Body—has structural and energetic similarities to what happens at the microcosmic level for sentient beings like us.

The saying continues with "as within, so without," which invites us to play with the possibility that whatever is going on inside of us is structurally and energetically similar to what goes on around us, and likewise, that what goes on outside of us relates to what goes on within. As such, as you tinker with living astrology, you might feel supported and take pleasure in building an outer world that reflects the inner growth you're calling in.

Think about how we already do this. We wear red to feel powerful. We lower the overhead lights and set out candles to create a more diffuse space for shared romance. We gather objects of a theme to create seasonal displays on our mantles.

As you create a rhythm around the exercises for each chapter, I encourage you to look for ways to make this cyclical practice exciting. In order to get to the point where you can't imagine living without these rituals, it helps to reward yourself for showing up with beauty.

Here are a few ways you can make your work with living astrology a more heightened experience:

- Use different colored pens in your journal.
- Wear a robe or necklace that you put on specifically for engaging with the practices.
- Ask yourself what each sign tastes like and feed yourself the sign.
- Create a chant or poem to invoke the planet you're working with.
- Watercolor your feelings with each sign and then bedazzle your space with your creations.

The most powerful way to engage physically with astrology in your living space is to create an altar to the sign each month. If calling it an "altar" feels uncomfortable for you, you can think of it as a sacred space, a special nook, or gathering spot for what excites you. The purpose of an altar is to create a designated zone for devotion to the relationship you're cultivating between yourself and astrology. Think of it as an externalization of your inner landscape as you contemplate and dream with the cosmos.

Aesthetics matter here—in the sense that you are calling in an embodied, lived experience. Anesthetics numb you. Aesthetics enliven you. Let altar creation be an exercise of delight more than anything. The more you delight, the more you will be enlivened.

An altar can be a table, corner, windowsill, ledge, or other nook for holding items you gather that correspond thematically with the sign you're studying. These might be:

- Colors
- Crystals
- Flowers
- Herbs
- Fruits and vegetables
- Spices
- Representations of gods or goddesses
- Tarot cards
- Any object or photo that represents that sign's themes, feelings, or elements

Suggestions that correspond with each sign are included in each chapter to get you started. Your altar becomes an externalization of the energy that you're calling in psychologically, emotionally, somatically, and spiritually.

Approach altar objects as you would any sacred relationship. If you're just getting to know a specific crystal, flower, or deity, invite yourself to be patient and open to listening. You may feel frustration and grief if you are just beginning this process and are just learning how to work with plants, deities, and ritual objects. But be gentle with yourself and keep practicing. We are in this repair and remembering together.

Here are a few ideas for approaching altar gathering with respect, care, and love:

- Research folk medicine practices of your ancestral lineage. The urge to appropriate another cultural tradition can begin with good intentions, but it will end up creating harm for you and for others.
- Beware of hoarding tendencies with ritual tools. Ask yourself why you think you need another crystal. There could be something tender there for you to hold with care.
- Be curious and respectful about the ethics of where objects come from and the path they've taken to land in your hands.
- Do not presume altar objects are separate from you and have power over you, or that you have power over them. It is the relational synergy between your loving intention for working with the objects and the objects' own animated intelligence that creates a space for growth and empowering change.
- Remember that your body, too, is an altar, and you can relate to your body with the same reverence and care as you would the altar in your space.

If you've never created an altar, it can feel strange and even ridiculous—especially at the start. Let it be something you experiment with. Make sincerity, pleasure, and beauty the driving desires behind this practice. Then you can spend a good part of your time with the exercises and rituals sitting in the glow of your altar. As your practice grows, your altar will too. Over time, you will begin to intuit which items correspond best for you and which ones heighten your unique power and connection to each sign.

Season

Seasonality is key to the turning of the wheel. Just as astrology is a study of cycles, so *living* astrology is attuning to the cyclicity within us and around us all the time. The wheel of the year is the most fundamental cycle because it relates to the cycle of the Sun. As the Sun moves through each sign of the zodiac and the four seasons, it illuminates the part of us that is each sign. This is an extension of the theme: "As above, so below; as within, so without."

In this way, each sign is a way of expressing a season. Your natal Sun sign is the sign the Sun was in the moment you were born, and that sign is part of a larger season of the wheel of the year. While the gifts of all signs exist within you, your Sun sign illuminates a natural capacity to express the inherent beauty and dignity of that season. For example, if the Sun was in Capricorn the moment you were born, then the idea follows that you are gifted in the beauty and dignity of what winter is.

Originally, humans lived by the shifting seasons, their bodies tuned to the rhythm of spring ushering in warmth and new growth, summer radiating in the fullness and warmth of peak bloom, autumn offering the harvest and death, and winter providing time to rest, endure, and dream for fresh life. For most in our modern society, life doesn't revolve around the need to grow crops, and we have lost our connection to the ceremonial magic of the seasons.

But no matter where you live, the seasons are present in some way, and they are certainly present within you, if you choose to listen. This book explores the seasons as they connect to the signs, each season containing three signs for the beginning, middle, and end of the season. The specific way each sign relates to the season they're in is important and meaningful. The beginning of spring (Aries) is very different from the end of spring (Gemini).

Astrology teaches us that these subtle distinctions matter. Astrology wants us to pay attention to the nuances of distinct invitations throughout the year. In noticing, we become conscious about different aspects of ourselves and develop a more expansive repertoire of responses to the human experience.

Noticing what's happening around you as you live astrology is an invitation to participate in a core teaching of this book: you do not exist in isolation from everything else. You are nature. And just as you are not separate from nature, so astrology isn't separate either. Astrology is in relationship to the trees, to the insects, and to the fungi in your ecosystem. Humans don't have privileged access to the planets. If you want to connect to a sign, all you have to do is be present to whatever is emerging in your midst wherever you are.

Element and Modality

We can organize the signs of the zodiac into two groupings: elements and modalities.

There are four elements, which are the basic building blocks for life on Earth and tell us about the energetic quality of a sign:

△ FIRE: our creativity, zestiness, inspiration, ecstasy, vitality, bravado, adventurousness

▽ EARTH: our steadfastness, stability, practicality, sensuality, structure

△ AIR: our meaning-making, communication, ideas, relationality, mental frameworks

▽ WATER: our emotionality, intuition, feelings, instincts, inner worlds

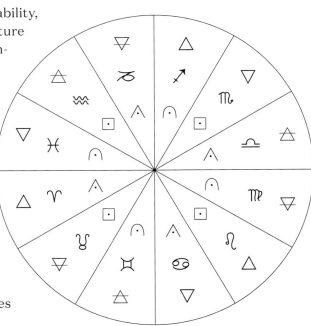

The twelve signs are divided among the elements:

FIRE: Aries, Leo, Sagittarius

EARTH: Taurus, Virgo, Capricorn

AIR: Gemini, Libra, Aquarius

WATER: Cancer, Scorpio, Pisces

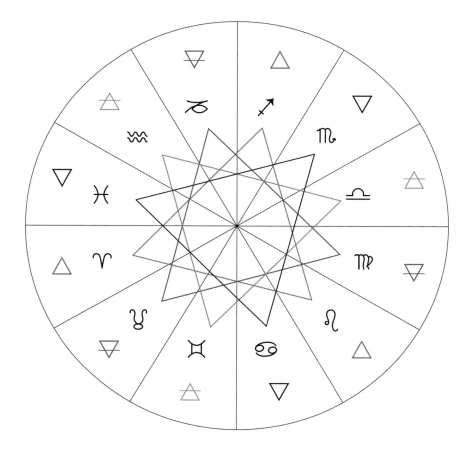

Signs of the same element are always 120 degrees from one another in the zodiac. If you were to draw a line between each sign of an element, you'd create an equal-sided triangle inside the wheel of the year.

Another way to group the signs is by modality. Modality refers to the energy direction and movement style of a sign, and then the needs, motivations, and interests of that directionality. There are three modalities:

CARDINAL: starting-initiating-searching energy
FIXED: rooting-stubborn-assured energy
MUTABLE: dispersing-processing-distributing energy

Modality always relates to where a sign falls in a season. Cardinal signs start a season, initiating the qualities of what the season will be. Fixed signs are the middle of the season, rooting into the quintessence of its energies. Mutable signs are the ends of a season, moving around and integrating all that the season was and preparing the way for the next season to come.

	SPRING	SUMMER	FALL	WINTER
CARDINAL (beginning)	Aries	Cancer	Libra	Capricorn
FIXED (middle)	Taurus	Leo	Scorpio	Aquarius
MUTABLE (end)	Gemini	Virgo	Sagittarius	Pisces

Signs of the same modality are always ninety degrees from one another in the zodiac. If you were to draw a line between each sign of a modality, you'd create a square inside the wheel of the year.

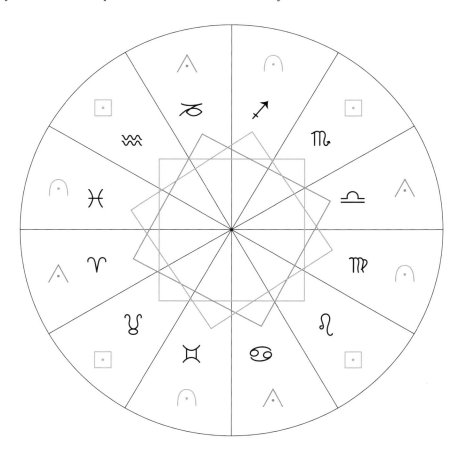

So while each sign shares an element or modality with other signs, no two signs have the same *pairing* of element plus modality. For example, Sagittarius shares Fire with Leo and Aries, and Sag shares mutability with Gemini, Virgo, and Pisces, but Sag is the only sign that is mutable Fire. To be mutable Fire is quite different from the fixed Fire of Leo. The former is passion that is constantly moving and shifting and reaching, the latter is stable, centered, and rooted where it is. To be mutable Fire is also very different from being mutable Earth of Virgo. The former illuminates the upward movement of excitement and conviction, the latter moves slowly, discerningly, carefully.

Human beings do whatever they can to meet their unmet needs.

As you will learn, so much of what you want to know about a sign you can understand by studying each sign's specific pairing of element and modality. This is such a profound and rich zone for contemplation because each unique pairing reveals the underlying needs and motivations for different parts of us. I'm reminded of the psychotherapy technique known as Internal Family Systems (IFS) where you learn to speak to facets of yourself—some of which may have unmet needs, fears, biases, and narratives in direct conflict with what your ego-driven self wants and desires. We feel shame when we don't understand why we do things that undermine what we consciously want. And so compassionately identifying and relating with those more hidden versions of ourselves can support us in seeing those blocks and resistances and opening them up.

Likewise, the unique needs of each element and modality pairing can help you speak to the part of yourself that may feel unseen. If you don't spend much time relating to your Fire self, or you don't feel you have permission to be fixed in your self-expression, then you might have an unseen Leo (fixed Fire) within you. Human beings do whatever they can to meet their unmet needs, even if it means acting or thinking in ways we regret. Listening to the elemental and modality needs of each sign inside of yourself will open lines of communication to all facets of yourself. When you live astrology, you get to bring a permission slip to any zones where you haven't felt you were allowed to have needs in the past.

Symbol

Each sign is associated with a specific glyph (graphic character) and symbol, which corresponds with the constellation and mythology surrounding each.

The stories of the constellations are part of specific human histories and lineages. The symbols of the zodiac I share with you here come from Western astrological storytelling traditions. The zodiac is itself a belt-shaped region of the sky that extends approximately eight degrees north and south of the ecliptic, which is the apparent path of the Sun across the celestial sphere over the course of the year. The orbital paths of the

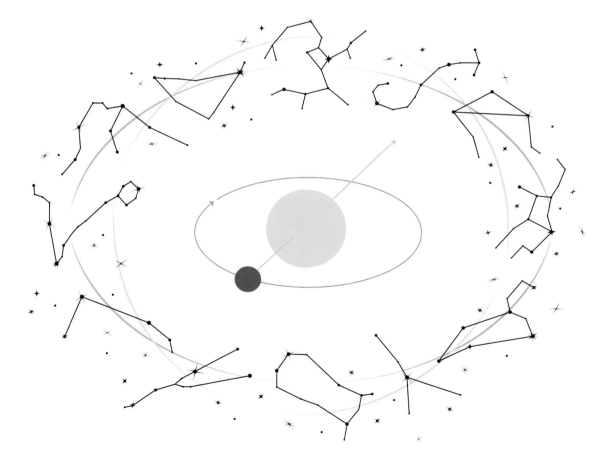

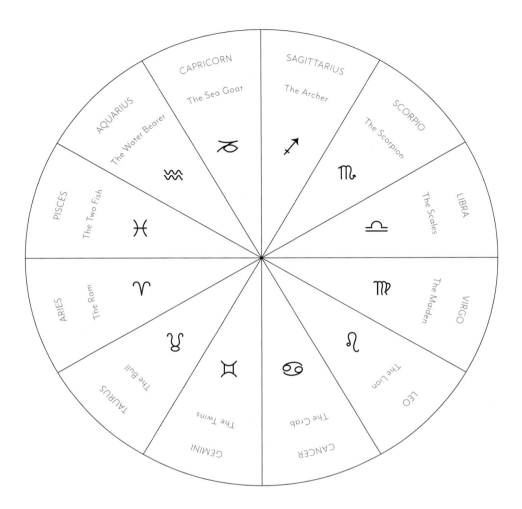

Moon and major planets are within this belt. The word *zodiac* comes from a Greek word meaning "cycle or circle of little animals." This division of the ecliptic into zodiacal symbols originated with Babylonian astronomy during the first millennium BC and continued evolving into what we recognize today during the Hellenistic period.

Eleven of the twelve signs of the zodiac have a living being as a symbol. Libra's symbol is the Scales, the only symbol to represent a principle rather than a being. Three of those eleven are human (the Twins of Gemini, the Maiden or Virgin of Virgo, and the Water Bearer of Aquarius). The remainder are living or mythological animals.

The symbol for each sign activates what I think of as the archetypal consciousness within you. What I mean by this is that as humans, we innately understand the archetypes of the oldest stories. *Archetype* at its root means the original of something from which copies are made, suggesting a primordial example of the thing. From a Jungian perspective (Carl Jung was an astrologer in addition to being a psychoanalyst), archetypes are universal and innate thought-forms, or mental images, inside the imagination of all of us. Archetypes can be found across history and culture. Examples include the old wise man, the trickster, the hero, the coyote, the raven, the sequoia, or the butterfly. We feel into the layers of knowing activated by the symbol of the archetype and experience it inside our bodies. The archetypes of astrology pump blood to the stories of the constellations because we feel them alive in our bodies.

While we can't trace every thread that connects the symbols of different times and places, there is remarkable symmetry and kinship across stories. There is a whole world for mythology and cosmology lovers! In this book, I will share what has resonated most for me and for my client-student community about the stories of the symbols. If you love what you read, keep researching to learn more. If you don't resonate with any one story, I invite you to seek out a different version—for example, the mythology from your own ancestry.

I take it to be true that as you open your ear to the stories, you activate the part of you that is actually in the story. To me, we are not separate from these stories. The more you open up to the feeling part of you that knows yourself to be a Ram or a Lion or a Fish, the more you enliven astrology in your body and live it. To embody astrology is to enact the truth in the essence of it, and much of the essence of that truth is in the symbols.

Polarity

It is my experience from working with clients and students that the six polarities of the zodiac are the most profound tool for wholeness that astrology offers. These are the six axes created by the twelve signs as they oppose one another on the wheel of the zodiac:

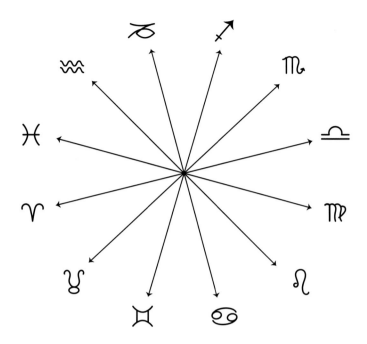

Aries ←→ Libra
Taurus ←→ Scorpio
Gemini ←→ Sagittarius
Cancer ←→ Capricorn
Leo ←→ Aquarius
Virgo ←→ Pisces

Each axis has a major life theme it represents, and the signs at either end of the pole symbolize one way of engaging with that larger theme. These signs may feel like they oppose each other, and the tendency is to compartmentalize one from the other. But, really, they are like two sides of the same coin. They need each other for balance.

For example, Aries is a portal to understanding how to cultivate personal agency in the world, go after what you want, and trust your self-sufficiency. Libra, Aries's polar sign, is a portal to understanding how to be in a relational world where you are constantly recalibrating relative to someone else's needs and desires. In Sun-Moon-Rising astrology, if neither of these is one of your Big Three, then you're ignoring these portals that are so crucial to being and relating here. And if only one of these is in your Big Three, then you're ignoring the other end of this spectrum, which leaves you unbalanced.

Think of the polarities as a system of spectrums to help us appreciate how the self is not one way or one thing but how the self is actually an entire ecology:

Aries (self in the monad) ←→ Libra (self in the dyad)
Taurus (self in the seen) ←→ Scorpio (self in the hidden)
Gemini (self in the village) ←→ Sagittarius (self on the mountain)
Cancer (self in the mother) ←→ Capricorn (self in the father)
Leo (self in the center) ←→ Aquarius (self as collective)
Virgo (self in the moment) ←→ Pisces (self beyond time)

The polarities of astrology may feel like binaries, but not in the sense that we're used to in our culture. The polarities help us to welcome home and integrate our wholeness rather than fragment or separate us into categories. This is why understanding that you are all twelve signs is so transformational.

To live astrology is to practice letting yourself be the part of you that feels most resonant, liberating, and appropriate to the moment you're in. It means cultivating self-trust that allows you to know how to tap into each expression of your own astrological ecology.

Ruling Planet

A powerful way to understand the signs is to know the planet that is associated with each. The planets that govern the signs include the seven traditional planets, meaning the celestial bodies that have been studied since ancient times: the Sun, the Moon, Mercury, Venus, Mars, Jupiter, and Saturn. In modern astrology, we also include Uranus, Neptune, and Pluto as rulers.

The ancients called the Sun and Moon planets because they had a different definition for planet than we do today. *Planet* originally meant "wanderer," and the Sun and Moon, like the modern planets, appear to wander

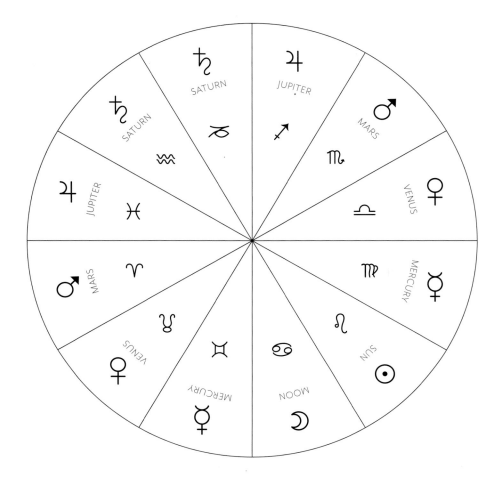

against the fixed background of the stars. Modern astrology preserves this piece of ancient language.

We turn to the planets to help us build the skills their sign represents. They are the teachers for all of life's diverse experiences. The planets impart their interests, styles, motivations, talents, quirks, and wisdom on the signs they "rule," which means they govern, shepherd, and look out for those signs.

For example, the Sun rules Leo. Leo is fixed Fire. As a way of being, fixed Fire is a bonfire. Leo invites you to be the center around which everything else gathers. As such, Leo's way of being and doing things feels like the Sun. The Sun knows what it means to be the life-giving center and bestows that knowledge upon the sign of Leo. To understand the essence of Leo and to grow skill in being Leo, we thus look to the Sun for wisdom.

An analogy that my students have enjoyed is thinking about astrology as a stage performance. The planets are the actors and the signs are the costumes. Planets have their favorite and most appropriate costumes for the roles they play. It helps you understand the costume if you know about the character it is for.

You are both the actor and the costume in this scenario. And over the years, you have likely developed an inclination to stick to certain costumes and avoid listening to certain characters in yourself. For example, maybe you reject certain aesthetic styles as "for other people." But I'm here to tell you: as long as you don't give yourself the chance to be all of it, you will be suppressing a part yourself. The goal of living astrology is to practice being the whole show as a way toward integration and pleasure.

Traditionally, the two luminaries—the Sun and Moon—each only look after one sign, Leo and Cancer, respectively. But the other five planets each rule two signs. Mercury rules Gemini and Virgo. Venus rules Taurus and Libra, Mars rules Aries and Scorpio, Jupiter rules Sagittarius and Pisces, and Saturn rules Capricorn and Aquarius. But what about the last three planets, you may ask? Neptune, Uranus, and Pluto are much further away from Earth and difficult-to-impossible to see with the naked eye. As such, they weren't "discovered" until later and therefore weren't originally included in traditional astrology. Many modern astrologers now include them, with Pluto ruling Scorpio, Uranus ruling Aquarius, and Neptune ruling Pisces.

As with a lot of astrology, what might feel like a contradiction or a problem (like that there's no hard rule about the rulers of Scorpio, Aquarius, and Pisces that everyone agrees to follow) gets resolved within the integrity of the system of the individual astrologer. It's mysterious how it works that a reading with one astrologer using one set of systems can feel as powerful as a reading with another astrologer using a different set. For my part, I primarily follow traditional rulerships while also acknowledging that the outer planets have a lot to teach us. In this book, I discuss both.

When a planet rules two signs, its teachings come from different aspects of the same teacher. First and foremost, the two signs have different elements and possibly different modalities. Mars feels different as the barreling force of early spring in Aries (cardinal Fire) than it does as the darkening penetration of mid-autumn in Scorpio (fixed Water). And yet, both signs describe Mars.

A special note about Cancer and Leo: as these are the only signs ruled by the luminaries, I take it as important that we understand Cancer and Leo as crucial parts of ourselves. I do not mean that people who have a lot of Cancer or Leo placements are luckier or better. I mean that for all of us, the luminaries offer a huge invitation to understand our unique experience of being human. Those two chapters are two of the longer ones in this book.

Another point to make about the planets is that they have been assigned genders based on their mythological lineage. I invite you to see both and all genders in yourself, and thus to see all planets as parts of you, regardless of your gender identification. I also invite you to see each planet through any and all pronouns as a practice of expanding what's possible in your relationship with them. I use the pronoun "it" in this book for consistency, but in my personal practice I change it up depending on what comes through. This is one way we can untangle from the biases of patriarchal conditioning.

For example, I know for many it is incredibly helpful when working with Saturn to open up to relating to Saturn as a strong older woman—the Crone archetype—instead of as a male god. If you don't resonate with the vibe of a planet, you can always change the gender, age, and look of the planetary archetype and see what shifts for you. Let this be emergent, always open, and flexible depending on your mood and needs. This is *your* relationship!

Skillful Sign

In living astrology, the signs are less like adjectives to tell you who you are. Instead, they become more like *ways of being* that you can choose to participate with or not in any moment. You have a way of being that's Gemini. You have a way of being that's Capricorn. And to know yourself more consciously and compassionately when you are in a Taurus way of being, you can enter the portal of Taurus inside yourself to notice what you need, what you want, and what will nourish you from the inside and outside. To me, this could not be more relevant, interesting, and helpful.

In popular astrology, there is often a shaming way of framing the signs; they are "good" in certain ways and "bad" in others, which doesn't resonate as helpful to me (though I do love a clever meme). For example, Leos are accused of being self-centered divas. Gemini are considered flaky as friends. Scorpios are vengeful and dominating. What has been helpful to me is to reframe the signs as having expressions that we might call "skillful" or "unskillful." At the heart of this perspective is the generosity to see that unsavory expressions of a sign are evidence of lack of skill in meeting the needs and desires of that sign, not questions of someone's inherent character.

Astrology helped me to un-shame my stories.

In life, we each have access to some forms of skills-building and not others. You may have skills you wish you didn't have, such as the Virgo "skill" of being crippled by self-doubt when you have an opportunity. We will call these *unskillful expressions*, in the sense that most of us wish we didn't have them. Of course, who decides what is unskillful? And what systems, structures, relationships, and conditions contributed to the lack of that skill? I am not interested in participating in further shaming. The goal is self-noticing with compassion so you can support yourself better. You will grow skill in expressing a sign differently by noticing where you have an unmet need or desire and giving that your loving attention. This is pattern breaking.

As an example of unskillfulness: I am a very Pisces person (a VPP I like to joke). And Pisces is known to be escapist, which I identify with strongly. I have a long history of bonding with alcohol, spending hours in daydreams, and zoning out with screens. Whatever it took to not feel the harshness of my pain. None of this is "bad" by itself, but my habits did increase the shame I carried. I felt like a failure for giving so much of my time to altered states instead of "reality." Astrology encouraged me to ask myself what my escapism wanted, and I saw that I wanted to feel a dream and live it. I wanted to trust that all possibilities exist for beauty, love, and renewal in this world. I wanted to feel that I was allowed to be otherworldly and mystical. These wishes are at the heart of the Pisces in each of us.

Astrology helped me wonder what the unmet needs were behind the unskillful manifestations. Astrology gave me a system for hearing myself that felt wondrous and magical rather than punishing. Astrology helped me to un-shame my stories.

And so I grew skill. Not just with Pisces, but with all the signs, as they each have guidance for building skill for different parts of yourself—especially those that have long been repressed, denied, or otherwise unseen. You are more than one, two, or three ways of being yourself. Accessing all twelve signs gives you permission to be the complicated, contradictory, fascinating person you are. Someone who has competing needs and preferences. Someone who can't be predicted or cornered or minimized.

So for each sign, I've offered ideas for what the skillful expression of each can be as well as how to go about fostering that during the season. Noting where you are currently at regarding the skillfulness or unskillfulness of each sign only gives you more information, more data, so that you can repair that relationship and grow with it.

Practices

Each chapter offers a different practice for deepening your lived relationship to the signs. Some of these practices are meant to be enacted out in the world, some of them are more quiet, more internal. Whatever they seem to be, I invite you trust that in a fractal way, whatever you're doing within you will shift what's around you, and whatever you're doing around you will shift what's within you.

As I shared earlier, we tend to think about practice in a negative way in this culture. As a burden. A chore. What I am calling "practice" has the energetics of play, curiosity, care, and most of all, devotion. In this way, practice is a very magical thing. When something is magical, to me it means that it brings the unexpected, even the impossible. If you have a belief about yourself that has calcified in such a way that you have zero hope for change, and then you do a practice for a while just for fun and to experiment, you may eventually discover that the belief you had no longer feels true to you. That is some potent magic.

For certain practices and sections in part two, I encourage you to begin with a grounding meditation. Almost all intuitive practice begins by ensuring that you are connected to planet Earth. Part of this is very practical: trancelike states can leave you feeling confused and out of it if you don't begin by connecting to an anchor.

Grounding

Here is a simple grounding practice you can do as an entry to other exercises:

- Be seated. If you're in a chair, make sure both feet are on the ground. If you're on the ground or prone, try to have a straight spine.
- Take a few deep breaths in and out on purpose, focusing on the act of breathing. Say hello to your in-breath and out-breath. Ask your breath for support in inhaling what supports your presence and exhaling what doesn't.
- Scan your physical body, top to bottom (or bottom to top if you prefer). Say hello to each part of your body with your attention: Hello, head. Hello, neck. Hello, shoulders, and so on. Notice if there are any parts of you holding tension, wanting to twist or move or stretch or craving massage, and give that to yourself.
- Scan your mental body. Say hello to any thoughts or voices that feel present for you right now. Ask any thoughts or voices not relevant to your grounding meditation to move out of your space for the time being. Say goodbye to them.
- Scan your emotional body. Say hello to any feelings that show up. You might feel supported to put one hand on your heart and/or one on your belly. Tell your feelings that you see them.
- Ask yourself to become aware of the contact points between you and the ground. See these points as apertures and ask them to dilate a little more so that you can be in deeper connection with the planet.
- Notice the ground beneath you. Say hello to the planet—hi, Earth! Ask yourself to see, feel, hear, or have a knowing trust that you're creating a conscious bond between you and the planet by dropping a cord from the base of your spine down down down to the center of the earth, like a plumb line. Trust that this is happening. You may even feel a tug as your grounding cord reaches the core of the earth and tethers to it.
- Ask the energy of the planet to move up up up through your grounding cord and up through the contact points between you and the ground and up through your spine. You might imagine the sensual qualities of soil or plants or sand or stones infusing your body with their qualities.
- Take a few deep breaths and ask yourself how you feel.

Everyone will experience grounding differently. My method focuses mostly on the energetics of visualization and intuition. For a more physical experience, you can also try grounding by going outside. Say hello to the earth below you as you stand or walk, barefoot if possible. Or try sitting outside on the grass, on a rock, or anywhere in nature. In addition, using tuning forks or crystal bowls can be incredibly supportive to help you feel grounded. Find what works for you, and then practice giving it to yourself when you're away from those physical tools or places.

In general, most people report that grounding exercises help them feel calmer, rooted, and more inside themselves. The more you practice grounding on your own time, the more you will be able to ground yourself in situations that and with people who tend to leave you feeling chaotic, confused, and outside yourself.

Grounding exercises do not need to be time consuming. The more you practice, the more you can facilitate grounding on the go, in the moment, whenever you need it.

Tarot Card

Tarot is a separate but adjacent discipline to astrology, another form of symbolic language. It is incredibly potent as a vocabulary for psycho-spiritual-intuitive awakening because it is anchored in visual form. Many astrology lovers never work with tarot, and many tarot lovers never learn the basics of astrology, which is completely fine. But there is overlap in the symbology, and many individuals play with, enjoy, teach, and read in both disciplines. I am one of those, as are most of my students, and I feel that building a relationship with tarot will enhance your understanding of astrology and yourself.

For a brief introduction, the tarot deck is divided into twenty-two major arcana and fifty-six minor arcana cards. The major arcana cards are the core of the deck; the images represent life lessons and archetypal themes. The minor arcana cards represent daily life and are divided into four suits, generally called Wands, Pentacles, Swords, and Cups. Together, the seventy-eight cards represent the entirety of the human experience.

Each sign of the zodiac has a corresponding tarot card from the major arcana, and this is what we'll investigate in each chapter. Along with information about each card and ways to work with its energy, I also provide a spread, or an intentional layout of cards, to help you dig deeper into that sign and card.

You do not need to have any background with tarot to appreciate this part of each chapter. Explore the possibility that what you read about each card will open doors in your heart, mind,

Tarot will enhance your understanding of astrology.

and spirit, and in turn, will expand what you think you know about each sign. For this book, I mostly refer to the traditional imagery from the *Smith-Rider-Waite Tarot Deck*, though you are welcome to use whatever deck speaks to you. Before engaging with the tarot section on any sign, I encourage you to find the representative card in your own deck or pull up a picture of it online so you can refer to the symbolism as you contemplate it.

Buying a Deck

If you do not own a deck, you will want to invest in one to fully participate with this book. The best deck to begin with is the one that feels most compelling, intriguing, and resonant for you personally. Approach the purchase of your first deck as you would the meeting of a new friend.

If you want a deck that will help you speak the "common tongue" of the tarot, then I recommend getting the Centennial version of the *Smith-Rider-Waite Tarot Deck*. If you want a deck that has evocative imagery with non-humans, I recommend the *Brady Tarot* by Emi Brady or *The Wild Unknown Tarot Deck and Guidebook* by Kim Krans. If you want a deck by a living, independent artist, check out littleredtarot.com for a range of choices. If you want a deck that doesn't center white, cis, young, skinny, hetero people, check out the options at www.asaliearthwork.com. I also recommend *Next World Tarot* by Cristy Road, *Sasuraibito Tarot* by Stasia Burrington, or *Modern Witch Tarot Deck* by Lisa Sterle.

Personally, I started with *The Wild Unknown* and moved through many decks. For a couple of years as of this writing, my primary deck has been the *Thoth* by Aleister Crowley.

Pulling Cards

There can be a lot of fear and even shame around approaching tarot. For example, you might be intimidated by the complexity of the cards or fear that you won't be "good" at it. You might be afraid that people will judge you for being into something metaphysical or that you'll feel ridiculous or that it's meant for some people and not others. You might be nervous that you'll find out about bad things that will happen to you. I encourage you to release these fears—especially if you are just beginning. No one needs to know about or understand your tarot practice but you.

There's no wrong way to approach the cards. To begin your relationship, get to know the deck in your hands in a sensual way first. Notice what it feels like to hold and move the cards around. Maybe lay the cards out face up and study them, say hi to them, and wonder about the images or symbols you see.

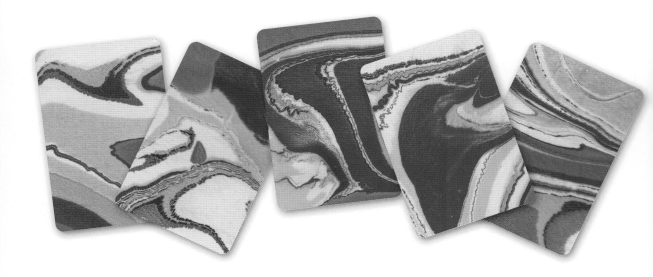

When you're ready to pull cards, you can shuffle the cards however works for you, whether a bridge shuffle (like card players do) or an overhand, where you hold the cards in one hand and lift them to shuffle with the other (this is what I do). You can also drop them in a pile. You can spread them out in a line face down. It's up to you. The main purpose of shuffling is to take a moment to center yourself and connect physically and energetically with your deck. There are several things to consider naming at this point in order to set the space:

- Notice and identify your intentions for going to your deck. What do you want to find there?
- Call in any guidance to support you—your higher self, your ancestors, your spirit guides—whatever feels resonant.
- Set your boundaries. Perhaps you only want guidance that is loving and compassionate to you and all sentient beings. Recognize and embrace this.

When ready to tune in and pull, notice a feeling, a sound, a visual, or an internal knowing about where to cut or which card to pick up. It will take practice for you to come into your way. No one can tell you what your way is but you (this is part of how it's empowering). Personally, I overhand shuffle until I hear a number, and then I go down from the top that many cards, and that's the card I pull. I only came to this method after much practice.

Interpretation

Each of the seventy-eight cards has a set of meanings, invitations, concepts, and vibes that are generally agreed upon, though they are also much disputed and discussed. Slowly, with patience and practice, you will begin to learn these. If you're just starting out, my advice is to unlearn the conditioning that urges you to memorize all seventy-eight significations on any kind of timeline. Take one card at a time, day by day, pulling just one and asking a simple question like: *What is the most compassionate invitation for me to be with today?*

Let the imagery bring up thoughts, visuals, feelings, and knowings in your mind, heart, body, and spirit. Let the artist's choices be as important as what any guidebook might say. Once you have a sense of what the card seems to say to you, then turn to your deck's guidebook or another resource like Rachel Pollack's *Tarot Wisdom*, which has support for each card. My favorite resource for daily pulls from a compassionate lens is *Tarot: Mirror of the Soul* by Gerd Ziegler. It's primarily designed for the *Thoth*, but the spirit of the message could apply to other decks.

After pulling, sit with the card and come back to this idea: What comes up with a question is more important than an answer to the question. If, for example, fear is the first thing that comes up, it's not a problem; it's simply your data to work with for now. You don't need to go any further than compassionately wondering about the fear and asking it to talk to you about what it wants. If you feel disappointment or wish you had gotten a different card, notice that and go from there.

Your deck may even tease you and make you laugh.

Humans are motivated largely by parts of us we are unconscious about. There's a broadly used saying that is often misattributed to Carl Jung which reads, "Until you make the unconscious conscious, it will rule your life and you will call it fate." Living astrology through tarot is helpful because tarot offers you a way to access whatever is going on beneath the surface of your automatic experience. Tarot helps you hear yourself and call unconscious parts of you back home.

Each card is a symbolic, visual, and nonverbal experience. They pair and intermingle with questions you have asked, where you are in your life right now, and other factors. The image on each card then gives you a range of options for understanding meaning, not one single answer. Within the holographic possibilities each card presents, you attune to your truth from the feel of the visual language. And this in turn supports you in accessing the truth behind any blocks, fears, or resistances to living each sign.

Over time, you will pull the same card a second time, a third, and so on, and you will start to notice a pattern. Your deck may be reminding you of that last time you pulled the card and helping you connect dots in a storyline. Perhaps you often draw Cups but never Swords. This is a chance for you to get curious. Your deck may even tease you and make you laugh. Trust that the relationality of that connection is actually your most crucial access to wisdom with the tarot.

Ritual for the New Moon

The New Moon initiates each sign's season. In the physical sky, the New Moon is when the Moon is located exactly between Earth and the Sun, making the Moon appear dark. Astrologically, it is when the Sun and the Moon are together in the same zodiac sign. The Sun takes about thirty days to move through the thirty degrees of a sign. The Moon takes about twenty-eight days to move through all signs. So a New Moon in Libra always happens in Libra season (late September and early October) when the Sun moves through Libra and the Moon catches up to the Sun.

Since the Sun and Moon represent the conscious self and the unconscious self, then the idea with the New Moon is that all of oneself is in alignment with that given sign. Thus, the New Moon signals a beginning, an initiation into a new sign's energy. It is an invitation to journey with the part of you that is that sign for an entire lunar cycle. So, for each chapter, I've included a ritual to explore for the New Moon in that sign.

Every twenty-eight days, rather than just at the New Year or at your birthday, you can start anew. How refreshing is that? I find it much easier to set a goal for one month than for a whole year. The chances for feeling good about myself in the end are much higher, and I can avoid unrealistic resolutions and self-defeating attitudes in favor of the momentum of empowering change.

It is helpful to liken the New Moon to the concept of the void. The void—like a blank page—is all possibility. It's a non-space for dreaming. It is liminal, meaning it is an in-between space, outside of the norm. Liminal spaces are inherently exciting, magical, and liberating because they resist categories, labels, and boxes. In the liminal, we can be anything.

What makes all rituals so powerful is that they dilate time with your conscious attention. And the more you pay attention to something, the more it magnifies for you. Most rituals happen in the small daily ways you attend to your life. Some rituals, like the ones you will find here for the New Moons, ask for more time, preparation, and focused attention. It's rare in our world to give anything that much of ourselves, and because you do it for you, you demonstrate to your unconscious and to the universe that your life is important to you. Every insight feels new when you greet yourself in the ritual dimension.

Make a big deal about these rituals. Show up as if your life depends on it. See what happens.

Setting Intentions

Consider yourself in the liminal at the New Moon. The possibility for the emergence of empowering change feels palpable. We feel into the courage to dream new ways of being for ourselves and our world.

In the broader wellness community, there's a lot of talk about setting intentions at the beginning of the lunar cycle. Living intentionally is a beautiful thing. It calls to our consciousness what we want from an experience and what we will take responsibility for bringing to each unfolding. What I've seen in myself and those I work with is that because of our conditioning, we often can't help but bring an attitude of disciplinary shaming to our intention process. Because we've been taught that something is wrong with us and that we should be able to fix ourselves if we apply enough willpower, there's this whole vibe of control and self-loathing that can slip into the intention process. Earlier I shared my view that potential is a fantasy that shames the present moment. In the same way, intention can be harmful when it's crafted from a place of hating who we are now.

For these lunar rituals, I invite you to practice calling in a *protected present*—a present moment made of compassion. One that doesn't cringe at the past or fear the future. This compassion is radical because it might go against all the terrible things you were told to believe about yourself. From there, ask yourself what you dream of in your heart, for yourself and our world. Call in intentions from this space, where all possibilities exist. This is a practice and will feel more comfortable over time, each cycle.

The Moon can help us cultivate a repertoire of skills for relating to our intentions as well as replacing the old paradigm of grind and hustle with practices that feel soft, present, and loving. But please consider too that the Moon does not exist to be our manifestation machine. Be curious about teachers who make manifestation the whole purpose of intention-setting at the New Moon. The Moon is your loving, encouraging witness and compassionate, honest ally. The Moon helps you resource yourself to meet your needs as things come up in the process of being human. Sometimes the Moon might want you to de-manifest, to stop trying to make things happen for yourself and just be. To just listen.

One of my core teachings is "Intentions as sentient beings." When you see your intentions as sentient beings, you externalize your intention so that it's not all about you. You liberate it from fear of failure and self-mistrust. When your intentions are treated as sentient beings, they are independent spirits that have chosen you to care for them. And you are free to decline if you don't have the capacity to care for them right now. This is rooted in the truth that everything is relational. When your intentions are sentient beings, your job is to listen and tend, not to manage or push. It becomes a relationship of attunement.

When I let my intentions come to me and commit to nurturing them, they come to life as if by their own spirit. Trying to push something through that isn't vitally alive is exhausting. The energetics of the pushed-through intention are just never as potent or interesting for others to experience. And then I end up feeling ashamed and disappointed on top of my depletion.

From New Moon to New Moon each month, you can practice rewiring your relationship to intention-setting. If you are interested in setting an intention in relationship to the sign the Sun and Moon are in at the New Moon, feel into the themes of that chapter—maybe just look at the Questions to Live Into sections—and listen for an intention that will awaken, practice skill, and meet challenges of the part of you that is that sign. For example, for the New Moon in Taurus, notice what resonates with you in that chapter as a growth edge. Maybe for you it has to do with a slower pace for sensual experiences. Perhaps for you, rushing feels safe. Your intention at the New Moon could be to give one hour of the day to slower experiencing, and then see how that goes. Let your intention come to you softly rather than grasping for or overthinking it.

The lunar ritual I share often suggests an intention, but not always. Please always work with intention in ways that feel resonant for you. Sometimes you might not even want to work with an intention related to the sign. I often set this simple intention: to listen and pay attention to what comes up in my life and be present with it.

May we all bring sincere love and respect to the Moon in our lunar rituals.

Creating a Ritual Container

For each ritual, I list a simple set of items for you to gather before you begin, along with a set of instructions for you to guide yourself through this journey. But perhaps the most important part of any ritual is bringing yourself into the ritual space in both body and mind. Rather than repeat the basic process for this in each chapter, I am sharing it here for you to refer back to as often as you need until you make a practice of your own. If you already have a process, feel free to disregard—or perhaps give it a try anyway and see what happens.

To begin, you will need to create a reverent, closed container for this exercise. A closed container is a set amount of time with a clear beginning and a clear ending. This is just as important as anything else you do here. No phone. No interruptions. No multitasking. This is your time; show yourself that you choose you. If needed, let people know that you need fifteen to thirty minutes uninterrupted. (If they don't honor this, then that's some good information for you.)

1. When you're ready to close the container, light a candle. This signals to the brain that you're beginning. Perhaps gaze at the candle awhile to let your eyes soften.

2. Then ground yourself (see page 57). Take some long, deep, purposeful breaths. Getting closer each time.

3. Connect with your deep inner guidance. Ask for help from any spirit guides, animal guides, ancestors, or deities that you know support your highest self and purpose.

4. Go about your ritual.

5. When you complete the ritual, conclude with gratitude and acknowledge that the ritual is over. Blow out the candle, and declare your container open. May your lunar practice support you in accessing the wisdom of your intuition. May you come to know your intuition as the moonlight revealing your path in the dark.

Chapter by chapter, Moon after Moon, give yourself over to the twelve signs inside yourself with a combination of sincerity and playfulness.

Let's begin!

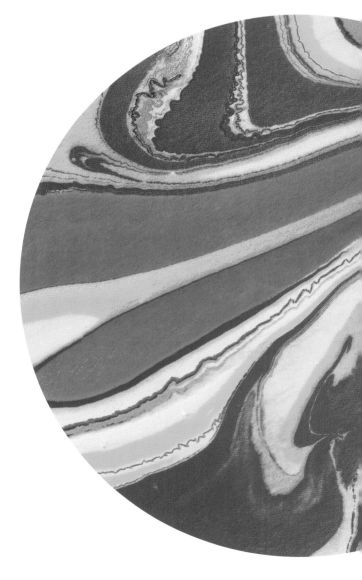

PART TWO

Living the Signs

Emergence never happens all at once. It is a slow stepping into the expanded capacity of your next self. You may need practice at releasing in those places you've grown accustomed to bracing which, like a tight swaddle, was comforting in its limits. But when the time to remain hidden comes to its natural end, you must begin to inhabit your new dimensionality. Breathe into the fullness of your gaining altitude and consider that what presents itself as fear may actually be exhilaration. As your future approaches you, worry less how it may receive you and say a prayer instead for your becoming approachable.

—Toko-pa Turner, *Belonging: Remembering Ourselves Home*

Aries

MARCH 20-APRIL 19

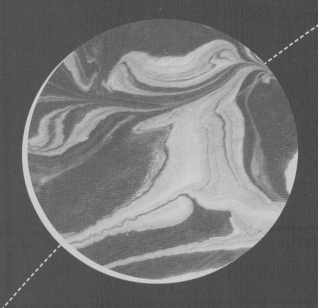

♈ ARIES

△ FIRE

⌃ CARDINAL

♂ MARS

Questions to Live Into

What bold actions can I take today
to serve what I want to see happen in
my life?

If nothing bad could happen and I knew
I had the full support of my loved ones,
what would be the most exciting thing
I could give myself full permission to
go for?

What are my frustrations, resentments,
or irritations teaching me about what's
blocking me on my path?

Altar

As discussed in part one, the purpose of creating an altar is to first prepare and then enjoy having a special space devoted to the themes and principles you're developing with each sign. The general qualities of Aries are listed below. I recommend you gather at least three items, but quantity isn't as crucial as choosing items of resonance for you. For example, this season, maybe you prefer to build an altar solely based on color. Your entire altar space could be full of only items with red and orange: candles, crystals, flowers, and art objects. Maybe you decide to wear more red this month. Take the suggestions that feel aligned and don't worry about the rest. As you read through the chapter, more ideas may come to you for your altar that aren't listed here.

Go for it!

COLORS
red, yellow

CRYSTALS
agate, bloodstone,
carnelian, fire opal,
garnet, red jasper, ruby

GARDEN
carnation, dandelion,
fennel, garlic,
honeysuckle

SPICES AND FLAVORS
allspice, cinnamon,
cloves, coriander,
cumin, frankincense,
galangal, ginger,
mustard, nettle, pepper

**GODS AND
GODDESSES**
Durga, Eris, Hestia,
Indra, Mars, Marduk,
Minerva, the Morrigan,
Ra, Sekhmet

TAROT CARDS
the Emperor, the
Tower, 2 of Wands,
3 of Wands, 4 of Wands

ITEMS
art, books, ceramics,
fabrics, food, incense,
magazine cutouts,
photographs, quotes
on paper, or anything
else that inspires you

RELATED THEMES
action, athletic ability,
courage, determination,
fire, growth, helmets,
power, rams, self-
sufficiency, audacity,
separating out what
doesn't serve you,
sharp objects (daggers,
knives, swords, pens),
sneakers, swagger,
trophies, Tuesday

SEASON

Beginning of Spring

After winter, Aries always comes. Aries is the first sign of the zodiac. This is important. Aries is the beginning, it comes first, it starts things.

There is movement and will to power inherent in the number one, and all of these speak to the essence of Aries. One is a number that signifies emerging unity from the void that is zero. All other numbers grow from one.

One emerges.

One becomes form.

One unifies.

One is independent.

One is self-sufficient.

The first day of Aries is the vernal (or spring) equinox. The equinoxes are the midway points between the winter and summer solstices—the shortest and the longest days of the year, respectively. *Equinox* means "equal night," for the fact that at the equinox we hold equal parts light and dark in that day. After the vernal equinox, we pass that moment of light-dark balance and move toward longer and longer days, with the approach of full-blown summer sun. The spring equinox is the time of the year when we shift from a more internal way of being (fall/winter) to a more external style of inhabiting our skin (spring/summer).

At the threshold of Aries, I often remember Clarissa Pinkola Estés's words in her classic must-read book *Women Who Run with the Wolves*: "And now comes the most important part of the story: spring approaches, new life quickens, a new turn, a new try is possible. The most important thing is to hold on, hold out, for your creative life, for your solitude, for your time to be and do, for your very life; hold on, for the promise from the wild nature is this: after winter, *spring always comes*."

Aries follows the winter sign of Pisces, sign twelve. Pisces symbolizes two fish swimming in opposite directions. After twelve, we can go two ways: we can start over at one, or we can slip into the mystery that is the number thirteen. Pisces is both the will back to one and the desire to know thirteen.

Aries then has something to do with what survives after twelve. In many ways, Aries is the dream of Pisces. Like salmon swimming upstream to spawn new life, Pisces stays alive to seed Aries. Aries is what drives you to start again. It is the spark of life that animates you.

I like to begin our study of Aries here because Aries is often perceived as blustery in its self-possession. It's important to understand that Aries is born out of the collective dream from Pisces. The precociousness of Aries grows from the wells of love inherent in the sign before it. We need the audacity of our springtime Aries self to catapult our dreams forward. It's the audacity of being a child of this world before we've known hurt or grief or danger. What would you do with such audacity? What would you do today if you could trust that you can always start again?

. . . .

MODALITY AND ELEMENT
Cardinal Fire

Like Cancer, Libra, and Capricorn, Aries is a cardinal sign and thus initiates a new season. It is the energy to pivot the wheel out of winter and into spring. That's a lot of force. The shift that happens between the equinox and the end of Aries is unmistakable.

Like Leo and Sagittarius, Aries is a Fire sign that cares about being creative, zesty, inspired, ecstatic, and adventurous.

The Fire of Aries is unambiguous in your presence. You can't miss it. All Fire has a heightened quality, but since Aries is cardinal, that means the majority of its potency happens at the start of that burst of energy. It's the power you see when you light a match. It's explosive and then softens out until it's gone.

In nature, Aries is a dicotyledon (or dicot), a flowering plant with two embryonic leaves in its seed that diverge into the two first shoots that we witness once the plant is above ground. To me, this is emblematic of the force of fresh spring. I think of the exuberant power of tulips bursting through the surface of the earth and pushing up toward the sun.

There is so much power in that Fire energy. There is so much courage. There is also so much hope: the hope to try and go for it despite all of the vulnerabilities, harsh conditions, and uncertain odds. Why do we do it? Why do we try? *Because we want to live!* We want to reach for the warmth of that sun and know life. The struggle of that reach is what tells us we're alive.

In human form, cardinal Fire is a runner leaping into a focused sprint at the start of a race. Imagine the swelling of power in their legs before launching into flight. Aries is a part of you that grows self-trust in your launching capability.

Cardinal Fire is the Hobbit Frodo volunteering to take the ring to Mordor before thinking about all that the journey entails. Hobbits are quite Taurus, the sign that follows Aries, as they are known for enjoying a quiet, simple life, not going off on adventures and risking the unknown. So it was very, very brave—and a bit impulsive—of Frodo to volunteer for a long perilous journey to save the world. Frodo said Yes to his Aries.

Cardinal Fire encourages you to first notice the Fire impulse as it burns into view. The impulse is a charge of adrenaline, your life force leaping with excitement. (We even associate the adrenals—which produce adrenaline along with other essential hormones—with Aries in medical astrology.) Then you ask the impulse what motivates it: Anger, frustration, competitiveness, inspiration, desire, passion, fun?

Sometimes a jolt of adrenaline is not something you want to honor. Often, it's just information for your data collection. "Oh, looks like something is annoying me. Hi annoyance! What are you trying to tell me?" It takes practice to become discerning about your patterns of adrenaline.

Many of us carry an excess amount of adrenaline because of past traumas. And lots of us are over-caffeinated (proud coffee lover, here). Excess adrenaline can show up as feelings of constriction and heat in the body when we're stressing. Harnessing cardinal Fire is also knowing when to practice releasing that stress.

Like all signs, Aries is a frequency you absolutely want to have for certain parts of your life, though it's not the appropriate force for all things. You may already have a sense for whether or not you feel like you're someone who has buckets of Aries quite naturally or if you wish you had more of it. Part of growing skill with Aries is accessing a pause button with your cardinal Fire in order to determine what to do with that power in ways that will feel empowering.

SYMBOL
The Ram   ♈

The Ram is the symbol commonly associated with Aries. Rams are male sheep, and they are known first and foremost for their defining feature: the large, curved horns on their head. When a Ram wants to win, it charges headfirst with a series of intense blows. Aries is the part of you someone might describe as "headstrong." The head is one of the body parts associated with Aries, and the brow plays an important role as the seat of your Third Eye, the site of your intuition. In addition, the word *helmet* comes from "helm," which is the front of a boat—the part that steers. Aries leads the way by your intuitive sight.

For the Aries in you, excitement often comes from the feeling of bumping into things. Life needs to feel a little like a battle, proving your ferocity to yourself. Aries is a go-getter. It's the you that "gets after it."

Every person will do the Ram differently. Maybe it shows up in how you experience relationships, create art, travel, court clients, or do research. We all have Aries, but it manifests uniquely in our personalities. This is why you have to talk to the Aries within. Find out what your Aries wants. What's worth pushing through the soil to reach for the Sun? What's worth charging toward?

As I like to say, "The energy has to go somewhere." So where do you want it go? Do you want it to help you set a boundary? Do you want it to burn away your fear and help you take a risk? Do you want it to work itself out by having a dance party in the kitchen? Do you want to channel it into a three-hour creative session? Remember also that Aries is a forceful energy, one that can do harm to others. So it's important to make sure you are directing your energy purposefully. But this power is not something to be afraid of. If you pretend you don't have it or you stifle it, it will only grow as resentment deep inside you and come bursting out in ways you later regret.

Aries is about participating in your life. The Aries in you has the initiative and the bravado to start whatever excites you and get it going. There is so much energy behind this part of us that we can truly make anything happen with our fiery passion.

What holds back your Ram? Usually, we feel debilitated by the phrase: "I'm not ready." But my hot Aries take on this is that "ready" is a fantasy. There is no ready. We like to believe there will be a future version of us who will have the expertise or the confidence to be ready for a new experience. And so when we say we're "not ready," what we mean is that we're afraid to try or trust because we don't think we're enough as we are now. The fantasy of a day when we're ready keeps us from engaging with the present moment.

This month, make a practice of working with any inner voices who insist you're "not ready" by befriending the fear behind this illusion. Have compassion for yourself that you've been culturally conditioned to think you have to be perfect or complete to be worthy. Behind the fear, listen for a desire that's trying to talk to you: a desire to belong, to participate, to offer something, to contribute, to play, to love, to explore.

Give your desire to the Ram inside you. Tell your Ram to take it and run.

POLARITY
The Aries-Libra Axis

All Fire signs are opposite Air signs, and all polar signs have the same modality. So cardinal Fire is opposite cardinal Air: Libra.

Aries evolves through Libra. Libra initiates the autumn season and its death processes. Libra teaches Aries to slow down, to reflect, to listen, and to appeal to good judgment before taking action. The Aries-Libra polarity tells a story about the spectrum between personal agency and interpersonal relationality:

- Aries pushes in one direction; Libra desires equal distribution of weight.
- Aries impulsively says, "Yes, I can do that!"; Libra says, "Hold up, I need to deliberate."
- Aries wants what it wants right now; Libra considers what's most in alignment for all parties.

Libra is about how you understand yourself relative to other people, something that independent Aries can often use. You can be so sure you know who you are when you're alone and practicing your ideas with your own self, but it's entirely another thing to witness how your words land on someone else and respond from there.

Think about the processes you go through when you want a person, an experience, or a goal. How do things shift when you begin thinking about strategies to communicate (Air) your impulse (Fire) instead of just acting on it?

This is the Libran part of you kicking in. Perhaps you will intuit how to smooth the pathway to what you want by calming the other person's possible fears or distaste for your plan. Perhaps you will discuss ways to guide the other person to your side or otherwise cooperate. Perhaps you will avoid the other person entirely so you can bypass a disagreement. Perhaps you don't care what the other person thinks, and you steamroll your goal through no matter what.

Aries can be brutish without Libra. Aries makes unilateral decisions without Libra. Aries forgets to enjoy the process without Libra. Aries neglects beauty without Libra. Aries is self-sufficient: "I'll just do it myself!" Libra responds with: "But doing things is more fun when we're together."

Libra's soothing Air cools off Fiery Aries, helping us cultivate patience, strategy, wit, and persuasion with all relational deliberation processes. It doesn't want to stop you from doing your thing—it wants you to make sure that your actions don't impede others along the way.

The truth is that "I" is not ever truly our own. Our sense of the Aries "I" can only ever come through the support and company of others. The myriad ways we are touched, handled, neglected, fed, attuned to, judged, and witnessed by others are how we constellate a self-knowing as "I" at all. The Aries-Libra polarity supports us in navigating the complicated and exciting ecologies of identity.

RULING PLANET
Mars

Mars is the planet that rules Aries, giving the sign its red-hot swagger. Mars is your capacity to go after what you want. Mars is your energy. It's your enterprising, active, and ardent will.

Mars is the teacher for you if you struggle with asserting yourself, if you feel stagnant, if you are lethargic, if you don't know what you're passionate about, if you're afraid to take a risk, or if you think you have to be 100 percent ready before you jump into things.

More than any other planet, Mars cares about the present moment. Mars isn't in the future, worrying about what might happen. Mars isn't in the past, remembering how things didn't work out the last time you tried something new. Mars is here now, wanting you to feel what it's like to make an impact on the world.

You feel Mars in you as a fervent impulse desiring direction and release. Mars wants to move in a clear, pointed path toward its purpose, and the glyph for Mars is the circle of spirit with the arrow of directionality. Thus, Mars rules all pointed objects, including the scalpel, the sword, and the penis.

Just because Mars is mythologically a male god, and just because a penis is associated with a male body, in no way is Mars only for people with a penis. Every planet is for every person's body. Something to consider with Mars is your relationship to "the masculine." This is such a fraught term that I usually don't use it. But in the case of Mars, it feels important to bring up as there is healing available here. Masculine does not have to be a permanent state of being related to traditional maleness; it can be an expression of qualities. I think of the masculine as the daytime qualities in each of us: more outward, externally moving, rational, visible. This is juxtaposed to the nocturnal, feminine parts of us that are more inward, receptive, mysterious, and unconscious.

Gender is a construct. Most of us—no matter how we identify—are actively healing the false bifurcation of gender qualities onto gender assignments given at birth. Acting as if we are only one gender is a mode of behavior we were conditioned to perform, not a natural extension of who we are. And this has made our relationship to masculinity feel toxic because it's fragile. Fragile masculinity defines itself in contrast with and seeks to dominate the feminine. Confident masculinity embraces its own femininity. Instead of being threatened by the feminine, confident masculinity looks to it as a source of power and strength. That power is in each of us.

For those of us turned off or terrorized by fragile masculinity, we might struggle to claim our Mars, fearing we'll participate in the same harm we've seen enacted in the world. But if you're not listening to the Mars inside you, then you will cede your Mars to an external authority. Thus, reprogramming your relationship to your inner masculinity can be a crucial part of falling in love with your Aries self.

You need Mars to stand up for what breaks your heart. You need Mars to be honest with your truth, even if others may not like what they hear. You need Mars to stop you from living automatically in a life without passion.

One of the most powerful ways to heal with Mars is to work with your reactivity, or how you react and respond to outside influences that trigger your Mars. Your reactivity describes how external factors are influencing your emotional state. We've all been around reactive people. They seem out of control. They are ungrounded. They could hurt someone. Working with your Mars in a skillful way has to do with controlling and protecting your assertive nature so that it grows and directs its force according to your will.

The number one goal when you begin working with your reactivity is to simply commit to noticing when you are reactive. *I am reactive right now.* That's all you have to do. The moment you consciously notice you're reactive, when you're feeling triggered, then you immediately begin to calm that response. It's when you don't notice the reaction is happening that you are controlled by its progress. When you give into your reactivity unconsciously, you lose your power.

SKILLFUL ARIES

Engage

Aries wants you to know: the most loving thing you can do is start before you know what you're doing. If there's something you're called to do—start a podcast, sell stuff online, write a book—you don't need to fully understand the thing to begin making it happen. Aries says: Learn by doing.

Thrival means getting in the game, I thought to myself one Aries season. To thrive—something this sign very much wants for you—you need to feel like you're participating in your life with vitality. This is a sign that likes athletics-based metaphors, but you don't need to be into sports to channel your inner Aries. "Getting in the game" means getting out of the spectator seat. It means not waiting for things to happen before you take risks. It means the audacity for self-permission. It means feeling the exhilaration of the momentum of the ride you're on.

Aries is the sign that follows Pisces, the last sign of the zodiac and a part of us that very much craves to feel in relationship to our dreams and ideals. Pisces then passes the baton off to Aries and says, now go do it. Aries has all the power and all the juice in its toolkit to make dreams happen.

Feeling skillful with Aries has to do with unlearning that sitting on the sidelines will keep you safe from life. It will not. Waiting for your life to happen only fuels resentment toward those who are participating in theirs, which will in turn breed shame because you don't actually want to judge people.

Unskillful Aries might feel bored and annoyed with you for not taking risks. You might make the mistake of presuming that passivity is part of your personality. Unskillful Aries might tell you that adventurous lives are for other people, not for you. This part of you might say Yes to playing the supporting role in other people's dreams to avoid growing your own. You might feel so exhausted from all the things you do each day to be the kind of person who helps out that you don't think you have the capacity to put your Fire behind your own dreams.

Getting in the game is about boldly making choices that eliminate other available options. Sometimes that might mean declaring, "I'm not doing this anymore." Participating in your life sometimes looks like insisting you need a rest. The spirit of skillful Aries has to do with being fully engaged with what's coming up for you, not numbing out.

Aries, I've learned, must be impressed with itself. If you want to tap into your Aries, go do things that impress you. Be startled at your swagger. Be tickled by your precociousness. Be turned on by your bold moves.

It's time to stop waiting for permission, says Aries. You *really can* be that person. If you hear a mean voice inside that says, "Who do you think you are that you could do that?" The response is simply, "I'm _____ (first name) fucking _____ (last name), that's who."

PRACTICE
Humpability

Healing with Aries is central to my story as an Aries Rising. From my perspective, your rising sign is the most important one for growing skill. I built my astrological practice on pure Aries pizzazz and razzmatazz. The more I impress myself, the more my work reaches new clients and students. And so it is with personal pride that I share my favorite Aries practice for jumping on the rocket of your Fire and living your dreams. The magical question: *Is this humpable?*

Aries is a very erotic sign. By erotic, I mean a broader definition than simply sexual energy. I am referring to channeling one's wild aliveness. Aries has a very thrusty quality about it. If you want to know what Aries feels like in the body, take a pillow and hump it until you come to the sensation of heat that arises. How you feel about humping will tell you a lot about where you are with Aries. If you feel like you're not allowed to tap into it, then perhaps that's your practice for Aries season.

A humpability practice is the practice of asking yourself how humpable something is for you. Examples: Does this collaboration feel like something I want to hump? Does this project have a fairly impressive humpability factor? Before I buy this house, do I want to hump the idea of living here?

You may be thinking that you can't literally hump a collaboration, project, or house, but the point is simply: Does this get you really excited? Does it ignite something in you that feels alive, stirring, and fun?

We live in a culture that is adrenaline-addicted and performance-focused where everything feels urgent. Urgency is one of the most pervasively harmful aspects of modern life. We push through things when we're exhausted. We demand things get done right now. We have no patience for wait times. If there's a mistake, we think it has to get corrected immediately.

Explore the idea that you have been trained to apply your beautiful Aries abilities to every little thing that feels urgent. This is a loss for the Aries part of you because it teaches you to confuse adrenaline-hyped drive with the raw power of the Fire you can create with your genuine excitement.

Here's the deal: Just because you can will something into being doesn't mean you want to hump it. Just because you can make it happen, doesn't mean it turns you on to do it.

Is it humpable, or is it the grind? Is it humpable, or is it urgency?

We're all very busy. The biggest struggle most of us have is feeling low on capacity—low on time, low on energy, low on attention. What I've found is that the humpable things are the ones you find the capacity to enjoy and show up for. Your attraction to it is what makes it happen.

The practice of asking "Is this humpable?" will help you determine pretty quickly if something is a Yes or No for you. Ask this every time you are faced with a decision to give your energy to an experience. Perhaps you're considering whether or not to offer something again that you did last year. Maybe you got a call from a friend who wants to collaborate on a project. If you don't know immediately that something is a Yes or No, then ask if it's humpable. Eliminate any options with a "should" attached because no one has ever been turned on because they should be.

Once you have your answer, honor it. Your Aries Fire deserves to be reserved for what really matters, and you don't want to run out of energy midway on something anymore. If that's not practical magic, I don't know what is.

TAROT CARD

The Emperor

The card in the tarot that we associate with Aries is card four: the Emperor.

In the *Smith-Rider-Waite* depiction, we see what looks like your typical old white dude in charge. The card can be understandably uncomfortable for people. Across history, emperors have amassed and hoarded resources. Emperors have dominated and suppressed challengers and their own people.

Thankfully, many folks are deciding not to ignore the violent legacies of colonialist nation-building and patriarchal hierarchies. Through this work, we can collectively mourn the unfathomable harm, loss, violence, oppression, and injustice of the Emperor's machinations. We can grapple with our role within the oppressed-oppressor matrix.

Since tarot is a tool for self-healing, growth, and empowerment, it's important to wonder how this card has medicine for us. The Emperor cannot only be about colonizing, dominating energy. This aspect of the card is, in Jungian phrasing, "shadow" Emperor. From a decolonial perspective, how can we imagine an Emperor that honors our interconnectivity and expresses power with the frequency of love?

The Emperor is a card that calls you to take up more space, more stature, and more expansiveness in order to give more of your unique light. Natural phenomena can help us imagine this archetype in a nonharmful way: the mountain, the sequoia, the redwood, the alpha wolf. We don't begrudge the mountain for taking up space. We don't resent the alpha wolf for their good stewardship.

Like flowers that burst forth during Aries season, Emperor energy can be about owning and activating your power in a nonviolent way. We love to see blooms in their full expression and vitality, and likewise, the world wants to see you activated. What if the flowers didn't show off for fear of taking up too much space? They would deprive us of their beauty and bees the chance to pollinate them and make honey.

The Emperor invites you to wonder about your personal power. Not to dominate, but to nudge you to sit more confidently in the throne of your own bright presence. To support your power you need energy, which you source through your daily choices like food, sleep, movement, meditation, and self-care.

The Emperor enriches our understanding of Aries because the Emperor weaves in stories about organization, structure, and responsibility that can buttress Aries's will, determination, and bravado. Just as the Emperor historically built bridges, roads, and aqueducts to last and to serve the whole, so you can channel Emperor energy to respond to your life in ways that offer underlying, long-term support to your many goals, dreams, and pleasures.

Note how "held in" the image appears. The figure is still and square inside its throne. When Aries is blended with skillful Emperor, we give our passions the structures they need to be more sustainable.

A Tarot Spread with the Emperor

See the chapter *How to Navigate This Book* if you're new to the tarot and seek support for pulling cards and interpreting them.

Take the Emperor out of your deck. (If you have more than one deck, you can pull the card from another deck so that the Emperor has a chance to "participate" in the deck from which you will draw.)

Feel into the visual inspiration of the card.

Take a few deep breaths on purpose and arrive to the reading. Connect into your intuition. Ask Emperor-Aries energy to help you with this reading. Shuffle according to your unique, never-wrong style. Center and focus your question thus:

With the most expansive levels of compassion for me and all sentient beings, what is the loving invitation to connect with the Emperor?

Pull seven cards according to your own unique process of knowing with the following prompts, and then sit with the cards and journal about them.

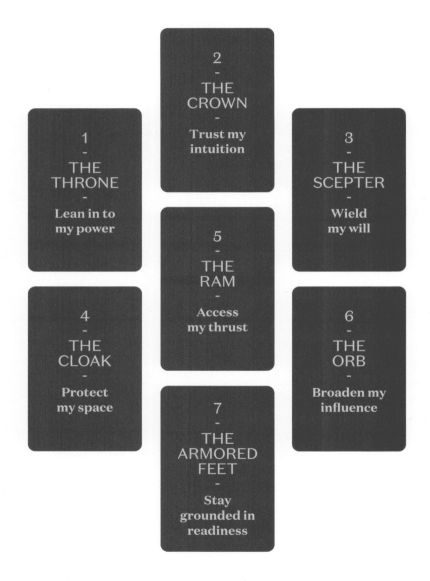

RITUAL FOR THE NEW MOON
The Helm of Awe

The days around the first official day of spring, the vernal equinox, and when the Sun officially moves from Pisces into Aries is like stepping onto a bridge. This bridge is a portal to rebirth in a new zodiacal year.

Aries comes in to create form out of the void. There's a serious shift in energy, made very visible and concrete in the outside world with spring's physical manifestations. Those first days of Aries season hold in that expansive fire like the high point of a big inhale. We intuit the expansiveness ready to burst forth as from a massive bellow inside the belly of a dragon. It is at the New Moon when this birth energy feels fully available to us.

The following ritual is designed to help you source your power and set potent intentions to unfold for you across this cycle and year.

The Vikings of my ancestral lineage had an ancient symbol for personal power known as the *Ægishjálmr*, pronounced "EYE-gis-hiowlm-er," or the Helm of Awe. The Helm of Awe has eight spiked arms ending in tridents that radiate out from a central point, as you can see in the illustration. In one of the Viking poems in *The Poetic Edda*, the dragon Fáfnir boasts about his strength and ties his invincibility to the magical powers of the Helm of Awe. The Helm of Awe helps him protect his treasure by being fiercer than all his enemies.

There are other folktales where the Helm of Awe is referenced in magical spells. For example, if one presses the symbol between the brows for protection and says aloud, "I bear the Helm of Awe between my brows!" then "awe" would overcome the minds of one's enemies so that they could not defeat you. The Helm of Awe is like a psychic shield, literally protecting the psyche from fear.

This idea of being able to fight and protect what you care about (Fáfnir's treasure) is very much tied to Mars, which rules all pointed objects and whose principle is about separating out what is not for you. Mars, through Aries, is the ability to say No.

What if the Helm of Awe serves us not just to induce awe in the minds of one's enemies, but to call in *self*-awe? At this New Moon in Aries, connect with your ability to sever what no longer serves you as you rebirth, gloriously thrusting into the new zodiacal year, and to protect you from fear of what's ahead. May you experience the self-awe to move through whatever comes.

Before beginning this ritual, gather:

- Candles, as many as you want, and a way to light them
- Something flat to paint or draw on that you can keep (paper, rock, canvas, t-shirt, pillowcase, etc.)
- Drawing materials of your choice that will mark on your flat surface (pen, markers, paint, etc.)

The Ritual

1. Sit at your Aries altar when ready. Set up your ritual container, light your candle(s), and come to a grounded, meditative state (see page 57).

2. Connect with your inner Fire. Let it grow from the root of your spine and emanate upward through your body with your breath. Feel into your animated spirit. See it. Ask yourself about it: color, temperature, sound qualities.

3. Bring your attention to your brow and forehead. Determine to set a psychic helm of protection there. Ask yourself to see the symbol of what your own personal psychic shield looks like.

4. Let this image constellate in your mind's eye, or let it emerge as a felt color or frequency vibration. Whatever you perceive first is perfect. There are no right or wrong answers here. Let this image or sensation sit at your brow, full of awesome power. Let it feel concentrated. Let it harden at its center. Let it radiate from a solid core at the center. If you don't see anything, just visualize the Helm of Awe.

5. Connect with the highest levels of trust that this symbol is infused with all of the self-awe that you need to protect your will, agency, and determination.

6. Say, "I wear a Helm of Awe upon my brow. I am strong. I am brave. I am protected."

7. Once you have an image, draw or paint it on your piece of paper or whatever you gathered. Maybe you prefer to dance with the vibrations of what the Helm of Awe feels like to you. Enjoy your process.

8. When complete, write down three goals that feel exciting to reach for across the spring season. Experiment with trusting in your Helm of Awe to support you over the months ahead. Set out your drawing or painting at your altar or wherever you can see it regularly to remind you of your self-awe.

9. Conclude and open the ritual container (see page 66).

Happy New Moon in Aries!

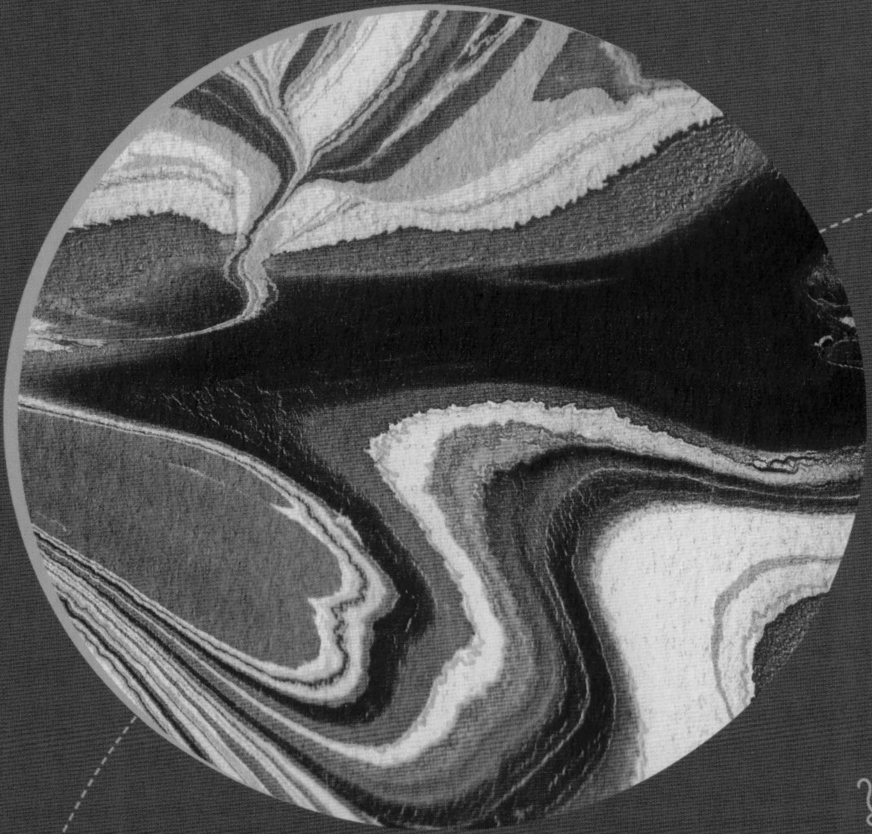

♉ TAURUS

▽ EARTH

⊡ FIXED

♀ VENUS

Taurus

APRIL 19–MAY 20

Questions to Live Into

What can I commit to doing slowly today, letting myself more fully receive the sensations of my experience?

What would I do differently if I trusted that I can't miss what is meant for me?

What desires am I ready to have the audacity to name, and how can I call in more assurance that I deserve to receive them?

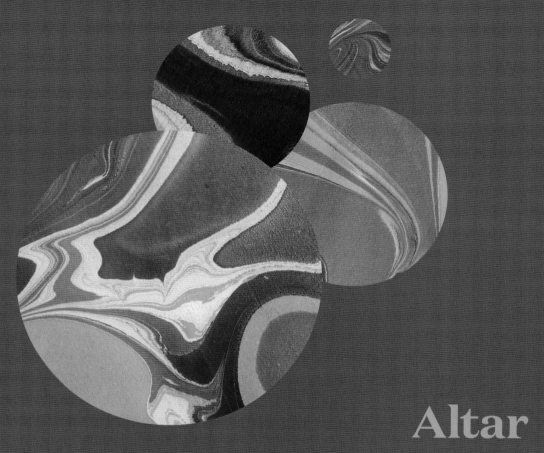

Altar

As discussed in part one, the purpose of creating an altar is to first prepare and then enjoy having a special space devoted to the themes and principles you're developing with each sign. The general qualities of Taurus are listed below. I recommend you gather at least three items, but quantity isn't as crucial as choosing items of resonance for you. For example, this season, maybe you prefer to build an altar solely based on sensual touch. Your entire altar space could be full of only items with exciting textures: honeycomb candles, gorgeous crystals, velvety flowers, rich woods, and objects that feel decadent to touch. Take the suggestions that feel aligned and don't worry about the rest. As you read through the chapter, more ideas may come to you for your altar that aren't listed here.

Go for it!

COLORS
green, light blue, light yellow, mauve, pink

CRYSTALS
diamond, emerald, peacock ore, ruby, sapphire, turquoise

GARDEN
gingko, hibiscus, orchid, rose, ylang-ylang, oatstraw

SPICES AND FLAVORS
bourbon, cardamom, cinnamon, maple, vanilla

GODS AND GODDESSES
Aphrodite, Dionysus, Gaia, Inanna, Isis, Hathor, Lakshmi, Osiris, Venus

TAROT CARDS
the Empress, the Hierophant, 5 of Pentacles, 6 of Pentacles, 7of Pentacles

ITEMS
art, books, ceramics, fabrics, food, incense, magazine cutouts, photographs, quotes on paper, or anything else that inspires you

RELATED THEMES
beauty, chocolate, comfort, dedication, design, Friday, garden flowers, grounding, home, honey, juicy fruit, love, lust, money, pleasure, the senses, stability, strength, tree roots, wealth, yummy textures

SEASON

Middle of Spring

After so much birth and growth energy over Aries, Taurus is the energy called upon to make sure what has grown will survive. Those first green shoots that burst forth from the ground with so much power now crave a thicker trunk so they can support what has been initiated.

While in many parts of the world Aries season looks and feels a lot like an extended Pisces season, Taurus brings more clarity about the swing back to warmer weather and longer days. And for most of us, we want it to stay that way. The Taurus in you wants certainty that winter is over. The Taurus in you doesn't want to doubt in spring's hold.

Setting up your life so that you can trust in it is a large part of what motivates Taurus. And this includes being resourceful and gathering what you need to get spring activities into a sustainable rhythm and reliability.

Taurus builds, sustains, steadies, and roots. This is the part of you that wants a long-range plan to ensure things last.

Taurus feels into the structure of things for security. This is the part of you that wants to know the fridge and the bank account are both full.

Taurus gathers what it needs for sustenance and dependable rhythm. This is the part of you that falls into rituals and routines that you can count on.

Taurus understands and deeply cares for the physical body. This is the part of you that attunes to your needs and meets them.

Aries sets us off on a journey at dawn, the start of a new adventure. Taurus finds a place to stop and build a stable home with a flourishing garden.

For some, the invitation to un-shame a slow pace might feel incredibly liberating. For others, it might be a challenge. I get this. I like to jump on things at the last minute and let my ADHD brain be brilliant when cornered. What I have found is that allowing myself to live my Taurus has softened some of my adrenaline-pumped determination to go hard and fast. Let other parts of you be in charge of quick moves. Today, listen to your Taurus. If you've created an identity around being free to change your mind at any time, then who would you be if you practiced committing to what's right in front of you to tend?

. . . .

MODALITY AND ELEMENT

Fixed Earth

Like the other fixed signs (Leo, Scorpio, and Aquarius), Taurus is the middle sign of the season. It roots into the essence of what spring is. The fixed signs help you feel the scaffolding of who you are—those parts of you less likely to change position.

Like the other Earth signs (Virgo and Capricorn), Taurus cares about being practical, dependable, and grounded. The Earth parts of you feel present to your experience in a body.

In nature, fixed Earth is a large boulder that has settled into its place. In human form, fixed Earth is a gardener with dirt under their nails from working with the soil or a baker with flour caked in their skin from kneading dough. There's a sense that they are one with their work and materials.

Fixed Earth is a parent rocking rhythmically while making eye contact with their baby drinking milk. This person isn't going anywhere. They are right where they are. It's as if the motion of the rocking chair is all that there is and ever will be.

The Taurus part of you is the part with strong opinions, the part least interested in changing things up. This is because Earth is the most slow-moving element, and fixed is the most consolidated modality. So together, this is where you know what you want, like, and value, and you won't likely be swayed.

Fixed Earth encourages you to notice your preferences and relate them to your values. For example, "I would rather go without coffee than abide the dark roast and sad aesthetic of Starbucks." Naming your preferences to yourself and others is an important part of fixed Earth. Taurus isn't afraid to have a stance that other people might disagree with. It's how you clarify who you are. Living your preferences is the boulder of your fixed Earth; the one others can lean back on and trust.

Fixed Earth wants you to know it's not only okay to have preferences, you should make them a crucial part of who you are in the world. The part of you that is fixed Earth is content just as you are. You built a symbolic home there and feel a resistance to the vulnerabilities of the unknown. You may cling to and insist upon repetition, longevity, and possession here because there is pleasure in not having to worry about change.

The beauty of your fixed Earth is that this is the part of yourself that you (and others) can count on. When life forces you to make shifts in your Taurus ways (which is not always fun!), you will have the strength to enfold those changes into your steady reliability and restabilize.

. . . .

SYMBOL

The Bull   ♉

Taurus is commonly associated with the Bull. A Bull is strong-willed and resolute in its purpose. In your mind's eye, you can just see that Bull, so solid in its form, standing there, immovable.

My younger daughter is a Taurus Sun. As soon as she figured out how to get a blob of banana in her own mouth, she refused to let me feed her. I can still picture her sitting in her high chair with her hands, arms, chest, face, and hair completely drenched in mashed food. When I would sing and dance to get her to open her mouth and take a spoon, she would purse her lips together so tightly that there was no way I could get the food in. And then as soon as I pulled my spoon away, she'd happily feed herself again. It was the same with getting dressed. "I do by self" was her favorite thing to say to me with a look that meant business. And there was no point in negotiating with her. To this day, if you try to mess with her program, she becomes the Bull. (And she still gets food all over her face when she eats something she loves.)

Taurus is a sign that deeply speaks to the fertility and fecundity of spring. It is in this way that Taurus also relates to the cow. Taurus ties back clearly to the cult of Hathor, the literal Holy Cow of ancient Egypt. Hathor is one of the oldest goddesses in the entire Egyptian pantheon, patroness of love, motherhood, birth, joy, and music.

Hathor means "mansion of Horus," and as she was the mother of the god Horus, the word *mansion* here refers to her womb. This is fascinating for Taurus both for the reference to the belly-home of creation and because so many architects, designers, and landscape architects have Taurus featured prominently in the chart. As a goddess of beauty, Hathor was also the patron of cosmetics. Wearing cosmetics was seen as a form of worship to Hathor, and offerings of mirrors or cosmetic palettes to her were common. Interestingly, I often see Taurus-dominant folks working in fields related to beauty and adornment.

How are architecture and beauty related? They are all about the sensual, and so is Taurus. The physicality of the Taurus archetype is tied to the multisensory symphony of body fluids, sweat, blood, breath, milk, and other excretions that are integral to the life cycle. To the Taurus in you, the embodied experience matters. You are the architect of your own space—how do you adorn it? You are designer of your own beauty—what message are you sharing? These are the things that connect you to this earthly experience and allow you to make your mark.

For millennia, the cow has symbolized motherhood, milk, and all that is life-sustaining nourishment for the community. Taurus has to do with the earthy, primal, gnarly business of breeding, pregnancy, birthing, and nursing. Notably, the symbol for Taurus looks like a uterus with fallopian tubes!

Whether we're birthing biologically or symbolically, the creative process is also messy, stinky, and bloody. It's exhausting, even painful, to gestate an idea while it kicks at our insides. It's vulnerable to spread ourselves open and expand into new territory to offer our gifts. Taurus holds space as the anchor for the creative process.

How can you incorporate and listen to more of your senses throughout your everyday activities this month? Stop to open every lid of every candle and breathe in. Eat slowly; let the food burst on your tongue. Get excited about the way a textile drapes on your body. Be picky af about the aesthetics of font choices.

POLARITY

The Taurus-Scorpio Axis

All Earth signs are opposite Water signs, and all polar signs have the same modality. So fixed Earth is opposite fixed Water: Scorpio.

Scorpio is a part of you that is deeply intuitive. It is a sign for the part of you that feels the leaves falling off their branches and the nights becoming increasingly long. Scorpio wonders about death. Scorpio wants to see in the dark, to peer behind closed doors, to be strong enough to stand the stench of decay. Scorpio has X-ray vision. It's the part of you that doesn't miss anything; the part that sees all.

- Taurus relates to the sensually felt experience; Scorpio connects to that which is emotionally felt.
- Taurus is concerned with mundane matters at hand; Scorpio is attuned to the hidden and mysterious.
- Taurus wants to know what it can count on in the whole ecosystem of support; Scorpio withdraws to the private realm where it can best count on itself and maybe one or two people.

No doubt, both are stubborn and self-protecting parts of who we are, which I know well as the mother of both a Scorpio and Taurus! My dragons are not afraid to say No.

The polarity between these signs tells a story of roots and fruits. Scorpio cares for the roots—hidden power beneath the surface. Deep emotional bravery. The willingness to be with the more gruesome and unsightly aspects of human relationships. A fascination with psychology and pathology and death.

Taurus cares for the fruits—what we gather around us for both pleasure and sustainability. Absolute commitment to cherishing life. The willingness to put in the work to care for what you have.

Scorpio helps the Taurus in you see behind face value. Where Taurus might take things literally, Scorpio encourages you to have a sense of humor, to clock what's false or dumb and make fun of it, to laugh at the taboo thing everyone's too afraid to say. Scorpio helps Taurus vibe the nuances of the references in a film and pick up on the inner subtleties in someone's behavior.

Scorpio also teaches Taurus that pain can be its own pleasure. You please your whole axis when you enjoy an experience not only for its pleasurable design but for its bravery to also be naughty and darkly funny.

At the heart of it, Scorpio helps Taurus soften into trust that death is an artist. Scorpio knows that destruction is an integral part of creativity. Relationships, projects, and ways of being must die off in exchange for wild aliveness. There's a part of Taurus that deeply fears change. Change feels like death to the Taurus in us, but *that's the whole point*, says Scorpio. Scorpio helps Taurus summon the audacity to bravely prune and compost that which, deep down, we know has grown cold for us.

· ·

RULING PLANET

Venus

♀

The planet that rules Taurus is Venus. Venus represents your capacity to attract, magnetize, and receive what you want and desire. In its Taurus guise, Venus is the Earth Goddess: the swelling, birthing, releasing, repairing, and resting of the planet's seasonal cycles.

Since Venus is between our planet and the Sun, the archetype operates as a key filter for your human experience of purpose, power, and radiance. The glyph for Venus depicts the circle of spirit above the cross of matter, reflecting Venus's great purpose for you: to help you discover yourself through embodied, sensual, material experience.

I believe the most important gift that Venus can give us right now is to help us return to the body, the pulse of the earth, and the sensory experience of being in and part of nature. As we slowly and consciously soften in practice with this return, we gently move out of the fear-brain and drop into deeper listening. Like the petals of a velvety flower unfurling, we open into the limitless layers of the heart. And the more we move from the heart, the more authentically we express our desire nature. Only then can Venus help us heal ourselves and others.

I was a few years into my astrology practice before I realized that I had a conditioned bias that Venus didn't matter as much as the other planets. If you're programmed to believe, as our society pushes, that productivity and achievement have the highest value, then relationships, beauty, and desire feel trivial. Venus felt like an enrichment class when I wanted to focus on my core subjects. I have had some profound realizations and awakenings with Venus since then, namely in healing my scarcity and abandonment wounds. And as I have been learning to trust in the inherent abundance of Nature, so I have come to know that everything is relational, that all systems are alive, that all meaning comes from that which we recognize as beautiful. Venus is absolutely central.

It's important to reclaim Venus's ferocity and fullness from patriarchal minimization. Venus is both provocative hair flips *and* ingrown hairs and stubble. Venus is both tilled fields *and* tangled overgrowth. Venus is that shiny new toy *and* an old lovey worn down to the nub. Venus is what we value.

Many of us walk around not realizing how deeply we grieve our conditioned separation from the fullness of Venus. A full relationship with Venus includes awakening to the anger under any numbing from the separation. When you submit to "how things are," you dissociate from your body in order to survive under the conditions. Being enraged at the sterilization and standardization of what is considered beautiful is a bridge to truly grieving.

This grief is holy. May your sacred rage and grief plow fertile ground for creativity and joy. May our shared refusal to participate in minimized Venus till soil for friendship and reciprocity.

SKILLFUL TAURUS
Resonate

Taurus wants you to know: the most loving thing you can do is to resource your wisdom from your body. Your body remembers way more than your mind does. Your body already knows your answers.

It's from this understanding that I created a new adage: *If it's not resonant, it's not fucking resonant.* We know something resonates because we feel it in the body. Sometimes we bend to make something resonate because the mind thinks it should be. But you can't make something resonate with your mind if it's not resonant in the body.

So, if it's not resonant, it's not fucking resonant. It either resonates or it doesn't—there's no in between. If it's not resonant, it's not for you.

It's a Taurean labyrinth to try to figure out all the reasons why your younger self learned to shut off wisdom from the body. But "why" is not an alchemical question, I like to say. The logical brain thinks that knowing our reasons for resonating or not resonating with something will help us come to a decision. But this is just our conditioning, which taught us to devalue our feelings. If you want alchemy—the exhilarating feeling of growth and aliveness through aligned change—then spending time wondering "why" you're unhappy, frustrated, or not feeling it with someone will not help much.

Resourcing the body's wisdom begins with the choice to stop and listen. Ask yourself, *Does this resonate? Does this feel true?* And tune in. The more you practice asking and tuning in, the more the parts of you that shut down this communication system will begin to loosen up. When your Skillful Taurus is listening, you will begin to receive information more directly.

As trauma educator Dr. Bessel van der Kolk teaches, "The body keeps the score." The body very intelligently helps us cope with overwhelming and terrifying events and experiences. Most people I work with don't realize until they get into the self-healing process that they have experienced some level of trauma. Self-healing involves a brave recognition of patterns of numbing and disassociating from the body (including one's bodily intuition!). We learned to disconnect from the body to protect ourselves from hard memories, invalidations, horrific incidents, a persistent sense of being unseen, and so on.

By returning to the body's information, we increase our capacity to feel not only our pain but also pleasure, joy, and love. In the process, we learn to trust that our bodies will tell us very quickly when something is resonant or not. And self-trust may be the single most important thing we can give ourselves.

Skillful Taurus is committed to being here in a body and remembering how to listen to what resonates with it. If you are at the beginning of your journey of learning how to reconnect to the body's information about resonance, I recommend beginning with the podcast Holistic Life Navigation

> ## Self-trust may be the single most important thing we can give ourselves.

from Luis Mojica, one of my mentors. I also highly recommend the work of Resmaa Menakem, Jonathan Koe, Natasha Levinger, and Leah Garza.

PRACTICE
Throat Work

In medical astrology, Taurus relates to the throat and vocal cords. When you speak your most authentic truth, you speak from the place inside where you connect to the weight of your presence. You express yourself in ways that honor your body, resources, and values. Speaking from this place requires Taurean self-care and grounding so that you know what it feels like to be securely in your own energy.

As the conduit to transport life-giving air to your lungs and rest of your system, the throat is a vulnerable part of the body, subject to violent silencing and death through strangling or hanging.

If you feel like you don't know what you want, if you feel like it's hard to name and claim your desires or values, if you have a Yes or No inside but don't know how to speak it, your throat is blocked.

Clearing and healing the power center at the throat can be a life-changing practice to reclaim your voice. Energetically, most of us have at least some blocks in this part of our body, often related to experiences of invalidation, intimidation, gaslighting, and other harmful forms of silencing. The throat is a portal into and out of our body (just as the genitals are, which are the part of the body that correspond to Taurus's polar sign Scorpio). Whenever rage, shame, self-judgment, or fear hide truth inside the body, there's stress on the throat portal. The throat longs to be a vessel for the release of your embodied presence through honest words and sounds.

From my view, what we most long for in the throat space is a sense of full sovereignty. The sovereign is the supreme chief and lord. The sovereign is the ultimate authority. There's no question about who's in charge: it's the sovereign. But so many of us do not feel sovereign in the throat. We hold back. We question ourselves. We doubt. We worry we'll say the wrong thing. The most insidious form of control is the kind that has us question our right to speak from our truth place.

Throughout Taurus season, try to pay conscious attention to your throat, vocal cords, and the quality of your voice.

I invite you to try one or more of these practices:

- Savor a cup of hot tea first thing in the morning and before bed. As you feel the warmth of the liquid move through your throat, ask it to support you in clearing out anyone else's voice but your own.
- Try a chanting or humming practice for one minute before you go into every phone call, meeting, or recording space. Hum for the deeper parts of yourself and then try to speak in a voice that comes from that depth space.
- Turn up the volume and sing in the car. Consciously notice the experience of your vocal cords expanding and contracting in a dance with the spirit of the music.
- Once a day, put a hand on your heart and another on your belly and ask yourself: *What do I need right now?* Ask this out loud so you can hear yourself. Then answer out loud.

Check in lovingly with yourself to find if you're speaking from a place of sovereignty, and notice if the command of your voice changes depending on who you're talking to. If you feel you need support, working with an energy healer to open up your throat can be a powerful way to begin your reclamation.

TAROT CARD
The Hierophant

The card in the tarot that we associate with Taurus is card five, the Hierophant.

Traditionally, the Hierophant is associated with religious or other institutional leaders, speakers, and teachers who teach from a position of expertise, training, certification, and other forms of culturally determined positions of authority. In the *Smith-Rider-Waite* deck, we see this Pope-like speaker standing before two figures whose backs are to us. From their frozen positions, we presume they are intently listening.

Hierophant is a funny name, and it doesn't appear to be visually related to themes we think about with Taurus. A way into making connection is to break down the word. *Hierophant, hieroglyphics,* and *hierarch* all share the common root *hieros,* a Greek word meaning "sacred." Joined to a derivative of *phainein,* which means "to show," the Hierophant shows and speaks what is sacred.

The original hierophants were priests of the ancient Greek city of Eleusis who performed sacred rites. They oversaw the rituals for understanding the mysteries of life, death, and rebirth, one of the primary themes of the Taurus-Scorpio axis.

The Hierophant in you speaks your wisdom, which is a journey because it's a dogma-removal process. To speak from a Hierophant place is to clarify what you believe because of prior conditioning versus what you believe from your sacred knowing. The Hierophant asks you for humility and to release hierarchies of authority. It asks: *What do you believe from your lived and embodied experience as a human being?*

The Hierophant prompts the questions: *What is the lineage of this idea, belief, stance, or opinion? How did these words come to live in me? Do they still resonate with who I am today? How can I say what I've learned in language that could come from no one but me?*

The Hierophant connects with Taurus in two important ways. First, Taurus relates to your values and the part of you that is most securely rooted. The Hierophant reflects and celebrates the Taurus in you that is loyal to your unique presence.

As discussed in the practice section (page 102), Taurus rules the throat and vocal cords. When you speak from your most authentic truth, you make choices and create influence in ways that honor your body, your resources, and your values.

The Hierophant explores the questions: *What if life, death, and rebirth are only possible when we act from the roots of our inner truth? What if releasing all programming that blocks truth is the path to sacred aliveness?*

A Tarot Spread with the Hierophant

See the chapter *How to Navigate This Book* if you're new to the tarot and seek support for pulling cards and interpreting them.

Take the Hierophant out of your deck. (If you have more than one deck, you can pull the card from another deck so that the Hierophant has a chance to "participate" in the deck from which you will draw.)

Feel into the visual inspiration of the card.

Take a few deep breaths on purpose and arrive to the reading. Connect into your intuition. Ask Hierophant-Taurus energy to help you with this reading. Shuffle according to your unique, never-wrong style. Center and focus your question thus:

With the most expansive levels of compassion for me and all sentient beings, what is the loving invitation to connect with the Hierophant?

Pull six cards according to your own unique process of knowing with the following prompts, and then sit with the cards and journal about them.

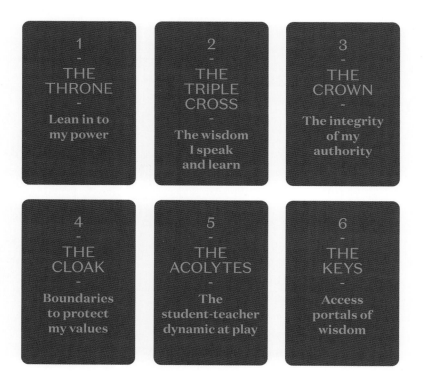

1
-
THE
THRONE
-
Lean in to
my power

2
-
THE
TRIPLE
CROSS
-
The wisdom
I speak
and learn

3
-
THE
CROWN
-
The integrity
of my
authority

4
-
THE
CLOAK
-
Boundaries
to protect
my values

5
-
THE
ACOLYTES
-
The
student-teacher
dynamic at play

6
-
THE
KEYS
-
Access
portals of
wisdom

RITUAL FOR THE NEW MOON

Open to Nourishment

You know the smell in the air when it rains, especially after a dry season? I love this smell. It's called *petrichor*, from the Greek *petra*, meaning "stone," and *īchōr*, the fluid that flows in the veins of the gods in Greek mythology.

This distinctive smell is created by oils that plants secrete during dry spells, which are absorbed by soils and clay-based rocks then released into the air with rain. The earth senses that the rain is coming and opens to receive the nourishing rain even before it rains—and then more intensely after the rain. As the water evaporates, the oils move through the air to our nostrils. One of the compounds that we're inhaling is called *geosmin*, meaning "earth-smell." Humans are apparently super sensitive to geosmin, which scientists believe is likely because our ancestors relied on the ability to sense rain coming in order to survive.

Can you pause to consider how beautiful that all is? I love to study how biological and physical processes reflect psychological and metaphysical ones. By analogy, consider how you prepare yourself to accept nourishment from the world. And contemplate how sometimes the gentlest gesture of kindness is more receivable than a deluge, especially if you have known any disappointment, cruelty, or betrayal in life and find it hard to trust in too much goodness at once.

The following ritual is designed to help you set an intention at the New Moon in Taurus but is appropriate for working with Taurus any time of the year.

Before beginning this ritual, gather:

- Candles, as many as you want, and a way to light them
- Your journal and pen

- A fresh bouquet of spring flowers
- A small plate of treats to enjoy: your favorite cheese, a glass of milk from a goat or cow, honey, fresh fruit, almonds, chocolate—or all of it!

The Ritual

1. Sit at your Taurus altar when ready. Set up your ritual container, light your candle(s), and come to a grounded, meditative state (see page 57).

2. Remember petrichor and how the earth opens up to receive the nourishment of rainwater.

3. Now ask yourself, taking time with each question so that you can hear the deep insight:
   - *In what ways do I open to receive nourishment from other people?*
   - *In what ways do I open to receive nourishment from my environment?*
   - *In what ways do I open to receive nourishment in exchange for my work?*
   - *In what ways do I open to receive nourishment from myself?*

4. Ask yourself:
   - *In what ways do I set limits on the amount of nourishment I am willing to receive from other people?*
   - *In what ways do I set limits on the amount of nourishment I am willing to receive from my environment?*
   - *In what ways do I set limits on the amount of nourishment I am willing to receive in exchange for my work?*
   - *In what ways do I set limits on the amount of nourishment I am willing to receive from myself?*

5. Ask yourself:
   - *Would I like to receive more nourishment from other people?*
   - *Would I like to receive more nourishment from my environment?*
   - *Would I like to receive more nourishment in exchange for my work?*
   - *Would I like to receive more nourishment from myself?*

6. Now center your heart and mind to what you would like, with no limits on the possibilities for growth here. Imagine all the ways you'd like to feel more nurtured by others, your environment, your work, and self-care, and let your answers magnify in your mind's eye. Let them burst like ripening fruit. Let them bloom like wildflowers.

7. Name your desires. Claim them. Write them down in your journal or on a piece of paper to save somewhere.

8. Sit as long as you like with whatever comes up with the ritual. When it feels right, give yourself spaciousness to enjoy the treat you gathered before the ritual. As you enjoy the yumminess, really feel your tongue receiving what you are giving yourself. Say to yourself: *I want nourishment. I receive nourishment. I enjoy nourishment.*

9. Conclude and open the ritual container (see page 66).

Across Taurus season, make a daily practice of giving yourself a treat and repeating the phrase: *I want nourishment. I receive nourishment. I enjoy nourishment.*

Happy New Moon in Taurus!

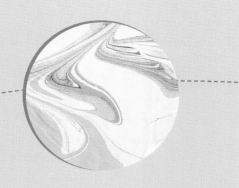

Gemini

MAY 20–JUNE 20

⊟ GEMINI

△ AIR

☽ MUTABLE

☿ MERCURY

Questions to Live Into

How can I approach everything I am learning with the curiosity and excitement of a child?

How would I speak to myself today if I trust that the words I use are spells that determine my experience of reality?

What would change in my life if I gave myself permission to be the multitudes of all that I am?

Altar

As discussed in part one, the purpose of creating an altar is to first prepare and then enjoy having a special space devoted to the themes and principles you're developing with each sign. The general qualities of Gemini are listed below. I recommend you gather at least three items, but quantity isn't as crucial as choosing items of resonance for you. For example, this season, maybe you prefer to build an altar based on the Gemini symbol, the Twins. Your entire altar space could be full of items that come in pairs or have mirroring resemblances. Take the suggestions that feel aligned and don't worry about the rest. As you read through the chapter, more ideas may come to you for your altar that aren't listed here.

Go for it!

COLORS
blue, brown, green, orange, pink, silver, turquoise, violet

CRYSTALS
diamond, emerald, peacock ore, ruby, sapphire, turquoise

GARDEN
fenugreek, lavender, lily, lily of the valley, linden tree

SPICES AND FLAVORS
anise, clove, marjoram, and mixtures of salty, sweet, spicy, and sour

GODS AND GODDESSES
Artemis, Hermes, Inanna, Mercury, Odin, Thoth

TAROT CARDS
the Magician, the Lovers, 8 of Swords, 9 of Swords, 10 of Swords

ITEMS
art, books, ceramics, fabrics, food, incense, magazine cutouts, photographs, quotes on paper, or anything else that inspires you

RELATED THEMES
adaptability, the androgyne, bees buzzing, butterflies, Castor and Pollux, cleverness, communication, creativity, data, facts, games, ideas, intelligence, the language of birds, magic, multitasking, nonbinary thinking, pollinating winds, relationships, TikTok, twins, words

SEASON

End of Spring

From the perspective of the northern hemisphere, each sign reflects the essential beauty and dignity of the time of year it represents. Gemini is about extending the possibilities of what Aries initiated and Taurus consolidated. In this way, Gemini both integrates all that spring was and looks ahead to make way for the potential of the coming summer.

Gemini is the energy of pollinating winds and buzzing insects that disperse life from trees and flowers, cultivating diversity in the ecosystem. The days stretch out before the summer solstice and the temperatures warm the land. The world becomes increasingly noisy and active. The dips and turns of a butterfly and the breeze-borne seeds of a dandelion reflect the nonlinearity of the Gemini approach to life. It's a style that is unpredictable but proliferating with life!

There's an excitement to the zig and the zag that isn't right or wrong but simply what happens when we're in a period of mad growth. Gemini can feel "all over the place" to those who want straight lines and known destinations.

To embrace the Gemini in yourself must involve allowing yourself to be nonlinear. Linearity is predictable to Gemini, which feels boring and uninteresting. Our culture has taught you to ask yourself, *Where am I going with this? What is my point?*

Gemini is a part of you that needs the freedom to not know the point or destination. Gemini wants to embrace the fun of exploring options. Gemini wants you to choose your own adventure forever.

For some, the invitation to un-shame nonlinearity might feel incredibly liberating. For others, it might be a challenge. I get this. I am naturally someone who thinks in a clear outline format. What I have found is that allowing myself to embody Gemini has softened some of my mental and conversational rigidities. Let other parts of you worry about the objective. Today, listen to your Gemini. If you've created an identity around being linear and to the point, then who would you be if you practiced not knowing where you're going?

. . . .

MODALITY AND ELEMENT
Mutable Air

Like the other mutable signs (Virgo, Sagittarius, and Pisces), Gemini closes the season and helps you integrate everything you've been learning in spring during Aries and Taurus. It's adaptable and helps you process.

Like the other Air signs (Libra and Aquarius), Gemini is the part of us that communicates, relates, and makes meaning. Gemini is your mental realm—the words, ideas, and choices that excite and describe how you think and learn.

Mutable Air is Air that moves things around. In nature, this looks like dandelion seeds carried by the wind. In the human world, Gemini are the pollinators: the silver-tongued podcaster who asks engaging questions of their guests and spreads good conversation over the airwaves, and the astrologer who synthesizes their many modalities and interests in the work they share. My mutable Air comes through in this book as I share ideas about astrology woven with concepts from psychology, mythology, art history, energy healing, tarot, and anything else I find interesting.

Mutable Air encourages you to notice the impulse to make a connection between one thing and another, and then follow that connection with glee, even if you don't know where it's going. Gemini loves to talk, so I encourage you to share your interests with someone else or in your social media feed. It's fun to give ideas to others and see what happens.

Your Gemini goes where the Air takes you. It's you resonating with the world around you—whether excited by a new book on your bedside table, following an account your teacher thought you'd like, or sharing hilarious inside jokes with friends that make you snort out your nose. What you find mentally stimulating is unique to *you*.

Mutable Air is another way of working out preferences. And the mutability of this energy is inherently free to move on when you're no longer interested. Some subjects might be fun to explore for just a season. Others will fascinate you for life. And even within the fields of learning you deeply love, the specific topics you'll want to explore will shift and turn and even fall away over time.

Friendships are also mutable Air. Some friends you want to talk to forever. Some friends are special to you while you have a specific shared interest. Gemini says that all friendships are beautiful. Letting friendships be mutable is not being disloyal or fickle to them but rather true to the spirit of the impulse that connected you. If the friendship is meant to last, then you can trust you'll be reconnected when the winds of shared interest bring you back together.

The Gemini in you has a high tolerance threshold for mutability. It's quite powerful to un-shame this if you've been judged for your Gemini. Let Gemini do what Gemini does best: follow where it goes with an open and curious mind.

. . . .

SYMBOL
The Twins

The constellation Gemini appears as two figures standing beside each other, their arms around each other's shoulders. It is tied to the Greek myth of Castor and Pollux, twin brothers born of the same egg from their mother, Leda, but with different fathers. Castor was the son of the king of Sparta, while Pollux was the son of the god Zeus. Thus, Castor was mortal, while Pollux was immortal. Though they appeared identical, their destinies were separate.

Castor and Pollux were each other's favorite person. They did everything together. That is, until Castor was fatally wounded. His death was excruciating for Pollux, and he was left with the feeling of being incomplete, fractured, and lost. Pollux turned to Zeus. On his knees, he begged to go to the Underworld to rejoin his brother. Ultimately, a compromise was made, and the two were able to live together forever as the constellation Gemini.

Within this myth, we learn much about the nature of Gemini. The Gemini story in you is often infused with a quest to find a lost self in order to recover wholeness.

Gemini is the sign that first feels what it means to be separate, to be an individual. In childhood, we negotiate this with our siblings, close cousins, or friends. Anyone who has a sibling knows that there's a wide spectrum of felt experience in this relationship, including rivalry, resentment, enmeshment, and confusion about lines of separation. It's hard to know the self without considering one's relationship to the sibling. And the entanglement is then mirrored in other friendships as they develop.

Though we eventually find some kind of differentiation and individual self, the Gemini in us carries a longing to find "the other" in adulthood. The other might be another person or a group of people, but it can also be the next big idea. This is a playful longing, the excitement and trepidation of hide and seek. Sure, there are some stakes, but it is also a game, and the joy is in playing it.

Whatever it is that calls to you as just the thing you need for completion in the moment, that is your Gemini twin. The chase begins, again and again. *Maybe this time I will feel whole.* There's a poignancy and a melancholy in this framing of the Gemini self that I find incredibly beautiful because it feels true. Becoming aware of this helps explain the uncon-scious restlessness and the anxiety of the quest. What if we're never alone because we're always in partnership with Spirit (or the universe or what-ever we want to call the energetic web of connection between all things)? What if we're always whole? What if the feeling of being incomplete is just the space between now and the next moment?

That longing is at the essence of the Gemini path. This month, how can you play hide and seek? How can you trust the fun is always in the process? We are forever young as long as we enjoy the game.

. . . .

POLARITY

The Gemini-Sagittarius Axis

All Air signs are opposite Fire signs, and all polar signs have the same modality. So mutable Air is opposite mutable Fire: Sagittarius.

Sagittarius helps us access the light and warmth of hope in the long night before the winter solstice. In the dark of late autumn, we look to the cosmos for aspiration. We long to see our struggles reframed as constellations—stories with meaning. We tell tall tales around the fire, eyes sparkling with mulled wine. Sagittarius is a broad laugh. Sagittarius has another helping of what sounds fun. Sagittarius twinkles like stars. Sag is your inner Santa Claus.

The Gemini-Sagittarius polarity tells a story about the spectrum between thinking and believing:

- Gemini communicates, learns, and thinks with the mind; Sagittarius does the same with the animating spirit.

- Gemini can get caught up in the mental realm, darting sometimes anxiously between thoughts; Sagittarius tends to trust that everything will be okay. Sag tells Gemini not to worry so much.
- Gemini is neck-deep in every specific detail; Sagittarius takes the bird's-eye view.

In the body, Gemini rules the hands. The hands are the body's Twins of Gemini. Gemini relates to what you can grab with your hands—that which is close, nearby, and around your space. There is so much you do with your hands. It's worth spending time this Gemini season to notice what you do with them. "I don't know what to do with my hands," we say when we feel highly stimulated, restless, or nervous—all related to Gemini energy.

In contrast, Sag rules the legs, especially the thighs. Sag learns from the feeling of broad movement and the experience of traveling distance. We don't grasp details with our feet. We don't write from our toes.

The polarity of these signs speaks to different forms of learning. In research, you first channel Gemini. Maybe you cover a wall with sticky notes. Bits of data and quotes from different sources, all nonhierarchical with no overarching narrative. Sag, on the other hand, is more inspired by the big picture than the detailed evidence. Eventually you start to see a pattern. Sag is the part of you that takes the data points and creates a narrative in order to come to a thesis.

Sag helps Gemini find a larger philosophy to protect you from a nihilistic perspective that everything is ultimately meaningless and noncoherent.

. . . .

RULING PLANET
Mercury

I like to think of Gemini as one of two costumes that the planet Mercury offers us to wear (the other being Virgo). To live in your Gemini costume fully, you need to better understand its ruler. Mercury is the planet of the mind, communication, word-making, idea exchange, and creative intelligence.

I shared in part one that the word *planet* comes from the Greek term for "wanderer." Planets wander the sky in contrast to the fixed stars. Mercury is the closest planet to the Sun, and as it whirls around in its orbit, Mercury appears to us as the fastest-moving planet. Sometimes we see Mercury before the Sun rises. Sometimes we see it after the Sun sets. And sometimes we don't see Mercury at all. The god Mercury is known to be fleet-footed; the one of winged sandals.

This quickness of Mercury is felt strongly in Gemini. In Mercury's other sign, Virgo, its response time is much slower and more deliberate, reflective of Virgo's earthiness. The Geminian Mercury is everywhere all at once, just like Air.

Mercury has a secret for you: The way you *interpret* your reality is central to the way you *experience* that reality. As the brilliantly mercurial ethnobotanist and mystic Terence McKenna wrote in his book *True Hallucinations: Being an Account of the Author's Extraordinary Adventures in the Devil's Paradise*, "The syntactical nature of reality, the real secret of magic, is that the world is made of words. And if you know the words that the world is made of, you can make of it whatever you wish."

Your words are spells. You spell with your words.

To become a magician with your reality (and Mercury is even represented by the Magician card in tarot), you begin by getting third-party positioning with the way your mind automatically operates. What are the old grooves? You can send your Mercury outside your patterned thought processes to get a look. Mercury moves between realms and passes information. Mercury likes these kinds of assignments. It's really good at noticing where you're stuck.

According to Roman myth, Mercury once used his wand to resolve a conflict between two warring snakes. The conflict seemed destined to end with one or the other snake's death, but Mercury stepped in to offer a third option: resolution. That's why the caduceus he carries has two snakes winding around it.

As in the story, you can work with your Mercury self magically by trusting always in a third way. So often we get stuck in a binary. We think the crossroads only has two options. But Mercury breaks binaries and destabilizes stagnation. A third way is more thrilling than a compromise; it is a possibility that didn't exist before you called it in. This is the imaginative capacity we need to build a new world with more enlivened timelines.

To play with Mercury is to look for doorways to opportunity. The word *portal* is from the Latin *porta* meaning "passage through." To be portal-seeking, you stay as nimble and flexible as an octopus to slip through any hole in the net or chink in the chain. And in this way, working with Mercury helps you grow trust that you can slither through or around whatever life puts in your way.

. . . .

SKILLFUL GEMINI
Quest

Gemini wants you to know: the most loving thing you can do is to embrace the erotic impulse. It's okay to be relentlessly curious. It's okay to flirt with whatever you're into.

The erotic is not the same as the sexual, though that is one facet of it, of course. The erotic really relates to a sense of wild aliveness. And that aliveness comes from engaging with the spirit of anything or anyone around you. With that definition, every sign is erotic in its own way.

As psychotherapist Esther Perel teaches, "Eroticism thrives in the space between the self and the other." Gemini's version of this is a mental charge in the space between you and whatever you're attracted to. The other can be another human, but it can also be a tree, painting, book, or cup of coffee. From an animist perspective, everything is alive, and we can engage in erotic aliveness with anything we want to. The other is whatever and whomever you're into in a given moment.

Why we aren't all skillfully Gemini has a lot to do with the fear of feeling and looking silly in the early stages of gaining fluency in something. Gemini has a lot to do with language. And it can be frustrating to learn another language (like astrology!) if you judge yourself for being a beginner. Gemini shows up with the frequency of the beginner's mind, always turned toward the wonder of the process, available to the truth that we can't ever know everything and expertise is only a construct.

The fear of looking dumb or clumsy or confused might also keep you from getting to know someone you're curious about. Or from visiting a place you've never been. Or from changing career fields midway through your adult life. Or from asking questions.

You can also block your Geminian impulses if you feel like you're not allowed to change your mind or go another route. Maybe you were taught that it's untrustworthy or unreliable to redirect. This is only true if you believe that you're not allowed to evolve. But living astrology means trusting what the sky and the earth constantly teach us: that cyclical change is the only true thing there is.

Permitting change means allowing yourself to let go of the effort to maintain how others experience you. Without skillful Gemini, your desire for consistency risks an entrenchment that might ultimately feel stifling and irritating. This is why Taurus flows into Gemini. Mutable Air helps open the flow.

As we discussed with the Twins, the quest for the thing matters as much as the thing itself. Skillful Gemini is about staying nimble and fleet-footed as you follow the impulse of your curiosity and stimulation, while also moving with your inner voice. Sometimes Gemini can feel scattered too wide, overwhelmed from saying Yes to so many fun options. Trusting your inner resonance helps you know when something's truly for you.

. . . .

PRACTICE

Mindful Distraction

Gemini is known for its distractibility. Like an octopus's arms moving independently around it, Gemini's mutable attention disperses across many areas of life. This month, I invite you to try out a mindful distraction practice.

Our capitalistic culture encourages distraction and also shames us for it, telling us that we're supposed to be grown-ups. We're supposed to be above being enticed by the bounty of endlessly fascinating information and content paraded in front of us every split second. We're told we're supposed to work on this problem—but only on the distraction side of the equation.

What if we allowed ourselves to consider that the more important work may in fact be on the shame side of the equation? What if we permitted ourselves time to indulge in guilt-free distraction regularly? This kind of practice could be considered learning, engaging with the world, curiosity, and even self-care.

A lot of our distraction shame comes from the education system. This gets further policed in the workplace. Looking back, we may wonder: Was it really such a bad thing that I liked to look out the window during social studies? Was it so wrong for me to joke with my friend during lab? Was there really such a problem with my desire to take a break from emails and move my body once an hour? The result of distraction shaming is nothing less than a mind at war with itself.

I submit that distraction is magical. The most wondrous connections flow in when I just let myself follow the urge to go with my mutable Air. And the more I shamelessly get distracted, the more I find what I needed, whether it's just the word I was seeking for my writing project or a resource that ends up influencing me in profound ways. When you approach your mind's wanderings with trust in the wonder of synchronicity, then it is synchronicity that you find. Trusting this, you honor your innate mutability.

The *practice* of distraction looks like *consciousness* of distraction. It's mindfully getting distracted. Whether this means investigating a Reddit thread, indulging in social media, or any other form that catches your attention, the point this month is to notice when, how, and why you are distracting yourself.

Bring self-compassion to the fact that reaching for your phone is often a trauma response. We reach for it because something about the present moment is uncomfortable, and we look to the phone to distract us from just being in our bodies. From a shaming perspective, the grown-up thing is to heal yourself out of this impulse. From a data collection perspective, the practice is simply to ask: *What is coming up for me right now as I reach for my phone?* Notice the answer. And then go ahead and check out that text or Google that question.

I suggest setting timers as part of your mindful distraction practice, something I do so I don't get lost inside my indulgences and forget about my to-dos. Set one as a check-in to see how you're doing. Give yourself a chance to notice if you're still pleased with your distraction impulse. If no, is there something else you need right now? If yes, then set a second timer. Until the timer goes off, fully and completely submit to shame-free curiosity.

Trust that your distraction is important. Trust in the inevitability of the delights and insights finding their way to you as you drop down the rabbit hole.

. . . .

TAROT CARD

The Lovers

The card in the tarot that we associate with Gemini is card six, the Lovers.

In the traditional *Smith-Rider-Waite* depiction, we see a man and a woman, and an angel overseeing both. I see the figures on this card as the Self, the Not-Self, and the Cosmic-Self. This can mean a lot of things:

- The Self: The person I think I am, including all of my limiting beliefs, internalized biases, long-running narratives, perceptions of failure, and unprocessed shadow work.
- The Not-Self: The thing, person, identity, or lifestyle that I think I need to feel complete, better, whole, or more aspirational.
- The Cosmic-Self: Who I am at a spirit level, at the level of universal love and cosmic consciousness.

Just as Gemini medicine is about learning that the quest for the thing *is* the thing we're wanting, so the Lovers card teaches us to recognize that everything we call "Not-Self" that we love, feel attracted to, and want so badly to complete us, is actually already in us. The reason we are attracted to people, things, places, and ideals is because they resonate with something we always have within.

The three figures on this card form a triangle, a very dynamic and strong shape. Much like the "third way" discussed on page 119 about Gemini's ruling planet, Mercury, the triangle is a magical form to invoke because it breaks the binary of two. Whenever our Self feels a lack of something, we're in a binary with the Not-Self. A third option gives us the possibility to see a portal of opportunity for the imagination. Through the dynamism of the triangle, the Lovers card returns us home to ourselves. We hold all of the love we need already.

1
-
THE
SUPER-
SELF

VI

THE LOVERS.

2
-
THE SELF

3
-
THE NOT-
SELF

The Lovers is a card the speaks to your capacity to vibe with what's in affinity with you, to attract what's interesting to you, to be stimulated by anything or anyone, to be curious about engaging and learning with the world, to notice what you're into, to flirt, and to engage with the erotic impulse everywhere.

A Tarot Spread with the Lovers

See the chapter *How to Navigate This Book* if you're new to the tarot and seek support for pulling cards and interpreting them.

Take the Lovers out of your deck. (If you have more than one deck, you can pull the card from another deck so that the Lovers has a chance to "participate" in the deck from which you will draw.)

Feel into the visual inspiration of the card.

Take a few deep breaths on purpose and arrive to the reading. Connect into your intuition. Ask Lovers-Gemini energy to help you with this reading. Shuffle according to your unique, never-wrong style. Center and focus your question thus:

With the most expansive levels of compassion for me and all sentient beings, what is the loving invitation to connect with the Lovers?

Pull three cards according to your own unique process of knowing with the following prompts, and then sit with the cards and journal about them.

. . . .

RITUAL FOR THE NEW MOON

Court the Wild Twin

In his book *Courting the Wild Twin*, mythologist Martin Shaw taps at the essence of the archetypal truth in all myths and stories about a lost and forgotten wild twin. He prompts us to remember the old tale, shared across many cultures, of "the other child" who was chucked out the window or into the forest at the moment of birth. This twin is the part of ourselves that we banish because we're too gnarly, undomesticated, twisted, or otherwise perceived as unlovable.

Shaw encourages us to invite our wild twin back home: "I'm not sure we ever really, properly, catch up with our wild twin, buy matching sweaters. The pursuit is the thing, the glimpse is the thing, the jolt of their quixotic nature may be barometer enough for one lifetime. But never to search? Well, that's missing out on life altogether."

What is especially exciting about Shaw's framing of the lost twin paradigm is his emphasis on the idea that—until you become conscious of them—your twin is looking for *you*, not the other way around. As Shaw describes it, "It wanders the woods and the prairies and the cities, lonely in its whole body for you."

In this way, all that stimulates us, all that we quest for, all that we seek with our Gemini self—consciously but also unconsciously—are searching for us, too, just as tirelessly. For the New Moon in Gemini, I invite you to "court your wild twin" back to you. As you practice this and get comfortable feeling your wild twin's energy, you can begin to practice doing small and large things as them, from cooking dinner to ordering coffee to sending an email. Before long, you will absorb and integrate a lot of your wild twin as your actual self—and feel zestier for it! May you conspire together for the days, months, and years to come!

Before beginning this ritual, gather:

- Candles, as many as you want, and a way to light them
- Your journal and pen

The Ritual

1. Sit at your Gemini altar when you're ready. Set up your ritual container, light your candle, and come to a grounded, meditative state (see page 57).

2. Ask yourself, *Who do I think I'm not allowed to be in front of other people?* Write down everything that comes up. You can list adjectives. You can list behaviors. You can list professions.

Name the various ways of being that felt and continue to feel off limits to you.

Examples include: "I'm not allowed to be selfish." "I'm not allowed to openly talk about how I'm into past life regression therapy." "I'm not allowed to want to make boatloads of money." "I'm not allowed to say 'no.'" "I'm not allowed to dress like that." "I'm not allowed to say I'm bisexual." "I'm not allowed to be basic." "I'm not allowed to be someone who posts selfies."

3. Once you feel you have ample material to work with, begin to develop a character for yourself—an alter ego who has granted themselves full permission to gleefully do what you think you can't get away with. See them in your mind's eye. Be playfully Gemini and have fun with this. Give your alter ego a name. Give them a wardrobe, a job, a lifestyle of preferences, a public presence. This is your Wild Twin. Write down everything that comes up so you have a record.

4. Now return back to a more meditative state. Ask yourself to see your Wild Twin on an invisible movie screen outside your aura. Once you have a sense them so strong they could almost be literally in front of you, invite the frequency of your Wild Twin's energy to float from that screen to the top of your head and down into your body all the way to your toes and fingers. Feel them in your body. Say hello to your Wild Twin in your body. How do you feel? What comes up for you?

5. Ask your Wild Twin to help you set a few intentions for working with them across the coming lunar cycle. Perhaps some ideas may feel like a stretch for you but are no problem at all for your Wild Twin. Write these down.

6. When you feel complete, thank yourself and the Moon for this time, and open the ritual container (see page 66).

Happy New Moon in Gemini!

⊙⊙ CANCER

▽ WATER

△ CARDINAL

☽ MOON

Cancer

JUNE 20-JULY 22

Cancer

Questions to Live Into

What needs are present for me to notice today so that I can be the one who always has my back?

What boundaries do I want to set so that tending to what I love becomes my most important work?

What forms of nurturance feel most in affinity with my innate capacity for care?

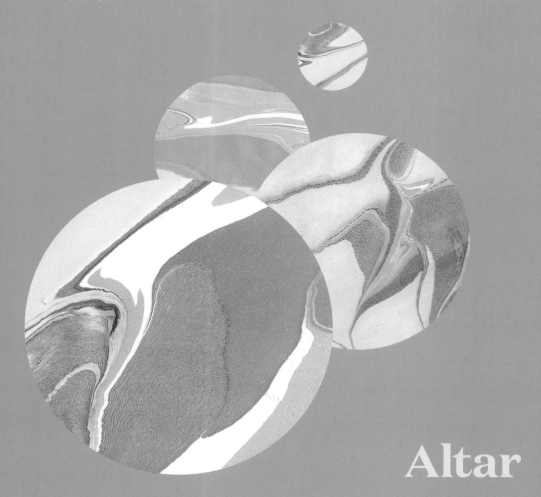

Altar

As discussed in part one, the purpose of creating an altar is to first prepare and then enjoy having a special space devoted to the themes and principles you're developing with each sign. The general qualities of Cancer are listed below. I recommend you gather at least three items, but quantity isn't as crucial as choosing items of resonance for you. For example, this season, maybe you prefer to build an altar to the Moon. You could place a photo of a Moon you've known, gather objects that reference one or several phases of the Moon's shape in the sky, or lay out iridescent objects that suggest moonlight. Take the suggestions that feel aligned and don't worry about the rest. As you read through the chapter, more ideas may come to you for your altar that aren't listed here.

Go for it!

COLORS
blues, purples, pearlescent shimmering surfaces, silver

CRYSTALS
pearl, moonstone, blue chalcedony, pink calcite, selenite, rhodonite

GARDEN
chamomile, gardenia, geranium, honeysuckle, jasmine, lemon balm, lotus, moonwort, mugwort, water lily

SPICES AND FLAVORS
ones that grow in the lands of your ancestral lineage

GODS AND GODDESSES
Artemis, Ceridwen, Demeter, Diana, Hecate, Isis, Persephone, Rhiannon, Selene, Yemaya

TAROT CARDS
the High Priestess, the Chariot, 2 of Cups, 3 of Cups, 4 of Cups

ITEMS
art, books, ceramics, fabrics, food, incense, magazine cutouts, photographs, quotes on paper, or anything else that inspires you

RELATED THEMES
amniotic fluid, belonging, breastfeeding, breasts, caves, chicken broth, coves, cozy nooks, crabs, family, home, your inner child, your inner mother, intuition, love, magic, the Moon, Mondays, nourishment, nurturing, psychic abilities, shells, soft blankets, the uterus, whirlpools, and objects of the sea such as driftwood, kelp (or a kelp rattle), sand, and shells

SEASON

Beginning of Summer

Cancer ushers us into summer season. We made it through spring's massive shift from winter's end.

The first day of Cancer season is the summer solstice, which brings us fully into the time of year for weddings, gatherings with the people we call family, sun-drenched holidays at the beach, making and cherishing memories, reaching out for hugs, and cooking for long outdoor dinners. Cancer is the part of you that absolutely lives for opportunities to gather with loved ones. Cancer wants to attune to that sense of belonging we get with tradition.

The summer solstice is a wildly exuberant threshold that marks the longest day and shortest night of the year. My maternal line is from Sweden, where the solstices are extreme. In the summer, that means there is sunlight around the clock. I have been lucky to travel to Sweden at Midsommar, their term for the summer solstice. What a surreal experience for the body to have the Sun never set.

Midsommar is a raucous few days of singing, hair-braiding,

flower-crown making, feasting, drinking, dancing, and merry-making in honor of survival, sunlight, community, love, and persistence. Participants celebrate what it means to hold onto each other. They know that the light cannot last and that the dark will take hold in the months ahead.

This is Cancer. It is what and who we belong to. It is the rituals of caretaking as well as caretaking through ritual.

Cancer is braiding your daughter's hair the same way your mom braided yours, and her mom braided hers.

Cancer is a recipe passed down from kitchen to kitchen, covered in marginal notes from different bakers, and stained with splatters of butter from a cake made decades ago.

Cancer is every time you sit next to your grandmother at the piano, watching the curves of the wrinkles in her fingers, knowing you belong to them somehow, and that one day your hands will look like hers.

Cancer is every large popcorn you ever ordered with your dad and the ones you order after his death, because that was part of your love language.

Cancer is any tradition you create with the family you make across your life, biological and otherwise. But because Cancer relates to the past and to our roots, it's also a part of us that holds tenderness and pain. We won't be bypassing this part of the sign's wisdom. What comes up for you as you reflect on this time of the year? What rituals or ceremonies feel important to notice and honor at this time?

MODALITY AND ELEMENT

Cardinal Water

Like Aries, Libra, and Capricorn, Cancer is a cardinal sign. It initiates a new season, which means there's forceful movement in its energy.

Like Scorpio and Pisces, Cancer is Water. It cares for the emotional realm. Water is the more primordial and mysterious aspects of your human experience, the deep wisdom of your ancestral lineage, the power of your intuition.

Cardinal Water in nature looks to me like a whirlpool. With centripetal direction, you reach out with your arms and then pull toward you what you want to care for, love, nurture, and give your attention. And as you only have two arms, you can't save or please everyone. You can't be all things. You can't do everything for those you love. The whirlpool analogy helps you visualize calling your energy back home to you, turning away from whatever isn't yours to carry.

In human form, cardinal Water is the parent deeply attuned to their child who scoops them up when they need encouragement. This is an art form. For some, cardinal Water from their parent felt like a deluge—too much attunement. For others, it was a drip. Not enough. Part of growing skill with your Cancer is wondering how your own cardinal Water expression is influenced by the experiences you had with your caregivers as a child.

Not everyone wants to give their cardinal Water to family, and that's fine. Cancer listens and gives its full emotional self to whatever it wants to: You can give Cancer to your service. You can give Cancer to your hobbies. You can give Cancer to your health.

> You can't be all things. You can't do everything for those you love.

Most of us were not taught how to notice our moods. And since we weren't taught, our emotional world can feel out of control. We can be shamed for being in a "bad mood," as if emotions have to be positive or locked deep inside. Sometimes the mood we feel might not be ours as we empathetically pick up on the moods of others.

What if your feelings are your superpower? Your cardinal Water is capable of sending energetic feelers into the world and can actually feel what other people are feeling or what they need—*in your own body.* You don't even have to be in sight of what you're picking up on to do this! We do this all the time, but most of the time we aren't aware it's happening.

As a culture, we are relearning how to engage the psychic system and the energy body in order to heal ourselves and our world. It can feel strange to be the one in your lineage who takes on this learning, and it can feel sad when family members don't want to learn how to care for themselves or others more skillfully. I decided it's not my job to wait for permission. I'm inviting you to do the same. In this way, cardinal Water encourages you to attune to what is going on in your emotional and energetic body. *Hello feelings! I see you. I'm listening.* Cancer asks your feeling realm what it wants you to know.

SYMBOL

The Crab

Traditionally, we associate Cancer with the Crab. Crabs are versatile, living in oceans, in fresh water, and on land. They are notable for their thick exoskeleton and pincers. The Crab works well as a symbol for Cancer because the Cancer in us wants to protect our sensitivities. These sensitivities are those of your inner children, the younger versions of you (even those from pre-memory and in utero) who are part of who you are today. Across your childhood and adolescence, your younger self had episodes, perhaps chronically, of feeling unseen, invalidated, or even unloved. Cancer is a healing revolution for you when you lean into its capacities to repair from any mis-attunement or severed belonging you experienced growing up.

The idea with the Crab then is that we developed an outer armor and defense system (the exoskeleton). We discovered what felt scary to that innocent child inside, and so we took on specific personalities or a sense of humor to deflect what might hurt us. Cancer is known to be defensive when triggered. This is when the competitiveness and fighting words (the pincers) come out. But what if the real point of the pincers isn't self-protection, but to show our inner children we have their back?

Crabs are also a species that molt. Molting is the process of sloughing off layers of skin in order to move into the next stage of life. We molt because the carapace has become too tight and we are ready to expand. This is a crucial aspect in the process of nurturing the wealth of emotional resilience for your Cancer. The female molts before she's ready to mate, and her softer shell makes her more accessible to the male. Molting makes deeper connection possible.

Molting happens when you intuit that you no longer need the defense systems you once developed. And in this way, you open your heart for more care to find you. In the psycho-spiritual healing world, we call this molting process *emotional reparenting*. You reparent, as in, you parent again. Reparenting presumes that your younger selves are always still with you.

In modern psychotherapy, there's a technique known as Internal Family Systems (IFS) that helps you to access and relate with the various "parts" that live within and guide your emotional responses and needs in any given moment. For example, we often perceive the world through the eyes of various inner child parts, but it's not always something we're aware of. A clue this is happening is whenever you don't understand why you're having such a big reaction to something that comes up.

Cancer skill set building involves learning how to identify when an emotional trigger—the Crab's defensiveness—concerns the past or the present. It's a drain on yourself and the people you love when you get pulled into old patterns. My life has completely changed since I learned about reparenting. It's incredibly liberating to slough off old shells.

Reparenting doesn't mean a rejection or condemnation of your caregivers. It's a framework for being with the truth: you are the parent of your inner children. This month, how can you reparent yourself and molt those old defenses? Take time to lovingly meet yourself to care for the wounds of your inner child and take responsibility for healing your past pain points. In this way, you teach your unconscious that you are the adult in charge of your emotional well-being.

POLARITY

The Cancer-Capricorn Axis

All Water signs are opposite Earth signs, and all polar signs have the same modality. So cardinal Water is opposite cardinal Earth: Capricorn.

- Cancer is deeply personal, sensitive, and feeling; Capricorn is an energy that calls for dispassionate, impersonal focus.
- Cancer is happy to dreamily ruminate; Capricorn is here to get things done.
- Cancer is warm and nourishing; Capricorn is cold and discerning.

Capricorn is the goat, doggedly climbing the mountain path one foot in front of the other. Whenever you walk uphill, the tendency is to keep your head down in order to focus on what's right in front of you. Sometimes it feels safer to endure than to feel. The feeling swells of the Cancer inside can be overwhelming, especially in a world that privileges logic over intuition. The Capricorn in you will shut off the body's feeling information—like thirst, hunger, discomfort, loneliness, and fear—in order to get where you think you need to go. Capricorn is the part of you capable of tremendous concentration and endurance in order to accomplish the goals at hand.

Like all the signs, Capricorn is truly a superpower. It's that which you draw upon in the hardest of times. Capricorn is your root resources that keep you going when you're deprived of warmth and the world feels brittle and dry. The more intimate you become with these resources, the more you can apply them to what you want. Anything is possible when you apply your Capricorn!

Capricorn helps Cancer get distance from the feeling world of mood and sensitivity. It's not easy to get things done when you're worried about what someone else is going through or when you're merged with overwhelming sadness—either your own or someone else's. With a little of Capricorn's more detached levelheadedness, you can pull yourself out of the emotional whirlpool and make a plan to move forward.

This polarity is about fully belonging to your life. Balancing your attuned care with your devoted discipline means you build a home for those you love to thrive inside. Through the axis, you become your most wise inner parent: the archetypal caring mother and disciplined father of yourself. In so doing, you can give yourself to the world.

When I feel mired in Cancerian sensitivity and can't see a Capricornian road, sitting in meditation with my future self helps ground me. Sometimes I'm looking an hour ahead, a season ahead, or maybe even half a lifetime ahead. Whatever the perspective I need. I visualize and feel the presence of my future me; I see her as my parent giving me guidance. As I write this book, I am in close counsel with the future me who will be promoting and talking about *Living Astrology*. I ask her what she would like me to begin doing now to help her share offerings that will be helpful to readers like you. This helps me balance the parts of me that are scared people won't like the book or worried that it will be judged (totally valid Cancer parts) with the part of me that likes to build out a pathway to focus my service one day at a time (my Capricorn parts).

The Cancer-Capricorn polarity has helped me come to trust my future self more than any living guide. Time and again, I witness how these two signs support us in scaffolding a level of self-trust that no one can take away from us. If you can lovingly care for your younger selves and admiringly look up to your older selves, then you have truly built a home inside yourself where you can feel safe to emerge boldly, authentically, and honestly. How? Because you know all the way to the bone that you cannot be abandoned.

RULING PLANET
The Moon ☽

Cancer is the only sign that the Moon rules. It is the Moon that makes Cancer. You may remember that it was the Moon who claimed me first. While I have come to love and trust all the celestial bodies as cherished mentors and guides, my relationship with the Moon precedes them all.

I am not alone in this. The Moon is the closest to Earth. It literally pulls on the waters of your body. When you look up, you can feel that gravitational tide to the Moon's embrace. You can make eye contact. In the Moon's gaze, you're never alone. The Moon is always there, even when you can't see it. It checks on you at different times of day, every day. It always looks a little different. It feels haphazard and surprising to notice the Moon here and there until you practice consciously living the lunar cycle.

When the Moon is new and dark, it says, "Okay, here we go. So you won't see me for a few days, but I'm here. I'll meet you as a right-side crescent in the western sky, just after sunset. Until then, make a wish for us this cycle. What are you dreaming for your life?"

And then when you see the right-side crescent, the Moon says, "Great job! Now I'm going to get bigger and bigger across the first half of the night sky until I get so big, I rise full to the east just as the sun sets. Between now and then, listen to and support those wishes. Let them guide you." As you watch the Moon, let its growth inspire your own.

At the full Moon, when the night sky is fully illuminated, it says, "We did it! You're amazing! Let's celebrate! I'm so proud of you for staying with me! Check in with me in a few days when I will rise toward your bedtime, slightly diminished. We'll regroup then."

And then at the waxing gibbous, the Moon says, "How are you feeling? How has it been going? Talk to me." And this is when you realize you have a lot to share about all that's been happening with your wishes. The Moon listens as long as you feel like talking. Then it offers, "Alright, so in the coming week, I will be slowly diminishing so you just see my left side. You won't see me at night anymore, but I'll catch you in the morning. I want you to listen to yourself and release the things you told me were heavy on your heart or holding you back. Let yourself get soft and open up to let go. As the night grows dark without me, give yourself more rest. Meet me when you can't see me anymore." And so you release and surrender and let die.

In the dark of night, when the Moon is nearly new again—from a place you cannot see and can only trust—the Moon says, "You were very, very brave to care for yourself this cycle. Look at how you attuned to yourself, even when it felt hard. Look at how you held yourself. I'm so proud of you for listening. I'm so proud of you for staying with me. Now rest. Do nothing. Just be until it's time for wishes again, and I'll be here." And so, the Moon tucks you in.

In this way, cycle to cycle, "moon to moon" (the title of my podcast), you regulate your emotional world to care for your dreams. I often say, "The Moon is my co-regulator," because I synchronize my nervous system and feeling realm to the lunar cycle's rhythms in order to feel safe and held. You can too.

In astrology, the Moon represents your capacity for caring for your emotional safety and security. It's how you assure yourself that you are loved and validated. The Moon in your chart has a lot to say about what particular superpowers you've developed in order to ensure you feel okay in your specific circumstances.

But when we zoom out chartlessly, it's easier to see the Moon for what it is: the greatest caregiver there ever was and will be. It is constantly showing us how to love ourselves more compassionately as we hold its hand in lunar time.

SKILLFUL CANCER
Intuit

Cancer wants you to know: the most loving thing you can do is expand your capacity to give and receive care. This begins with growing a home inside yourself to hear your inner voice. Your inner voice is your intuition, and your intuition knows the kind of care you crave and deserve to give and receive. What that looks like is as unique as you are, and it may not reflect the care you have previously known.

Intuition is your sanctuary, a protected space in the present moment that's powerful without dominating or grasping. Like a great dogwood tree protected on all sides, intuition is both strong and soft. Skillful Cancer embodies this soft strength.

A lot people think intuition is a quality that some people have and others do not. This isn't true. Intuition is the practice of recognizing your own truth. As a practice, it means that you develop your intuitive capacities when you consciously show up to tend them. It involves recognizing yourself, consciously noticing, witnessing, and nodding to what you know you need, want, and desire.

Until I learned about working with my intuition, my default setting was always to jump to wondering what other people were thinking, needing, or wanting from me. I could only feel okay if I felt like I was okay with the people I cared about. If someone seemed mad at me, my whole day was thrown into chaos.

Going within to hear my intuition created a form of stability I'd never before known because intuition requires self-trust. If you struggle with self-trust, it's not your fault. Many of us have experienced invalidation, shaming, bullying, narcissistic abuse, or gaslighting. In all cases, we learn to outsource truth to others. We are conditioned to question our inner reality.

Intuition is so empowering to cultivate because it feels like coming home. Intuition is a practice for repairing breaches in self-trust. The more you act from that core place where you hear your truth, the more you see your intuition validated, which only causes it to grow.

From inside your intuitive sanctuary, you have the spaciousness to attune to your inherent lovability—*and then love yourself there*—with all the force and compassion you wish you had received from the outside world as a child. No one can do this for you. It is you who must build this inner cave space. That's how you come to trust it.

Living skillfully with Cancer means falling madly in love with yourself first, so that you are so full of your own life force that you have the patience, assurance, and perspective to nurture the world from your soft strength.

PRACTICE

Moon Attuning

The practice this month with Cancer is simple. Attune to Cancer's ruler, the Moon.

The invitation is both literal and symbolic. At a literal level, the assignment is to be sure that every day of Cancer season you track where the Moon is in the sky, noting the phase. For bonus points, note the sign it is in as well. I strongly suggest tracking this practice in a journal or the notes app on your phone so that you can track the ebb and flow of your experience. Any astrology app can tell you the sign of the moon and likely its phase in a given moment.

The Moon is always in the sky, and, depending on the phase, you can see it throughout different times of the night or day. Every time you go outside, try to find the Moon. You can even try to time your visits for when the Moon will be visible. Whether you see it or even if it's out of sight, I want you to wave or wink or smile to say hi to the Moon. Just see how that feels. Have fun with it! If you are in the northern hemisphere and it is summer, then when the Moon is full, I insist that you sit or walk outside for at least an hour in the moonlight and soak it all in.

At a symbolic level, I want you to "Moon with yourself," meaning, I want you to be your own Moon. Do this through a daily habit of sitting with yourself and tuning in to how you're doing. In astrology, we say that the Moon rules all daily habits and practices. This is a way to honor the rhythm of being alive and present with our experience in human bodies.

When you can, do this while you can see the Moon in the sky. Before beginning, please review my suggestions for collecting data on pages 38–39.

1. Get into a comfortable seat with your journal and pen, perhaps outside under the Moon or at your Cancer altar.

2. Decide up front what is the maximum amount of time you have for this. Maybe it's only five minutes. Maybe it's an hour. There's no good or bad amount as long as you show up at all. Then set a timer on your phone so that you can utterly relax into this and not have to worry about forgetting the time.

3. Begin by closing your eyes and taking some deep breaths with one hand on your heart and one on your belly. You might like to follow the steps for a grounding meditation on page 57.

4. Say hello to yourself as a divine spirit inhabiting a human body.

5. Ask yourself to do a check in. You are scanning yourself to see how you're doing at four levels:
    • Mentally (Air: your quality and force of thoughts. Anything nattering on?)
    • Physically (Earth: the body's information. Are you sore, tired, flexible, tense, jittery?)
    • Spiritually (Fire: your energy's information about your access to excitement, warmth, and expansiveness)
    • Emotionally (Water: your feelings that are present to notice and name. Are you sad, thoughtful, moody, at peace?)
    Do this practice in whatever order feels appropriate. Make this something that feels in affinity with you. At the beginning,

it may feel strange to separate your experience into four categories, but it will become more natural as you practice.

6. In your journal, write down the date and Moon phase (and sign, if you want). Start writing, noting how you're doing and anything else you want to capture. You don't have to write in complete sentences.

7. You may feel complete with the exercise before your timer goes off, or you may enjoy zoning out until the bell rings. Either way, close out with a thank you to yourself and to the Moon (and if resonant, a thank you to whatever else you trust is supporting you right now).

The Moon in astrology rules all daily habits, which for the most part, we do simply because we always do them. We're used to them and so they anchor and regulate us. Making this practice part of your habit is a Moon thing to do. Perhaps you already do something like this. In that case, welcome home! Perhaps this month you can look for a new way to stretch this practice. Maybe you'd like to try pulling a tarot card for wisdom on embodying each of the four elements in your daily activities.

What happens over time when you do this cycle to cycle is that you start to notice trends, such as feeling certain ways in different phases or signs of the lunar cycle. That way, you can begin to anticipate and prepare for your needs—one of the most loving gifts you can give yourself. Please treat yourself like a person with needs that matter!

. . . .

TAROT CARD

The Chariot

The card in the tarot that we associate with Cancer is card seven, the Chariot.

The Chariot is a card that references a triumphal march through the city after winning a battle, and thus signals the idea of victory. And, indeed, you may find that this card often talks to you when you're in a period of defining just what victory looks like to you.

The Chariot relates to Cancer when we remember the Crab and its exoskeleton that protects the crustacean's tender meat. We build our shells as humans do, with literal and metaphorical defense systems. We live in buildings with locks on the doors. We protect our inner vulnerabilities by designing storefronts like Instagram feeds and Christmas cards that showcase evidence we're living our "best life."

For the younger self, the Chariot is what you build to move you toward your ego's attachments. And yet, as we move further into adulthood, we begin to notice with gnawing dread that, as we check the boxes of the victory marches we had anticipated with such optimism, they do not fulfill us as we had hoped. "I thought when I got married, I'd be happy." "I thought when I finally made partner in the firm, I'd feel fulfilled." "I thought once I _____ (fill yours in here), I could relax."

We move into the higher vibration of this card when we drop into its primary teaching: the Chariot is not static; it moves. The Chariot shows us that there is no destination where we declare victory over change. There is only growing self-trust that your intuition will collaborate with the flow of your guidance to help you trust in your next loving step.

You are always on the move in some way, because life is change. This is what the Moon, as Cancer's ruler, helps you understand. Trust in your

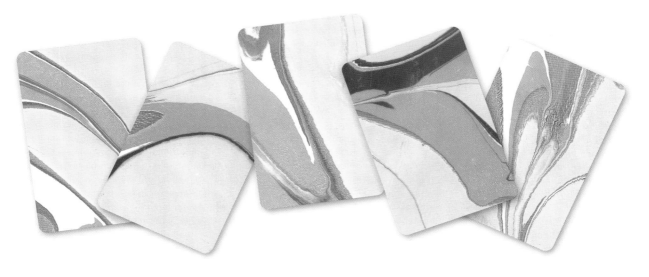

inner Moon means you know that you will molt and grow bigger whenever you are ready.

If everything is change and there is no real stopping at any destination, then what are we doing parading around this victory? To me, the Chariot is about embracing the ride and deepening into these kinds of questions:

- *How do you want the ride to feel as you're experiencing it?*
- *Who do you want to invite with you for a time?*
- *What does the overall vibe of this trip want to be about?*

Notably, the card is called the Chariot, not the Charioteer. The Chariot is that which carries you. Your physical body and its systems are a Chariot

for your soul and spirit. The Chariot teaches us how to sit at the helm of our life with more softness, more listening, and more trust in the desired flow of the intuitive, emotional, and physical body.

A Tarot Spread with the Chariot

See the chapter *How to Navigate This Book* if you're new to the tarot and seek support for pulling cards and interpreting them.

Take the Chariot out of your deck. (If you have more than one deck, you can pull the card from another deck so that the Chariot has a chance to "participate" in the deck from which you will draw.)

Feel into the visual inspiration of the card.

Take a few deep breaths on purpose and arrive to the reading. Connect into your intuition. Ask Chariot-Cancer energy to help you with this reading. Shuffle according to your unique, never-wrong style. Center and focus your question thus:

With the most expansive levels of compassion for me and all sentient beings, what is the loving invitation to connect with the Chariot?

Pull five cards according to your own unique process of knowing with the prompts above, and then sit with the cards and journal about them.

. . . .

RITUAL FOR THE NEW MOON
Triple Moon Self

In this lunar ritual, you will be invited to hang out with yourself across different ages. We're invoking an ancient tradition of depicting singular deities in tripartite form. Goddesses such as Hecate and Diana were known by three forms to emphasize their complex, mysterious, and manifold nature. In the twentieth century, the Triple Moon came to be associated more emphatically with the three phases of life: youth, midlife, and older age. These phases have often been referred to specially as Maiden, Mother, and Crone.

While I find these archetypes useful in some ways, I don't subscribe to the idea that the Triple Goddess belongs only to female-bodied individuals. And, since not all humans are on this planet to procreate, it's not very helpful that the keywords are all about the child-bearing potential of a body.

Please invoke the most inspiring and empowering version for each phase of the Triple Moon Self. Here's what I give to myself:

- For the Maiden, I see all versions of my younger self. I see her through the lens of radical compassion and impart on her the innocence of not having the wisdom I have now. I give this generously, especially to the memories of myself when I've been most pulled into my trauma, engaging in behaviors that harmed me or other people. For my Maiden, I trust that even in my most difficult or embarrassing moments, underneath there was a longing to hope for goodness in this world.

- For the Mother, I see the present moment, no matter what my actual age. We are all of us always mothers to the moment we're in. We're fertile with emergence. We're lactating for our joys, dreams, and our will to keep going. Every second is a birthing room. Life is a set of choices about what will receive our care today.

- For the Crone, I see any version of my older self. The Crone is the one who knows which fucks are worth giving and which are a waste of time. She throws her head back and cackles at the folly of this human experience. She's ripe with wisdom and gives guidance that resonates through to the bone. She cannot be intimidated or invalidated by anyone. Even if I never live to the age I sometimes see for my Crone, it's a comfort to know her the way she appears to me.

Release any pictures around age that feel shaming. Takes what's inspiring about the Triple Moon framework and leave the rest.

Before beginning this ritual, gather:

- Candles, as many as you want, and a way to light them
- Your journal and a pen; alternatively, paper and paint
- Anything else that feels important as you work with Cancer

The Ritual

1. Sit at your Cancer altar when ready. Set up your ritual container, light your candle, and come to a grounded, meditative state (see page 57).

2. Draw the Triple Moon on your paper or in your journal. Make it at least as tall as your palm.

3. Connect with your younger self:
    - Trace the lines of the crescent moon on the left and begin to zone out as you do this.
    - With great neutrality and self-compassion, invite yourself to contemplate whatever forms of your younger self want to bubble up, including the person you were yesterday. Let your calm intuitive mind recall various ages, moments, anecdotes, and also previous needs, vulnerabilities, fears, joys, wins, disappointments, grief, and anything else that appears.
    - With every image that appears, say inside to yourself: *I see you.* The key here is to let things just emerge and pass on. No judging, analyzing, fixating. When you feel complete with this, which will be an intuitive sense, you can say to your collective past self: *I see you. I honor all of you. I am here for you.*
    - Now ask a version of your younger self what they want you to know in the present moment. Then tell them something you want them to know to help them be the age they are. Write these down in your journal or on the left side of the piece of paper.

4. Connect with your future self:
    - Trace the lines of the crescent moon on the right and start to zone out.
    - With great neutrality and self-compassion, invite yourself to see various versions of your future self, including the one tomorrow. Let images bubble forward of who you are becoming and will be, in various older stages. If your mind moves into something fear-based, re-center it back to neutral.
    - With every image that appears, say inside to yourself: *I see you.* The key here is to let things just bubble up and pass on. No judging, analyzing, fixating. When you feel complete with this, which will be an intuitive sense, you can say to your collective future self: *I see you. I honor all of you. I am here for you.*

- Now ask a version of your older self what they want you to know in the present moment. Then tell them something you want them to know to help them be the age they are. Write these down in your journal or on the right side of the piece of paper.

5. Connect with your current self:
   - Finally, trace the round full moon shape in the middle and zone out. With great neutrality and self-compassion, notice that you are here now. Here you are. You are nowhere else. This is the place where you always already exist and from which you have access to your past and future selves in any moment, though you are not defined by them. You can say: *I see you. I see you here now. I honor you here now. I am here for you now.* Be with that mantra as long as feels right.
   - Now ask yourself what you need to know about your life right now that's important for you to see here in the present moment. Write this down in your journal or in the middle of the piece of paper.

6. Ask if you feel ready to complete this ritual or if you want to spend more time with your inner guidance.

7. When complete, set an intention for the New Moon in Cancer that distills some of the wisdom you received here. Maybe one of your selves imparted a message that feels really important to spend more time with.

8. Conclude and open the ritual container (see page 66).

Happy New Moon in Cancer!

ʌ   LEO

△   FIRE

⊡   FIXED

SUN

Leo

JULY 22–AUGUST 22

Questions to Live Into

How will I release myself today from the expectation to always be doing and give myself some space to just be?

What if the most important work of my day is to create scenarios that open and swell my heart?

What would I do differently if I trusted that it's safe to let the world fully see me as my authentic self?

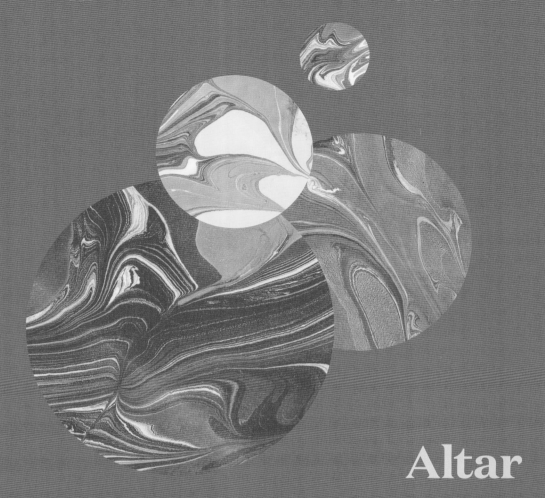

Altar

As discussed in part one, the purpose of creating an altar is to first prepare and then enjoy having a special space devoted to the themes and principles you're developing with each sign. The general qualities of Leo are listed below. I recommend you gather at least three items, but quantity isn't as crucial as choosing items of resonance for you. For example, this season, maybe you prefer to build an altar based on the theme of your inner child. Your entire altar space could be full of items that remind you of the things your used to love as a kid, including photos of you looking proud and bright. Take the suggestions that feel aligned and don't worry about the rest. As you read through the chapter, more ideas may come to you for your altar that aren't listed here.

Go for it!

COLORS
gold, orange, red, yellow

CRYSTALS
agate, amber, bloodstone, carnelian, citrine, garnet, hematite, yellow calcite

GARDEN
angelica, basil, carnation, dandelion, fennel, garlic, honey, honeysuckle, lemon balm, lemons, marjoram, peppermint, summer squash, sunflower

SPICES AND FLAVORS
allspice, cinnamon, clove, coriander, cowslip, cumin, frankincense, galangal, ginger, mustard, nettle, pepper

GODS AND GODDESSES
Apollo, Sekhmet, Sun

TAROT CARDS
the Sun, Strength, 5 of Wands, 6 of Wands, 7 of Wands

ITEMS
art, books, ceramics, fabrics, food, incense, magazine cutouts, photographs, quotes on paper, or anything else that inspires you

RELATED THEMES
acting, art, beating hearts, hugs, being, children, creativity, first harvest, flow state, joy, laughter, lions, love, outdoor shows, performing, play, pride, radiance, role-play, royalty, sheaves of golden wheat, summer, Sunday, sunlight, vacation, visibility, warmth

SEASON

Middle of Summer

Leo is the peak of summer. Leo *is* summer.

Almost everything you would want to know about Leo you can gather in this picture: Imagine sitting outside on a summer day when the temperature is just right and it's not humid. Everything in your life tunes out as you feel called to close your eyes, lift your head back to face the sun, and just let it warm your face. That sun on your face feels so good. You do this for no other reason than because it feels deeply delicious to do it. You swell with joy. That's Leo.

The middle of summer wants you to do whatever feels so good that you swell with joy. As you engage this way with life, the brightness of your delight becomes the sun for other people. When I receive your light, it warms my face. It soaks into my skin and lights me up. I cannot help but send my glow back your way. We become lights to each other, and there's this back and forth of delicious vitality. And we want to shout, "Fuck, I *love* being alive!"

In preindustrial times, this was the time of the first harvest. In many cultures, humans would walk through the town in a ritual procession, carrying the abundance of what they grew in their arms, showing it off, sharing. To be Leo is to process through your world, giving your abundance away through the light of your being.

The middle of summer is the exuberant peak of solar energy. Plants and grass and flowers are at their most vibrant and juicy. We dance, sing, perform, enjoy music, and make love outside more than usual. People want to play more and work less. Children run around the neighborhood, happy that adults are letting them get dirty outside and be imaginative in their games. Adults show more skin too, free to be their glorious selves. Romances peak with the passions of Leo season!

This is all Leo. It is you, whenever you embody the middle of summer.

MODALITY AND ELEMENT
Fixed Fire

Like Taurus, Scorpio, and Aquarius, Leo is one of the fixed signs in the middle of the season. All of these are the parts of you that root into who you are. Your fixed nature has preferences and isn't ashamed to name and claim them. Your fixed self will say No even if it disappoints people because you know what you're into and what you're not up for.

Like Aries and Sagittarius, Leo is a Fire sign. Fire is your energy that gets animated when you're excited, passionate, in love, creating, and letting yourself be into what you're into. Where Aries has the initiative and the bravado to start something, Leo has the pride and the self-esteem to tend the thing and let it grow and be seen. Then Sag brings the optimism and the trust to let it lead you into new territory and connect with other lights.

In nature, a fixed Fire looks like a bonfire. See one in your mind's eye. It's such a fun summer ritual to enjoy a bonfire with others. Everyone gathers around to enjoy one another's company. We relax in the presence of the bonfire and tell stories or break into song. Even in the hottest part of the year, humans still build fires. It's an abundance mindset. For Leo, there's never too much of a good thing.

You are the bonfire. It is your light that magnetizes those around you. It is your warmth that relaxes the space. A bonfire isn't going anywhere once it's lit. It has a clear position in space. And it more or less has the same glow while it's alive. Likewise, your Leo is reliable, steadfast, and loyal.

Living your fixed Fire has to do with holding and tending a strong, stable fire. This isn't difficult for the Leo part of you because you naturally give your Leo self to what lights you up. You cannot help it. It's obvious to anyone in your space when your Leo is vibing on something.

In human form, fixed Fire is the performer on stage you can't take your eyes off of. It's the leader you appreciate because they always show up and inspire you. It's anyone who has a laugh you can count on.

Your Leo is not the same as anyone else's, so there's no wrong way to express fixed Fire. You're in your Leo when you can't help but sparkle with love for something or someone. And this cannot be forced. Leo simply is.

SYMBOL
The Lion

The symbol for Leo is the Lion. As an apex predator, it occupies the top of the food chain and has no natural predators. Humans have sought symbolic alliance with the Lion since the age of cave paintings, tens of thousands of years ago. To declare connection to the Lion is to step into the skin of the alpha. This is Leo.

The Lion is also a keystone species. Just as an arch will collapse without the keystone, so the ecosystem would be negatively affected without the keystone species. The keystone species supports the biodiversity of its ecosystem. Thus, to connect with the Lion is also to participate in the role of sustaining the whole community. This is also Leo.

Lions are social beings that live in synergy with their "pride," their family group. Their pride is their pride, so to speak. This double meaning is purposeful to the archetype, as Lions are proud creatures, and so is the Leo within. Self-pride and pride in one's family and life are inherently beautiful and supportive qualities. Especially if you've known bullying or invalidation energy, growing pride is crucial to rebuilding self-esteem.

Originally, Leo was associated with the Nemean Lion of Greek mythology. It was said that the golden fur of the Nemean Lion was impenetrable, so when Heracles (known as Hercules in Roman mythology) went to confront the beast, he had to be clever. After defeating it, Heracles wore the Lion's skin and mane as a sign of his cleverness and strength; it is his identifying feature in ancient Greek and Roman art. With this mantle, he became impervious to the elements. The golden fur of the Leo inside of you can be imagined as a glimmering shine that radiates around your physical body. Leo deflects against all the weather life brings us.

Lion energy is also royal energy. This is not the ruler up in a fancy castle separated from the peasants below. The root of the Latin word *rex*, which means "king," has a derivative meaning of "to direct in a straight line," suggesting that the nature of rulership is in clear guidance. "King" may be a masculine concept, but our gendered ideas break down when we remember it's the lionesses who rule their prides and do the hunting. Even if Heracles is depicted wearing the mane of the male lion in art, the Heracles archetype would have absolutely worn lioness skin.

To guide like a Lion is to care for the pride. It is to be a big-hearted, warming leader, whose charisma and whose smile inspire others to trust their strength. This leader has to be okay with being witnessed, appreciated, celebrated, and honored in order for this ecosystem to generate energy. This is pride, which is bright and clear and nourishing.

What thoughts or feelings emerge as you read about the Lion here? Remember one of the core teachings in this book: what comes up for you with the information is more important than the information. If there is a part of you that doesn't feel access to the Lion, or resists taking it on as an identity, or thinks it's for someone else and not you, then this is a potent zone. A small daily gesture you can offer yourself is to put a hand on your heart and say, "I'm proud of you." Let whatever critical parts quibble about this if they want to, but continue to locate pride in your body. Let it suffuse your heart space with a warming sensation.

The Leo-Aquarius Axis

All Fire signs are opposite Air signs, and all polar signs have the same modality. So fixed Fire is opposite fixed Air: Aquarius.

- Leo sees you as the center, the bonfire of your life; Aquarius sees you as a bonfire in a world of billions of bonfires.
- Leo is passionate and speaks from the heart; Aquarius stays dispassionate and speaks from objectivity.
- Leo is the relatable and charismatic leader; Aquarius allows room for the unique perspectives of every member of the group.

When Leo is all in and hands-on, the Aquarius part of you maintains distance so they can deliver feedback that feels true because it seems to come from an unbiased place of an outsider looking in. Aquarius is an outsider genius. Aquarius is an alien that landed here to whisper helpful tips to us funny humans.

Aquarius supports Leo because Leo's job is to keep you personally invested in your pride so you can continue to love and work and show up from the part of you that is fiercely loyal. Your Leo needs to be committed to tending your ecosystem. So your Leo is *deep* in it. Leo cannot access the perspective your Aquarius is designed for. Like all Air signs, Aquarius moves through your mental realm. Aquarius is your gift of seeing all the dynamics at play in a situation, and the aerial view is difficult to comprehend when you're so deeply inside something.

Thank the stars we're all twelve signs, right? The heart of this polarity has to do with balancing your relationship to centering and decentering yourself. You want the bright light of Leo to be eager and proud to participate in the genius of a shared Aquarian economy.

Leo and Aquarius want you to know that you are a divine being among divine beings *and* you have a right to be seen joyfully sharing the best of yourself. We are the starring role in a movie being made about us, says Leo. But we're also a key supporting actor in our loved ones' lives, as well as characters with only a few scenes in others. For most people, we're only extras in the background, but Aquarius helps us remember that those roles matter to the larger collective too. We can build a future from the present moment when we participate in our lives through the multiple perspectives of our role.

. . . .

RULING PLANET
The Sun

Leo is the only sign that the Sun rules. This makes Leo a really important sign to study because the Sun is essential to life on Earth. We literally wouldn't be here if we didn't live on a planet perfectly distant from our star, such that we don't burn from its unfathomable heat or freeze in its shadow.

We might ask: What is the responsibility of a star? It is to surrender to its own nature, the fact of its aliveness. The star's own being makes fusion inevitable, which creates light and powers all the life in its orbit.

If we see the sky as ancient civilizations did, the sun is this glowing orb that rises in the east, peaks at the top of the sky and then descends to the west, where it disappears and is gone. And the cycle repeats, again and again, bringing light and warmth and then allowing darkness to have its time. Though there are aspects of this dance with the Sun that may feel limitless, this is not true. The Sun teaches you something crucial with its rise: the only sure thing is that you have this day—this moment.

The Sun is precious. It is your treasure. It is the animating force of your life. The god associated with the Sun in ancient Greece was Apollo, whose epithet *Phoebus* means "bright."

I propose that the Sun is your spirit, which is unfathomably old and undying and also confined to a human body with its own rise, peak, and descent to the underworld. Your responsibility to your Sun self is to surrender to being who you are.

You can't experience the magnificence of your spirit all at once, in its totality. It's the same with the Sun in the sky: we can't look directly at it. In the same way, your ecstatic spirit is caught in glimpses: When your eyes sparkle. When you throw your head back genuinely laughing. When you speak to someone from a place of direct presence and authenticity. Thank you for letting others see you. When I see your spirit, I wonder if it might be safe to show you mine.

> Your ecstatic spirit is caught in glimpses.

This issue of safety is central to the Sun's expression. When the spirit experiences theft of innocence and absurd unfairness across childhood and adolescence, we begin to cultivate patterns of blocking our Sun from giving itself to a world that might not appreciate it. The world would be a different place if we were all shining our Sun on each other all the time. It feels like part of my work in the world is to help my clients and students trust that it's safe to let their Sun out. I task you with the work of healing and reprogramming these patterns.

For your spirit to shine, you build a home inside yourself. Your Temple of Apollo. One of Apollo's maxims was *know thyself.* And from inside your temple, you practice knowing and being the Sun. Your Sun is unlike anyone else's. It only shines when you give it what delights you, what you love, what feels fun, what is exciting and giddy and exuberant. There is no room for judgment here. Your life force is at stake.

As you live the Sun inside yourself, you will become Sun-seeking, just like a plant. Leaves actually look greener on cloudy days because the chlorophyll in the plant is pushing to the surface to get closer to the sun's solar power—this is you as you live Leo. Seek sun-filled foods. Seek sunny music. Seek sunny people.

SKILLFUL LEO
Illuminate

Leo wants you to know: the most loving thing you can do is to have the audacity to adore yourself and be appreciated for all that you are and do. Leo wants you to be shiny—all the time. Whether or not there's an audience.

The reason Leo isn't easeful is because of our conditioned belief that a good person is a selfless person. When I think about how outrageous it is that we have been encouraged to be self-*less*—as in without a self!—I feel such sacred rage over it. And I have no shame about that rage. It's very healthy, and it's very good for your Leo. Let it light your fire!

The indignity of this cult of selflessness has really messed up our relationship to the solar expression of Leo. We've learned to swallow the desire to take up space so we can perform humility. We've learned to say No to our creative outlets because we don't want to be seen as selfish with our time. We've learned not to tell people about our wins to protect ourselves from being judged as bragging. As a result, a lot of us have a confused relationship to our ego. We crave being centered and valued, but we're practiced in refusing it. This creates unconscious, unskillful expressions that look like outbursts demanding attention, gossiping, or jealous judgment about someone who is expressing their Leo. These behaviors can be so pervasive in our families, social circles, workplace, and the world at large; is it any wonder that we've been told to shut down our Leo to be self-less? Your Leo cannot be stopped, and it's going to express itself however it can.

To support your Leo, consider this mantra: *Nobody's looking at you, and people want to see you.*

On the one hand, "nobody's looking at you"—as in, release yourself from fear that people are judging you. Maybe you hear voices saying, *What's the point? Who cares anyway? Who do I think I am, thinking people want to see me?* What would you do, how would you express yourself, how would you create if no one was looking? There is so much healing here.

But also: "people want to see you." They really do. People are so wanting to warm their hearts in the light of who you truly are. What would you do differently if you realized this in your whole body? How would you show up if you really let this in?

Something I've learned is to let people have their own experience of your Leo. Your only job is to not get in the way of running your light. You can't possibly know what the experience of your light is like for anyone else. If someone judges your shine, maybe it's a part of their own path to understanding. Since it's not your job to know or control, what others think of you is none of your business.

Practicing shining—whether people see you or not—is a beautiful way to get used to what it feels like to be in your luminosity. You are in the glory of your shine when the world is watching and when nobody is watching. You are the aliveness of that light, always and everywhere.

PRACTICE

Disrupt Limiting Self-Images

I have yet to meet a client who doesn't come to my space holding deep grief that they feel somehow disconnected from the radiance of their Leonine self. Earlier I shared how the responsibility of the solar self is to surrender to who you are, and yet, this is complicated. When people say, "You do you" or "Just be yourself," it can feel really confrontational because it's actually not that easy. We have been conditioned to take on identities and self-images that we're told are best for us. In some cases, we faced threats, oppression, ostracism, or even violence for disobedience.

This practice will help you to identify which identities are truly native to your being and which are those you took on for safety and validation. My thesis here is that you limit possibility and give over precious agency whenever you do things to keep up a self-image. And over time, the consequence of surrendering your agency is lack of self-trust. Repairing and revitalizing self-trust is at the core of this approach to astrology.

The practice for Leo season is to identify which types of self-images you are invested in and then, each day, do things to destabilize, disrupt, and disobey the rules of that self-image. What you're looking for is just to notice what comes up for you when you do this.

Here are examples of self-image types with suggestions for disrupting them. Feel free to add more for yourself and play around with the suggestions. Let this be fun! Leo loves to play and perform!

- Self-image as a "rule follower": show up late to the meeting.
- Self-image as someone who replies to emails promptly: don't check emails for a whole day.
- Self-image as a "good mom": don't go to your kid's game and do something for your own self-care instead.
- Self-image as a "great guy": say you can't help when you're asked if you can.
- Self-image as a "wonderful host": do nothing in advance to prepare and just order pizza.
- Self-image as a "hipster": be basic.
- Self-image as "always smiling": let your face drop to a resting place, no masking allowed.
- Self-image as "agreeable": disagree, interrupt, don't nod, don't linger around to chat.
- Self-image as "advice-seeking": go on an advice freeze and don't ask for anyone's opinions.
- Self-image as "wise": don't offer insights or prepare something profound to add.

So the first part of this practice is to pick a different self-image each day and then disrupt it. The second part is to be willing to notice how it felt and what came up mentally, emotionally, physically, and spiritually. If you were worried about people not understanding you, not liking you, or being mad at you, then you're learning that the self-image is limiting. It is limiting because it's a performance for safety rather than possibility. Performing for safety will obstruct your solar shine. If you felt liberated and energized, then keep leaning into the disruption in different environments and with different people.

Please always bring a spirit of fun, curiosity, and compassion to this practice. It's not here to shame you or others. It's here to help you understand yourself so that you can call back your power, agency, and life-force energy that might be leaking out with the effort to perform.

. . . .

TAROT CARD

Strength

The card in the tarot that we associate with Leo is card eight, Strength.

In the traditional *Smith-Rider-Waite* version of Strength, we see a woman draped in flowers who gently leans over to caress (and close?) the muzzle of a lion. The beast appears to be smiling up at her face, submitting to her calm presence with his tail between his legs. Strength, in this depiction, is not about physical force or power over anything. Rather, the illustration offers us the quiet power of nonviolent strategies to subdue the beast.

Strength comes from leaning toward what frightens you with an open and undefended heart—which is the anatomical structure Leo rules in medical astrology. When you route a fear or judgment through the heart, you completely change its frequency and vibration. You drop your weapons and move into (self-) compassion. Usually when you block anything from heart connection, it's because you're afraid of leaving your vulnerable heart—that emotional and live-giving center—undefended. It takes courage to cozy up to what scares you in yourself as well as to people who seem threatening, chaotic, or out of your control.

It's worth remembering that the word "heart" is *cœur* in French and *corazón* in Spanish. These are from the Latin root *cor-*, which is the same root word as "courage." Interestingly, "courage" initially referred to the heart as the seat of one's emotional strength and passion.

My favorite depiction of the Strength card is actually titled Lust in the *Thoth* deck. In the card, we see a young woman riding a multi-headed lion-hybrid beast. With her legs on either side of its neck, she leans back across the back of the animal with an open, bare-breasted chest. Her head turns away from the viewer to gaze at the fiery uterus-like chalice she holds up in her right hand. In her other hand, she pulls gently at the beast's leash.

This is a very erotic image. It throbs with desire, appetite, and unashamed pleasure. This is a Leo that purrs, moans, and roars.

It takes courage to give yourself the release that attends your lust. I know that for me, there's not a whole lot of difference between the facial expression I make when I orgasm, the face I make when I tap into previously repressed grief and cry, and the one I made when my daughters came out of me in childbirth.

We often fight experiences of wild, primal eruption because we fear the chaos. Strength to me is about meeting yourself at your own chaos. To live Leo means to be willing to lean into your own creative chaos, the kind that comes from trusting leaps of the heart. It takes courage to trust the heart's language because its vocabulary is not from the mind. The heart feels like chaos to the brain because we can't control or tame it. Your heart's beastly language emerges from the tongue of your wild self.

A Tarot Spread with Strength

See the chapter *How to Navigate This Book* if you're new to the tarot and seek support for pulling cards and interpreting them.

Take Strength out of your deck. (If you have more than one deck, you can pull the card from another deck so that Strength has a chance to "participate" in the deck from which you will draw.)

Feel into the visual inspiration of the card.

Take a few deep breaths on purpose and arrive to the reading. Connect into your intuition. Ask Strength-Leo energy to help you with this reading. Shuffle according to your unique, never-wrong style. Center and focus your question thus:

With the most expansive levels of compassion for me and all sentient beings, what is the loving invitation to connect with Strength?

Pull five cards according to your own unique process of knowing with the following prompts, and then sit with the cards and journal about them.

. . . .

RITUAL FOR THE NEW MOON
Play for Your Life

Legendary drag queen RuPaul Charles once said, "When you become the image of your own imagination, it's the most powerful thing you could ever do." RuPaul doesn't dress *like* a queen. RuPaul *is* a queen. And she coaches others to find this in themselves.

In his highly inspirational and influential reality TV show, *RuPaul's Drag Race*, contestants channel the image of who they can become in their imagination through the art of drag. They compete to see who most skillfully embodies that vision through different kinds of challenges, including design, acting, improv, comedy, dancing, singing, and more. Viewers watch them transform from normal, everyday people into larger-than-life queens, marveling at what happens when extraordinary make-up and costume are enlivened by pride, swagger, and showmanship.

Drag humor is camp humor. Susan Sontag said, "Camp is being-as-playing-a-role." Drag is camp in that it heightens reality by escalating—and often questioning—the performance of gender. Part of camp's playfulness is that it takes frivolity utterly seriously. We can't help but laugh at its sheer audacity of taking your creative vision all the way to maximum extreme. Laughter is the body's natural response in the face of such potent aliveness.

The iconic "lip-sync for your life" is a staple of the show, where the queens who performed the worst that week face off in a lip-sync battle to save their spot in the competition. On the one hand, the idea of lip-syncing like your life hangs in the balance is very silly. But at the same time, it zings with the heart of the whole show, which is to love yourself like your life depends on it—because it does.

All ritual is a form of theater; we set aside the "normal" flow of the day in order to experience heightened reality. We set the stage beforehand, sometimes just by lighting a candle, sometimes with a multiday set of preparations. There's a clear start and clear end. We invite in a focused state of listening, often in a dark room. And there's the excitement of the unexpected. You can't presume to know what insights will roll in, what visions will appear, what support you will receive.

There is great freedom in adopting a sense of self that embraces performance and role-playing. What if authenticity isn't a single thing but rather a skill at playing whatever role is most authentically appropriate to the moment you're living in? What if authenticity is always emergent? In this open space, we can discover who we are within the process of self-creation.

In this ritual, get serious about being playful. I invite you to see this ritual for what ritual always is: a performance that alters your experience of reality. Get into it. Prepare and show up as if your life depends on it.

Before beginning this ritual, gather:

- Wardrobe, makeup, and hair items that feel royal
- Set pieces to create a scenario where you are the sovereign (king, queen, or whatever title feels right for you)
- Candles, as many as you want, and a way to light them
- Your journal and a pen
- Several songs you know by heart, cued up
- A goblet filled something yummy to drink and a plate of an exquisite treat. I encourage you to be over the top.

The Ritual

1. Sit at your Leo altar when ready and dressed. Set up your ritual container, light your candle(s), and come to a grounded, meditative state (see page 57).

2. Ask your intuition to see a golden sun disc above your head. Let it appear, noting its size and qualities. Feel open to being surprised by how big it is. Sit for several minutes or as long as you desire in the glow of this bright, golden crown above your head. Ask yourself how it feels to connect with your divine sunlight. Ask yourself: *How would it change the way I want to move through the world if I were to trust in this sun disc in every moment?*

3. Sitting as you are with this golden sun disc, this regal crown, ask yourself: *Am I willing to notice that this light imparts upon me a regal bearing that is inherent and intrinsic to my being? Am I willing to notice that this part of me is royal and unfuckwithable?*

4. Now ask for drops of this golden light disc to gently move through the top of your head, all the way down into the heart. See and feel bright, golden light filling your heart and growing bigger and bigger as it fills your chest cavity and begins to radiate out beyond your physical body. Sit for a while in the glow of your shining golden heart. Perhaps lay your hand on your heart. Ask yourself how it feels to connect with your divine heart. Ask yourself: *How would it change the way I want to move through the world if I were to trust in this beaming heart in every moment?* Ask yourself if you are ready to understand that you are capable of the most fierce and brave love. If the answer is unsure or a no, ask for more information, and write down your answers. Part of your lunar intention can be to call in a brave, loving heart this cycle. Ask for support here.

5. Now visualize the golden light from your crown that now radiates at your heart and ask it to move down into your solar plexus, the power center below your diaphragm. Breathe that golden, bright light in and out from your solar plexus. As you do, imagine clarifying that light so that it distills your will and your leadership into a channel for your deepest truth. Sit in this for a while. Ask how it feels to connect with your power center. Now ask yourself: *What is my truth?* Let the answer roar out of your mouth. Ask: *What lights me up with healthy anger? What is the benefit and service of this sacred rage? How is my conscious will and determination supported by this? How would it change the way I move through the world if I were to trust more deeply in my sacred leadership?*

6.   Ask yourself if you are ready to understand that you are
     capable of defending and protecting your truth with the will of
     your leadership. If the answer is unsure or a no, ask for more
     information, and write down your answers. Part of your lunar
     intention can be to call in healthy anger and compassionate
     power. Ask for support here.

7.   Now take a few deep breaths, reconnecting with the ball of
     golden light above, throughout, and around your body. Ask
     for your guidance to support you in burning away what is not
     your truth.

8.   Take some time to write down any intentions you'd like to set
     for Leo season based on what came up in the ritual. Perhaps a
     yummy intention might be to practice attuning to your golden
     sun disc and letting yourself be suffused with the truth that
     you are a royal being.

9.   Optional but highly encouraged: complete the ritual by "lip-
     syncing for your life" to your favorite songs, while still in
     costume, as long as feels fun.

10. Toast to your sacred leadership with your much-deserved
     drink and treat.

11. Conclude and open the ritual container (see page 66).

Happy New Moon in Leo!

Virgo

AUGUST 22–SEPTEMBER 22

♍   VIRGO

▽   EARTH

☌   MUTABLE

☿   MERCURY

Virgo

Questions to Live Into

To what will I give the gift of my reverent attention today?

How can I more sincerely trust that there are no problems, but rather appropriate responses to whatever arises?

What if I looked at all experience as a daily process that guides me to become more specific in who I am, honoring both the Yes and No that emerge naturally from my intuition?

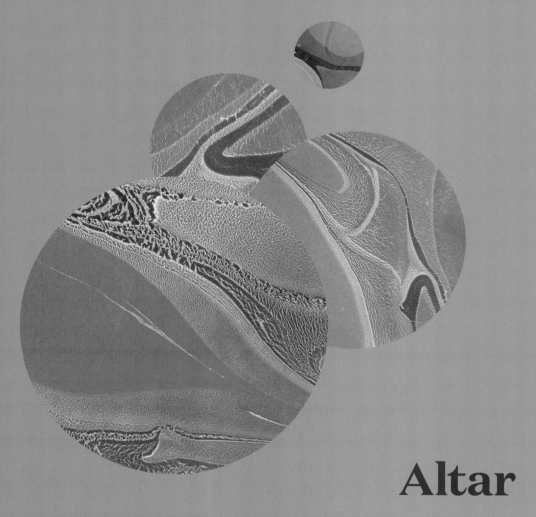

Altar

As discussed in part one, the purpose of creating an altar is to first prepare and then enjoy having a special space devoted to the themes and principles you're developing with each sign. The general qualities of Virgo are listed below. I recommend you gather at least three items, but quantity isn't as crucial as choosing items of resonance for you. For example, this season, maybe you prefer to build an altar based simply on the theme of the harvest. Your entire altar space could be full of only items with references to harvest cycles. Take the suggestions that feel aligned and don't worry about the rest. As you read through the chapter, more ideas may come to you for your altar that aren't listed here.

Go for it!

COLORS
gold, green, yellow

CRYSTALS
jade, moss agate

GARDEN
cornflower, fennel,
lavender, narcissus,
skullcap

SPICES
caraway, dill, marjoram

GODS AND GODDESSES
Artemis, Chiron,
Ceres, Demeter,
Hestia, Isis, Mercury,
the Moon, Vesta

TAROT CARDS
the Hermit,
the Magician,
8 of Pentacles,
9 of Pentacles,
10 of Pentacles

ITEMS
art, books, ceramics,
fabrics, food, incense,
magazine cutouts,
photographs, quotes
on paper, or anything
else that inspires you

RELATED THEMES
abundance, alignment,
the analytical mind,
appropriateness,
body health, cycles,
devotion, grain,
grounding, the harvest,
healing, intuition,
learning, organization,
purification, refinement,
responsiveness,
sexuality, well-
being, Wednesday

SEASON
End of Summer

Virgo is the bridge between the ripeness of high summer with Leo and the pivot into autumn that is Libra. This is the time of year in preindustrial cultures when folks were focused on tending to the harvest. It was a time to discriminate between what was good enough to keep and what wasn't, a quality we associate with the Virgo in ourselves.

Ultimately, this time of year invites us to develop skill in *preparation* and *preservation* so that we can be people who receive the harvests we want from life. The cautious, deliberate care of the Virgo essence has to do with the truth that it's at the precipice of the death phase of the wheel of the year. Virgo attends to the rituals and ceremonies for prolonging sustenance well into the future. The rigor of care that Virgo brings is rooted in deep love and respect for life.

In many parts of the world, including the US, we go back to school in Virgo season. There's a collective drive to get organized, clean up, clear out, and make way for a shift in energy. This is a powerful time to realign with yourself, reorient to the path you're on, and shake off other people's energies from your physical space.

Virgo season carries the excitement of fresh notebooks and new beginnings. You may be eager and ready for the darker days ahead. There can also be a sense of grief: the end of summer's decadence, the loss of daylight forthcoming, and the constriction of a return to order. Both can coexist, and this is okay.

How does this time of year typically feel for you? What patterns of experience, relational dynamics, or life questions tend to repeat for you in the season? The ways you personally connect to this time of year will inform how you experience Virgo.

· ·

MODALITY AND ELEMENT
Mutable Earth

Like Gemini, Sagittarius, and Pisces, Virgo is a mutable sign. It processes the experiences that came up across the first two signs of a season. In this case, Virgo helps us integrate Cancer and Leo, and looks ahead to prepare for autumn.

Like Taurus and Capricorn, Virgo is an Earth sign that cares about being practical, reliable, and grounded in the way you go about things.

In nature, I see Virgo like wet clay: a material of the earth that is shapeable and responsive to conditions. Virgo earthiness is loamy, as distinct from the rootedness of Taurus or the stony trails of Capricorn.

In humans, we see Virgo in the ceramicist at the potter's wheel, shaping the clay then fine-tuning the vessel with their tools into wabi-sabi beauty. I think of the Reiki healer tuning to the health of their client, noticing misalignments, and offering their healing hands. Virgo is in the writer editing their draft, tinkering and revising to eliminate the inessential and shape the flow into the most appropriate channel for the reader experience.

Mutable Earth encourages you to notice and listen to what's present in your life, including the asymmetries, gaps, and cracks. This is a part of you that *learns*. You learn from what you see with your Virgo. You learn so you can respond, adapt, and then realign. Virgo is a process-based part of you, focusing on cyclical refinement. Learn, respond, adapt, realign. Again and again. Again and again.

Virgo is radical awareness. When you're in balance during this season, you have dilated access to the details of your life. This is hugely eye-opening as you see all possibilities. But, for many, this can be an uncomfortable perspective. The Virgo in us can feel tyrannical, always adjusting toward a perfection we can't reach or sustain.

The medicine of Virgo is remembering that we are both the mother and the child of all of our experience (see more about Virgo's connection to this archetype on page 176). Whatever is happening at any time at any point in our lives, we are both the creator-nurturer of that experience *and* the novice learning from it. If the Virgo inside you feels hypercritical and shames you for perceived mistakes, then this is conditioning from over-culture that would have you forget that you are also a child, an innocent, a beginner at being human.

What would it be like this Virgo season to give yourself the generosity to always be learning?

For me, when I let myself have the space to not know, to be messy, to fail, then I am more willing to open myself to being a human who learns. This may not be easy, but it's what Virgo wants from you right now.

How can you expand your capacity for showing up to your life with more radical awareness to really be with it, listen to it, and learn from it, so that you can then adapt and refine with love, patience, and care?

· ·

SYMBOL

The Maiden

The symbol for Virgo is traditionally the figure of a young woman, a Maiden, often holding a sheaf of wheat. There are various associations for this figure. One of these is Astraea of ancient Greece, whose name means "star maiden." Known as the virgin goddess of purity, innocence, and justice, she was one of the last immortals to live among humans before the gods adjourned to Mount Olympus, hence the sign's association with the Earth.

When the Sun is in Virgo, it is traditionally the time of the grain harvest. The brightest star in the Virgo constellation is Spica, meaning "ear of grain." The ancient Sumerian goddess Shala was the goddess of grain and compassion, and she was often depicted holding lions or standing atop their heads, relating to the fact that Virgo comes after Leo. Grain was associated with compassion because a bountiful harvest was considered the compassion of the gods.

Since the Maiden in the symbol is often pictured holding wheat, we can also associate Virgo with the Roman goddess Ceres—the goddess of agriculture, nourishment, cereals, and the secrets of the earth—or the Greek goddess Demeter. It was Demeter who taught people how to grow crops, which changed the course of human history. Demeter is very often associated with her daughter Persephone, and the story of Persephone's abduction and descent into the Underworld as the bride of Hades (or Pluto). This myth, which also has strong associations to the Taurus-Scorpio axis, is essentially an explanation of seasons—the very cycle of life-death-rebirth at the source of all existence.

In the Middle Ages, Virgo was associated with the Virgin Mary, who gave birth to Jesus Christ. Since *Bethlehem* (the birthplace of Jesus Christ) means "bread," the analogy worked nicely. Like Mary, who mysteriously bears life in her belly to "renew" the world, so Demeter and Persephone evoke the principle of the earth's—and our own—regeneration.

But if we look to pre-patriarchal vestal practices, priestesses of the Great Mother Goddess served the Moon and tended the community temple fire with an oath that they would not let it die. They were not called virgins because they were sexually chaste but rather because they did not belong to nor were they defined by a man. They were sovereign, self-contained, and whole. Known to bathe in sacred springs, the purpose of their bath rituals was to come home to the body-spirit and replenish—that purification and self-renewal piece of Virgo.

In this way, the symbol for Virgo is a loving invitation to return to self. Notions of Virgo as related to prudishness or barrenness are incorrect and rooted in patriarchal responses to women's body sovereignty.

Across Virgo season, you are invited to seek opportunities to create sacred space for your body-spirit and clear out other people's energy. Notice whose thoughts, opinions, needs, and demands are in your space, and release these, as if placing them in a basket on the surface of a flowing river. Come home to yourself. Fill yourself up with your own essence. You are sovereign. You are whole. You belong to yourself.

POLARITY

The Virgo-Pisces Axis

All Earth signs are opposite Water signs, and all polar signs have the same modality. So mutable Earth is opposite mutable Water: Pisces. While both signs are known for being incredibly responsive to their environment (this is from their mutability), the elemental distinction is important. Earth relates to practical life and the material world. Water relates to the parts of experience that are invisible and often more subtle and mysterious to us: feelings, dreams, visions, and psychic energies.

Pisces is an oceanic part of us. Whether we feel like we're sinking, floating, or surfing, the Pisces experience is immersive by nature. When we're in a Pisces state of mind, we might look zoned out or like we're in some other channel to someone observing us. Pisces is the part of you that yearns for oneness with a song, with an ecstatic feeling, or with a dream that you want to see come to fruition.

Scratch the part of you that's Virgo hard enough and you discover the part of you that's Pisces.

- Virgo is details; Pisces is vastness.
- Virgo carefully lays out an appropriate crystal grid; Pisces feels the symphonic frequency of the grid in their auric field.
- Virgo is the appropriately modulated argument; Pisces is stream-of-consciousness poetry.

Pisces is that highly empathic, intuitive, imaginative self that can dissolve the hard edges of material life into the feeling world and all that is nonverbal and insubstantial: music, poetry, dreams, love, ideal feelings, the spirit realm. If you feel distant from your Pisces, that's okay. Of all the signs, Pisces is the part of you that overculture finds unproductive and labels a waste of time. You probably have not been encouraged to know this part of yourself.

The Virgo-Pisces polarity tells a story about being devoted to something greater than yourself. Virgo shows up in a practical way that can be noted with hard evidence. Pisces shows up with energetic and emotional support that often goes unseen. Both parts are doing important work for people and things outside of you.

The Virgo-Pisces balance is about playing with spatial dimension in our lives and psyches. When you chop wood, you are ostensibly doing something practical (Earth) with great focus on precision. But who's to say that chopping wood isn't as sacred as sitting in meditation (Water)? To magnify the grandeur of the intimacies of our daily life is to invite in wonder, gratitude, and spirit. If Virgo is a magnifying glass and Pisces is the Moon, the balance between these signs is seeing the Moon in a grain of salt. Both Virgo and Pisces are deeply spiritual parts of us that express in different but consonant ways.

Know what you need and how to respond.

Ultimately, this axis is a part of you that wants and needs to express love through service, balancing your practical Virgo side with your numinous Pisces side.

RULING PLANET

Mercury

Mercury is the planet of the mind, communication, word-making, exchanging ideas, and creative intelligence. In ancient Roman myth, the god Mercury is the messenger, the one who communicates and negotiates between realms.

Mercury rules two of the four mutable signs: Gemini (Air) and Virgo (Earth). Elementally, we can sense a significant difference between the two, as Earth moves much more slowly than Air. Gemini is a quick, mental intelligence. Virgo is more of a haptic form of holistic intuition: sensing vibrational energies of a system, whether abstract or right in front of you.

One of the reasons Mercury is so important and fascinating as a part of us to study is because the way we perceive and interpret our reality is central to the creation and experience of that reality. Thus, the more conscious we are about how the mind works, the more skillful we can be at creating solutions to whatever the brain considers a problem. This is no small thing.

One of my favorite things to say to questioning or conflicted students is "This is not a problem." Moreover, I often wonder: *What if there are no problems, only responses to what is?* For "what is" is all we really have. Mercury looks at what is and determines the most proper response.

Mercury teaches the Virgo in us that there's an important difference between reacting and responding. To react is to lose your power. Reactions are knee-jerk survival mechanisms that are rooted in biases, underlying beliefs, and unconscious assumptions. Responses are thoughtful and slower to unfold.

As the ruler of Virgo, Mercury bestows upon Virgo its qualities of discernment and discrimination. Mercury gives to the Virgo part of you the ability to sense the whole of any system, to identify where there's a misalignment, and then offer the most appropriate and thoughtful care to attend to realignment.

When you nurture your Virgo, you trust in your innate, instinctual, and intuitive capacities to know what you need and how to respond. This Virgo season is a great time to practice response-ability: your skill in responding to the stuff of life—which is often messy, weird, and triggering—with care.

Mercury also teaches the Virgo in us to be methodical. This Virgo season, even if you don't do it naturally, I am inviting you to fall in love with identifying and naming your processes. Here are some examples to get you started. Feel free to amend and add or delete so these work for your life:

- My process for making breakfast:
- My process for picking out accessories to my look:
- My process for deciding if I want to say Yes to a social event:
- My process for determining if I have time for playing around on social media:
- My process for selecting collaborators on a project:
- My process for leaving an event or ending an interaction:
- My process for coming into a state of grounded meditation:

SKILLFUL VIRGO

Sharpen

Virgo wants you to know: the most loving thing you can do is to get more specific about who you are and what you want and don't want. You're not limiting yourself. This will help you be more effective at becoming yourself.

It's like sharpening a knife. Our knife is dull when we could go this way or that way, when we don't really even know what is a Yes and what is a No, what is for us and not for us. Virgo wants a sharp edge. Virgo wants precision. Virgo wants effective and efficient moves. The knife cuts better when it's sharp, after all. Whatever it is you want, perhaps there's a way to get more specific in how you do it—and how you *are* it—so you can be precise, so you can do the thing you're doing, and do it well. And so, getting more skillful with your Virgo has something to do with getting more precise and specific, honing how you show up as yourself.

When you're unskillful at Virgo, you might feel like you're overwhelmed by how exacting the demands of your Virgo are. Maybe you wish your Virgo would chill out because your will for precision is relentless and tyrannical. Or perhaps your Virgo doggedly expects precision and perfection from everyone else, to an unrealistic degree. In these cases, becoming skillful with your Virgo involves honing who you're being specific for, and why. If you investigate this, you might find that the problem is that you're feeling a demand from authorities beyond yourself. That's when we start to feel resentful and are capable of inflicting our inner tyranny on the outside world.

Here are a few empowering questions you might enjoy playing with when your Virgo feels unskillfully "too much" or is demanding more than you want to give: *On whose authority do I have to show up so polished? On whose authority is my effort not good enough?* Clearing your Virgo of conditioning that says you have to be perfect or "ready" before you can be worthy of validation is a form of trauma releasing. Ask yourself: *Is that voice mine or someone else's?*

The problem is not the refinement process in itself, but rather the programming that tells you that if you aren't perfect then you won't be worthy of love and appreciation. Shame alchemizes into self-acceptance when you clear out the internalized critical voice that's not really you.

Skillful Virgo recognizes that the parts of you that you thought were self-sabotaging your efforts are actually very intelligent and wise because they don't want to see you bending over backward for authorities other than your higher self. This part of you is deeply unimpressed with the standard for excellence that you've been conditioned to work toward and is helping you resist playing that game.

Bottom line this Virgo season: It's your life, so you define the Virgo standard. "Too much" stories are externally defined. When you clarify what you want to devote your authentic presence to and gently release yourself from other people's judgment or misunderstanding of those choices, then you will show up like the Virgo you always already are.

There is no destination to living your Virgo. It's all process. It's all practice. It's all play. Every single day.

. . . .

PRACTICE

Deal Breakers

If Virgo were a verb, "to Virgo" would mean devoting yourself to distilling your own essence, eliminating that which is not you, reclaiming sovereignty, feeling wholly unto yourself, intuiting what you don't need anymore, cleansing your body-mind-spirit system, and regenerating and renewing yourself.

Often when people think of Virgo, there's this idea that they're cleanliness freaks, exercise fiends, or nutritional perfectionists. Maybe everyone knows one Virgo who is like this. But this stereotype is only a consequence of the Virgo desire to feel in service to one's wholeness, using elimination and purification as part of a refinement process that is always ongoing with no destination. The process is what's important.

What happens when you really lean into your Virgo self is that you begin to resonate with and magnetize people who are also holding themselves to their own Virgo. What I mean by that is that they trust in their own boundaries, their own emotional healing, their own spiritual path. People who hold their Virgo do not lean on you to process their emotional baggage. By holding your own Virgo, you attract people who hold theirs, and together you can create the foundation of a responsible, mature, functional relationship.

So your practice this month is a self-reflection exercise considering your boundaries in terms of *deal breakers*. A deal breaker is a clear line that you will not cross or allow others to cross. Below, you'll find categories of deal breakers and some questions to get you started in thinking about your personal boundaries for this topic. Once you name a deal breaker, you become much more aware of your boundaries and can protect yourself with them. The goal is to become more and more specifically yourself, to feel more whole and sovereign.

With that in mind, the more you approach this holistically, the more it will nourish you in a broadly sustainable way. Work with this practice however feels most right and good for your truth. Take what you like and leave the rest. You might journal on one deal breaker category each day and create a master list. You could make Venn diagrams or visual boards. And then begin to practice enacting them in the world. Spend time giving physical form to your deal breakers.

- Conversational deal breakers: What will you not discuss or engage in or abide hearing (perhaps with certain categories of people)?
- Physical deal breakers: What forms or places of touch are not okay for you so you can feel safe in your body?
- Relational deal breakers: What is not acceptable to you from a partner or close friendship?
- Media consumption deal breakers: What are the limits to what is good for you?
- Nutritional consumption deal breakers: What foods, beverages, or substances are not meant to walk with you at all in this life or at least not over certain clear quantities?
- People deal breakers: Name folks who are just not good for you. What are the qualities in those people that aren't healthy for you?
- Energetic deal breakers: What energies will you not tolerate? (For example, someone's energy of invalidation.)
- Shopping deal breakers: What rules do you need or want for spending money? What rules do you have around the ethics of brands?
- Anti-privilege deal breakers: What verbalized or enacted biases, slurs, ignorance, or aggressions against BIPOC, queer, nonbinary, ability-different, body-different, or other non-normative folks will you not tolerate in your presence?
- Self-talk deal breakers: What negative or harmful words will you not say or think about or to yourself as part of your self-care practice?
- Marie Kondo–inspired deal breakers: What types of things in your home do not bring you joy and need to be eliminated for your space?

. . . .

TAROT CARD

The Hermit

The card in the tarot that we associate with Virgo is card nine, the Hermit.

The Hermit is an archetype with which most people have some level of familiarity. The Hermit is a person who voluntarily undergoes a period of seclusion from worldly life with the intent to connect with either a spiritual path or way of living that promises to heal and evolve them through self-denial, silence, prayer, or meditation. The Hermit's devotion to self-knowing recalls the vestal virgins of Virgo.

In the traditional *Smith-Rider-Waite* deck, the card depicts an older man in a stark landscape. He has some of the classic attributes of the Hermit such as a plain hooded cloak and a walking staff. Head down, the figure holds up a bright lantern, emphasizing that the light itself is more important than the personal face of the one holding it.

The invitation of the card is to get away from the world in order to come back to yourself. With the Hermit, you are drawn into your own yearnings to know the Self that hasn't been so programmed by culture, family, and capitalism. In this quiet cave, we are more attuned to the inner voice. We

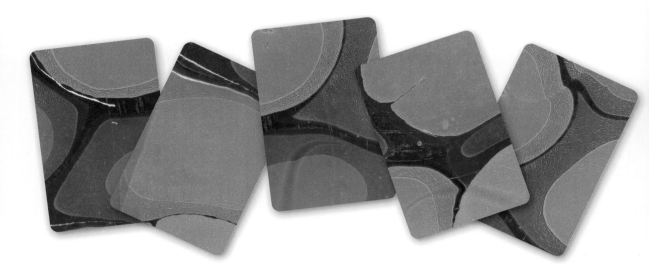

listen in the dark for our own answers: *Who am I away from all that? What am I capable of if I can only draw on my own will, courage, endurance, and other inner resources? What am I really made of?* Through this isolation and introspection, you retrieve parts of yourself that will be powerfully impactful when you go back out into the world.

The long, white-bearded look of the Hermit reminds me of the wandering wizard of great stories, such as Merlin and Gandalf. These types of characters spend a lot of time in study—learning and developing wisdom and skill in their arts. Yet they also spend a lot of time walking the land in order to serve others with their amassed knowledge. They put their studies to work in the world. This is the lantern in the image.

We live in a culture that applauds mic drops and hot takes, but truly profound insights come from cultivating practices of listening and contemplation. To live the Hermit is to live your own wisdom, a very Virgo sentiment. This Virgo season, consider what ways you might lean in to the Hermit in yourself. Perhaps, for example, you might want to go on an "advice freeze" and take thirty days to not ask for anyone's thoughts or opinions on your life.

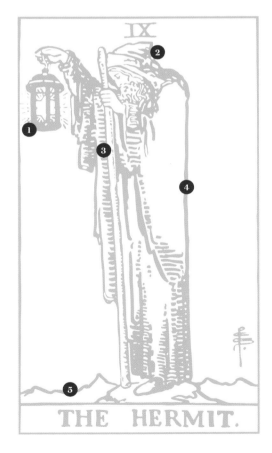

A Tarot Spread with the Hermit

See the chapter *How to Navigate This Book* if you're new to the tarot and seek support for pulling cards and interpreting them.

Take the Hermit out of your deck. (If you have more than one deck, you

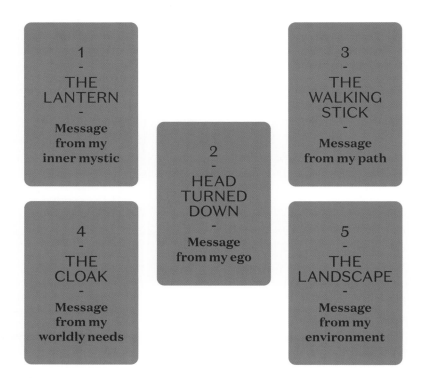

can pull the card from another deck so that the Hermit has a chance to "participate" in the deck from which you will draw.)

Feel into the visual inspiration of the card.

Take a few deep breaths on purpose and arrive to the reading. Connect into your intuition. Ask Virgo-Hermit energy to help you with this reading. Shuffle according to your unique, never-wrong style. Center and focus your question thus:

For my highest and best, at the highest levels of love and compassion, I want to know: What is the loving invitation to connect with my inner Hermit this Virgo season?

Pull five cards according to your own unique process of knowing with the following prompts, and then sit with the cards and journal about them.

. . . .

RITUAL FOR THE NEW MOON

Connect to and Refine Your Core Striving

As you've been learning, connecting with Virgo has to do with leaning toward the appropriate processes and practices in your life that protect, preserve, and honor what matters to you. Virgo is about refinement.

Part of refinement is elimination, so for this season's ritual, we'll be creating sigils. A *sigil* is a symbol representing a place, business, family, or any kind of outcome. In modern advertising, a logo is a form of sigil. Think of the Nike swoosh, the Starbucks mermaid, McDonalds' golden arches, the Mercedes star, or Chanel's double Cs. It's like a pictorial signature that distills the essence of what it represents in an immediately recognizable visual. Though there are many ways to go about sigil making, here is a simple method of elimination and refinement:

- Write out the letters of the topic (your name, your business, or whatever it is) in all caps.
- Cross out all of the vowels.
- Looking at the consonants left over, detach them from their meanings as letters and begin to see them as abstract patterns.
- Notice how some parts of letters repeat like the long straight vertical lines of an M or H, or the half-circle curve of a P or R.
- Start to move these common shapes around, totally forgetting their original order and eliminating any shapes that you want to edit, so that they begin to create a design that you find aesthetically pleasing or potent.
- Once you land on a final design, you have your sigil.

You can then play with your sigil in intentional ways as a form of engaging with what it represents and the outcomes you most desire. The sigil's power is in the refinement of its making. It holds the essence of what it is.

For this ritual, you will create a sigil from the letters of your full name as a form of Virgoan refinement in your life.

Before beginning this ritual, gather:

- Candles, as many as you want, and a way to light them
- Sheets of loose paper
- Your journal and a pen

The Ritual

1. Sit at your Virgo altar when ready. Set up your ritual container, light your candle, and come to a grounded, meditative state (see page 57).

2. When you feel relaxed and ready to receive, connect with a clear intention for refinement in your life.

3. Using the sheets of loose paper, begin to create a sigil with the letters of your full name, or the name of your business or handle, or the name you want people to call you. Follow the steps above. Get lost in the process of eliminating what is no longer needed to bring you to the essence of a design that feels complete to you. You can't do this wrong. It's an intuitive process.

4. Once you've reached a final design, put a copy in your journal, and then make a large version that takes up a whole sheet of paper.

5. With your finger, trace the outlines of your sigil while you focus your thoughts and say out loud, "I refine the processes and practices of my life so that I can protect, preserve, and honor what matters most to me." Do this at least three times.

6. Doing this may bring to your awareness anything you want to eliminate or do less of this month so you can feel more refined. If so, write these down and commit to honoring what you notice.

7. Determine to place this sheet of paper under your mattress and forget about it. Trust that at some point, your future self will remember that it's there.

8. Conclude and open the ritual container (see page 66).

Notice how you feel over the coming days. Be sure to circle back to journal more about any insight that rolls in later.

Happy New Moon in Virgo!

Libra

SEPTEMBER 22–OCTOBER 22

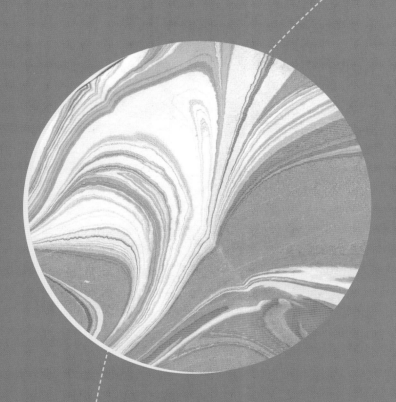

♎ LIBRA

△ AIR

◺ CARDINAL

♀ VENUS

Questions to Live Into

What can I do today to give the world more beauty?

How can I show up to my relationships in ways that prioritize reciprocity, where both parties give and receive in right balance?

What am I doing to live each choice from my most discerning place of truth and sound judgment?

Altar

As discussed in part one, the purpose of creating an altar is to first prepare and then enjoy having a special space devoted to the themes and principles you're developing with each sign. The general qualities of Libra are listed below. I recommend you gather at least three items, but quantity isn't as crucial as choosing items of resonance for you. For example, this season, maybe there's just one theme you want to focus on, such as beauty. Then create a space that represents what feels beautiful to you and your own unique taste. Take the suggestions that feel aligned and don't worry about the rest. As you read through the chapter, more ideas may come to you for your altar that aren't listed here.

Go for it!

COLORS
green, light blue, pink

CRYSTALS
copper, emerald, jade, jasper, opal, rose quartz, smoky quartz

GARDEN
damiana, hydrangeas, jasmine, passionflower, rose, violet, yarrow

SPICES AND FLAVORS
clove, garam masala, nutmeg, sandalwood, turmeric

GODS AND GODDESSES
Aphrodite, Astraea, Athena, Juno, Ma'at, Venus

TAROT CARDS
Justice, the Empress, 2 of Swords, 3 of Swords, 4 of Swords

ITEMS
art, books, ceramics, fabrics, food, incense, magazine cutouts, photographs, quotes on paper, or anything else that inspires you

RELATED THEMES
art, apples, beauty, balance, equilibrium, fairness, fall, Friday, Instagram, justice, law, nickels, pentagrams, reciprocity, relationships, relating, sword of truth, wabi sabi, wisdom

SEASON

Beginning of Autumn

Libra season is a time when the winds shift. The first day of Libra is also the beginning of autumn, what is known as the autumn equinox. The equinoxes are the midway points between the winter and summer solstices, the shortest and the longest days of the year, respectively.

Equinox actually means "equal night," for the fact that at the equinox the day holds equal parts light and dark. This is ever shifting. Once we pass the autumn equinox, that singular moment in time, we tip toward shorter and shorter days, the deep dark of winter approaching. In this way, the equinoxes speak to the times of the year when we shift from a more external way of being (spring and summer) to a more internal style of inhabiting our skin (fall and winter).

So it is an essential part of Libra to mark this tipping period of the year when we shift into fall. We activate a different part of ourselves.

The glyph for Libra looks like a horizon line with a sun either rising or setting. Sunrise and sunset are very wondrous times of day, but they are also profoundly disorienting. Our daytime self is totally different than our nighttime self, especially if you consider human life before electricity. In a much broader way, this represents the shift of the equinoxes.

Libra, while known as a sign drawn to the beautiful, is also a sign that works hard to smooth over the disequilibrium and messiness of life. Fall is a strange time. In Libra season, there are green leaves next to red ones. The shift is startling, and there is often a degree of grief that goes with it.

What does this time of year mean for you? What are the sensory qualities that you associate with Libra season? What are the rituals, the celebrations, the habits, the foods, and the libations for this period in your family and community? All of your feelings and associations regarding this time of year are important to your overall story with Libra energy.

MODALITY AND ELEMENT
Cardinal Air

Like the other cardinal signs (Aries, Cancer, and Capricorn), Libra initiates a new season. It is the energy to turn the wheel out of summer and into fall. There is so much power in this shift.

Like the other Air signs (Gemini and Aquarius), Libra is the part of us that communicates, relates, and makes meaning.

In nature, I see cardinal Air in cool winds that rustle leaves on their branches, some still green from summer's glow, some yellow with change. All beings respond to the crisp air and diminishing light in their own ways and with their own timing.

In the human world, we see cardinal Air in the diplomat who can sit with someone who has a very different agenda and help them relax into their humanity enough to find common connection. Libra is that person who always seems to possess beautiful words of sound judgment. Libra is anyone who must make art of their way of life.

Cardinal Air wants to initiate relating to someone or something, including different parts of yourself, through both verbal and nonverbal channels of communication. It encourages you to notice the vibe of the people and energy of the environment. You attune to what would be needed to bring more goodness to any space you are in. But just recognizing this need doesn't mean you have to feel it. A very important step that we often bypass is asking ourselves if we feel like turning on our Libran charm or if that would be draining. When you have your answer, then honor what resonates.

Honor what resonates. All the time.

Air is the space between. And the space between people is so often charged with something: desire, judgment, anger, annoyance, insecurity, confusion, projection. When we are totally neutral, then there isn't much to connect us or a reason to keep talking, is there? And so cardinal Air is the part of you that cultivates counterpoint awareness: your capacity to be aware of the viewpoint that is not yours in any given moment, whether it's complementary to yours or starkly different. We lean into engaging with one another while we're subtly reading the cues and negotiating both our point of view and our conversation partner's.

You need counterpoint awareness to be able to function as a human being living in social culture. You're all doing this all the time. The Libra part of you just does it with more finesse than other parts of you. The Libra part of you is the one you congratulate after a tough conversation went smoothly, and you feel proud of how fair you felt, how honestly you listened, and how loving but clear your boundaries were.

SYMBOL
The Scales

Libra is the only zodiac constellation in the sky represented wholly by an inanimate object: the Scales. It was the Romans who officially gave Libra the status of constellation, seeing it as the Scales of Astraea, goddess of justice.

The Scales are, of course, connected to the concept of the law: both divine law and also codes of law governed by a ruling body of some kind. Scales represent the idea of weighing the interests of one person or group's needs or actions against the interests of another person or group's needs or actions. How do they measure up? What is fair?

In medical astrology, Libra rules the kidneys. The kidneys are a pair of organs that regulate the electrolyte, acid-base, and salt balances of the body. The kidneys assess the fluids of the body and flush out toxins to restore equilibrium. This process exemplifies how Libra is a part of us that is able to pick up on subtle, unseen cues from within and around us that tell the body something is off. The Libran in us responds to these in order to restore the order we crave, whether it's a change in design aesthetic, an adjustment to the way we're moving through space, or a vibe shift we want to bring to a conversation.

The personification of the concept of justice and balance goes back to the Egyptian goddess Ma'at. Ma'at represented order, law, and harmony as the counterpoint to chaos, injustice, and violence. Ma'at is recognizable in art by the ostrich feather at her brow: the feather of truth. The most notable aspect of Ma'at's mythology is the legendary Weighing of the Heart ceremony. The judgment of the dead was a lengthy and very important process of the afterlife in ancient Egypt. The goal was to determine the worthiness of a soul based on how they had lived. This was done by placing the dead person's heart opposite Ma'at's feather on her set of scales. If the scale was balanced—meaning they had lived a just and truthful life—then the soul was allowed to journey to a realm of paradise. Any heart heavier than her feather was devoured by a demon, permanently destroying the soul of the deceased.

Ma'at was more than a goddess. Ma'at represented the entire principle of a way of life. She infused all social interactions, dealings and negotiations, seasonal cycles, rituals, and ways of showing up in the community. If there is harmony in the cosmos, so it goes, then one should act in harmony on earth.

Ma'at and her Weighing of the Heart ceremony help us feel the roots of the Libra archetype, which teaches us good and sound judgment so that our hearts will feel light. Here I don't mean *judgment* like being judgy or critical of other people's business. I mean *judgment* as the ability to determine what to do after wisely deliberating and weighing out the options, evidence, and possible consequences.

The Libran part of you values good judgment. What does it feel like in the body when you have acted in good judgment? How does it feel in your heart? What does it feel like in the body when you regret your judgment? How does it feel in your heart?

This month, I invite you to bring more conscious awareness to how the things you say and do, the choices you make, affect your heart. You might ask yourself: *Will my heart feel lighter or heavier?* I have learned that if I ignore doing the harder thing, such as having an honest conversation with someone that might be sticky, a part of me is relieved. But then there's an energetic drain and heaviness of knowing something isn't right or in balance by my avoidance. The heart knows.

POLARITY

The Libra-Aries Axis

All Air signs are opposite Fire signs, and all polar signs have the same modality. So cardinal Air is opposite cardinal Fire: Aries.

Aries initiates spring with one equinox just as Libra initiates autumn with the other. Aries and Libra turn the wheel of the year with such potency because both catalyze massive change in light and temperature that totally alter how we experience our world.

- Libra surrounds themselves with choices; Aries pinpoints a path with decisiveness.
- Libra savors the "we"; Aries focuses on "me."
- Libra softens into fall, enjoying the fruits of summer's labor; Aries kick-starts spring, revving up for a season of explosive growth.

As an Aries Rising, I always marvel at the charm of the Libra, their smooth way of speaking that puts everyone at ease. The Libras I've known have been quite popular people, very savvy and witty conversationalists, excellent at keeping their reputation sparkly and clear, and generally the ones in the room who everyone wants to talk to. If you need to raise money for a cause, ask a Libran person to do the soliciting. If you want to word an email in a way that won't rub someone the wrong way, ask a Libran friend to proofread it for you.

The Aries-Libra polarity tells a story about the spectrum between pure agency and pure dependency. While it is important to not make decisions lightly, the Libran part of you can get hooked in the deliberation process, wondering about how to make the best move when there are so many different factors to consider and so many ways to piss someone off. Aries is impatient with having to wait on other people and weigh all the options. Aries says, just do the thing.

Aries helps Libra move projects along. Aries doesn't get why we can't just be direct and blunt. The Aries in you finds small talk supremely boring. Aries doesn't have time for Libra's pleasantries and foreplay. Aries just wants to get to the point as fast as possible. Aries will kick your Libra in the ass.

In short, Aries helps Libra not only *get* what you want, but *know* what you want. Libra wants to please everyone so badly that you can lose your own compass. Aries never loses their compass.

. . . .

RULING PLANET

Venus

Like the fixed Earth sign of Taurus, Libra is ruled by Venus. Venus represents your capacity to attract, magnetize, and receive what you want and desire.

The overculture would like us to believe that Venus is a side teacher, a romantic interest to the hero, a pretty little ditty. What's missing in that characterization is the potent vitality and visceral generativity of this archetype. Venus is what yogis call *Shakti*: the primordial, cosmic energy that runs life-force energy through everything, including all creation and destruction.

Venus is an energy that makes everything in our lives feel more alive, animated, and fertile. Through Taurus, Venus teaches us about sensuality, tending and cultivating the garden, setting milk and honey for the table, and taking care of our bodies. Through Libra, Venus teaches us about the beauty expressed in relationship and in the environment.

Venus is in that Libran capacity to disarm people, as in quite literally, to lay down their arms, weapons, or defenses. When we lay down our arms, we are more likely to listen from the heart. Venus rules the heart chakra, the place in the body where it's safe to love and send compassion. Venus is the transporting embrace of the Libran presence in other people and in ourselves.

Venus makes things beautiful, which is why Libra is often tied to artistic sensibility. The origins of "aesthetic" lead back to the ancient Greek *aesthesis*, relating to the perception of the senses. Aesthetically, as an Air sign, the Libra in us aims to inhabit language and thoughts with beauty, wonder, and amazement. This reminds me of one of my favorite lines by poet Emily Dickinson, who had a Libra Moon, "The soul should always stand ajar, ready to welcome the ecstatic experience."

This isn't to say that your Venus can't sometimes be obsessed with aesthetic needs, stances, and opinions in ways that rule your life more than you want. I like to joke that my Venus can be tyrannical when I can't enjoy something because I don't like how it looks, or the color palette feels off, or the vibe isn't how I want it to be.

Venus helps you to identify and understand your preferences—and don't let anyone tell you that your preferences don't matter. Preferences are what make us unique and human. Yes, we are spirits inhabiting bodies and we have a right to enjoy how we do it. Thank you, Venus.

SKILLFUL LIBRA
Negotiate

Libra wants you to know: the most loving thing you can do is to deeply care about attuning to the relational dynamics of the environment. And it's also okay if sometimes what is most just and right and fair for you will bring disagreement and disharmony to the space.

When people talk about Libra being about balance, that doesn't mean the actual achievement of balance. Homeostasis is always fleeting, and the experience of balance is constantly relative to another person, stimulus, or external factor—all of which are out of your control. Skillful Libra is instead about negotiating *im*-balance, *dis*-equilibrium, *a*-symmetry. You can only control your own side of the scales, and what you do with your side matters.

For the Libra in us, everything is about contracts. There are legal contracts (remember that Libra relates to the law) where we create clear language with certain relationships and bind that in a document. However, many qualities of the felt relationships we have in the world are not clearly delineated in print. So I like to think of Libra as relating to our *energetic* contracts.

Energetically, we fall into patterns and ways of relating in the world that feel habitual and entrenched in a set of agreements that might not have ever been spoken. We have deeply rooted ways of relating to those we're in committed relationships with, and then we have ways of relating to friends, authorities, colleagues, and other folks in our various networks. It's a feeling of: "I agree to be like this (fill in the blank with behaviors, qualities, styles you feel allowed and encouraged to bring and not bring), and you agree to be like that (what the other person brings, is allowed to bring, isn't allowed to bring)."

In your desire to be liked, keep the peace, or not be seen as a "bad" or unfriendly person, you might sacrifice what you want, stay in a situation longer than is healthy for you, or participate in gossip you're not into—all in the name of keeping the scales balanced.

If you grew up feeling like love, safety, and validation were more achievable for you if you sacrificed your needs, wants, and preferences, then you may have developed what is called a fawning response. Fawning is an intelligent coping strategy for protecting the younger self from someone's anger, annoyance, or chaotic behavior. And it can continue into adult life and repeat in our partnerships and other relationships.

When we fawn, we stop listening to the body's information about our desires in order to maintain our sense of safety. We learn to wear masks that don't reflect how we actually feel inside. Skillful Libra notices and names that having to perform a specific way to keep someone from being upset with you is neither fair nor beautiful.

To stand inside your skillful Libra, you center the importance of the body's sensations and the voice of your intuition. This is a practice of listening, of unlearning the habitual response to fawn, and of growing trust that sometimes the most beautiful thing between people is for them to disagree while each standing in their own truth.

Love Notes to Yourself

The longer I've been devoted to my healing path, the more I come to see the truth that whatever limits I have on the amount of love, grace, and respect I give myself will be the same limits I place on the amount of love, grace, and respect I give to other people. If I want to experience more expansive generosity in my relationships, then I need to expand my capacity for self-generosity.

The Libra practice this month is to write yourself love letters. It may seem strange to have a self-focused practice for a sign that is very relational, but there's a logic at play. You are one side of the scales. Your partner (in any kind of relationship) is the other. There must be balance, and the only side that you can truly control is your own.

I'd like you to get a pack of sticky notes. Every day of the thirty days of Libra (and beyond if you like), I want you to write yourself a sincere compliment and then stick it on the wall some place where you can see them all together, maybe the inside of your closet door or on the bathroom mirror.

The only rule is that the compliment must be different each day. They can be simple: "My mole is really cool." "I bake excellent sugar cookies." "My laugh helps people relax." "My friends can count on me to be honest." They can also be specific rather than general: "I handled that conflict this morning with a lot of patience." "I showed up to my running goal this morning." "I looked hot in my new blazer today."

Warning: this may not be comfortable. Sincerity means that you really mean it and that it feels true to you. You might want to be ironic in your love note. This is an intelligent form of defense that we've been taught to deploy to seem smart and detached. If there are days when you truly can't find another compliment for yourself, then do it ironically. Play along as if you were serious even if and when you don't feel it. Put the sticky note on the wall.

Every five days, I want you to take a moment to read each one, and I want you to do it out loud. I want you to hear yourself.

At the end of the month, record a voice memo reading all of your love notes, and then take a photo. Ask yourself if you'd like to keep going. Ask yourself if you want to take them down and paste them in your journal. Do what feels resonant.

To close the practice, set aside some space to journal or talk about it with a friend you trust. Let yourself debrief the experience. Ask yourself what it was like mentally, emotionally, physically, and spiritually, since you might hear different answers for each of those ways of knowing yourself. Notice if this practice has shifted what you recognize and acknowledge about yourself. And, finally, notice if this practice shifts the way you talk to the people in your life.

TAROT CARD
Justice

The card in the tarot that we associate with Libra is card eleven, Justice.

Justice has clear ties to ancient archetypal depictions of Lady Justice, going back to the Greek goddess Themis. Themis was the goddess of divine order, whose attributes were the Scales of Justice, representing balance and pragmatism, and the Sword of Truth, representing the ability to cut through bullshit.

In the Justice card, as depicted in the traditional *Smith-Rider-Waite* deck, we see a robed, gender-neutral figure seated on some type of throne between two pillars, one of Themis's attributes in each hand. Behind the figure is a curtain that firmly foregrounds the figure. The throne is on the ground, but there is a sense of "no place" to the image, which is fitting because Justice is an abstract concept we inhabit, embody, inhale, and exude.

Justice is a card that invites us to look at what is. You can't change things (as in make them more just) if you aren't willing to look at them *as they currently are.* A phrase that embodies Justice is: "What you allow is what will continue." The only way to begin to create meaningful and nourishing shifts here is to cultivate clear eyes to see what we're "allowing" now.

You can't make your partnerships more equitable and loving if you aren't willing to be honest about the dynamics at play right now. You can't build a life of vitality and lusty well-being if you aren't willing to look at harmful ways you might treat or talk about your body. You can't entertain dreams for your community in the future without looking at how they actually are in present time.

Justice invites us to have the bravery and discernment to be with what is, so we can respond from grounded reality rather than a fantasy of future potential. Libra is an Air sign, so it helps us to hold the Sword of Truth, severing connections with the extraneous or unhelpful.

A Tarot Spread with Justice

See the chapter *How to Navigate This Book* if you're new to the tarot and seek support for pulling cards and interpreting them.

Take Justice out of your deck. (If you have more than one deck, you can pull the card from another deck so that Justice has a chance to "participate" in the deck from which you will draw.)

Feel into the visual inspiration of the card.

Take a few deep breaths on purpose and arrive to the reading. Connect into your intuition. Ask Justice-Libra energy

to help you with this reading. Shuffle according to your unique, never-wrong style. Center and focus your question thus:

For my highest and best, at the highest levels of love and compassion, I want to know: What is the loving invitation to connect with Justice this Libra season?

Pull seven cards according to your own unique process of knowing with the prompts above, and then sit with the cards and journal about them.

What you're looking for here is a message about how to connect with yourself with reverence.

RITUAL FOR THE NEW MOON

Update Energetic Contracts

The most regenerating gift you can give your relationships is the truth of being in the present, standing inside yourself as who you are right now and giving the other person full permission to be who they are as well. In the language of Libran energetic contracts, you should take the time to update your contracts regularly and rigorously so you can be totally clear with partners, friends, and others in your life.

The baseline for updating energetic contracts with people is to accept that relationships must shift, change, morph, realign, die, and be born again and again and again. By updating contracts regularly, shifts in your relationships feel flexible, nimble, and subtle.

It is wise, fair, and loving in any relationship for both members to be who they are with one another, trusting in each other's capacity to sit with potentially weird or uncomfortable conversations about your preferences. Of course, sometimes an updated contract results in the termination of the contract. This does not mean that you are or the other person is a failure, though it may be a sign that you could be doing more consistent rebalancing and updating of your contracts.

Before beginning this ritual, gather:

- Your journal and pen
- Candles, as many as you want, and a way to light them
- Something sweet to give yourself at the end of the ritual: a spoon of honey with apple slices and/or a piece of chocolate

The Ritual

1. Sit at your Libra altar when ready. Set up your ritual container, light your candle, and come to a grounded, meditative state (see page 57).

2. Call in guidance, asking to be supported in this moment as you magnetize more balance, harmony, beauty, and love to your life. Ask for wisdom, clarity, and discernment. Ask to be lovingly held as you shift into this new season.

3. Set an intention to practice updating a contract with someone important in your life right now, maybe pick one where the relationship feels out of balance.

4. Imagine or feel the presence of this person as if they were across from you in the room about five to six feet away. Say hello to their spirit.

5. Now feel into your energetic contract you have with them: the expectations, assumptions, attachments, and agreements that go into each of your roles and jobs in the dynamic. Is one of you assumed to be wealthier? Funnier? More fashionable? More educated? More direct? More skilled with romance or kids or work? Write down what comes up.

6. Ask yourself to notice if, in this contract, you:
    *   feel any resentment. If so, ask yourself for more information. What's under the resentment? (Write down anything you want to remember for these questions.)
    *   feel any frustration or anger. If so, ask yourself for more information. What's underneath?
    *   feel any intimidation or invalidation. If so, ask yourself for more information. What's underneath?
    *   feel grounded and safe. If so, ask yourself for more information. What supports the grounding and safety?

- feel seen and attuned to. If so, ask yourself for more information. What supports this feeling?
- wish you could do the partnership differently. Ask yourself if you feel it has old or stale energy in the way you operate. Ask yourself if it feels like one or both of you would benefit from making amends, coming clean, or saying something as yet unsaid.
- have any other questions you wish to ask.

7. Based on everything you've seen, felt, and heard, ask yourself to clear out whatever in the contract is no longer in alignment with your brightest, emerging self. Visualize or feel the contract recharging with the vitality of present time. Ask the contact if it would be helpful to have a conversation with this person sometime soon where you can speak your truth.

8. Now ask yourself if you feel complete. If so, say goodbye the person's spirit and—before leaving your meditative space—commit to following through with the update energetically and verbally, if needed.

9. Ask yourself if it would be supportive to you to do this exercise with anyone else across Libra season. Set an intention to commit to whatever feels nourishing for you relationally right now.

10. Feed yourself your sweet treat! How do you feel? What did you notice?

11. Conclude and open the ritual container (see page 66).

In the weeks to come, notice how it feels to be more updated in your relationships.

Happy New Moon in Libra!

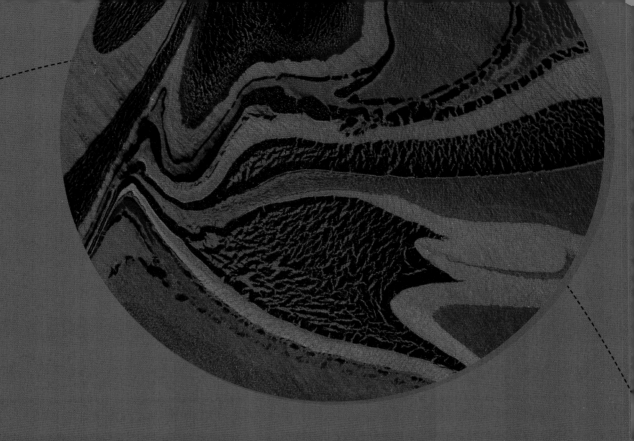

Scorpio

OCTOBER 22–NOVEMBER 21

♏ SCORPIO

▽ WATER

⊡ FIXED

♂ ♇ MARS AND PLUTO

Questions to Live Into

If my life is a Disney movie, what would it be like to walk through my day as the sassy villain who has all the best lines and most fabulous costumes?

How can I call in more trust that I am brave enough to see the hidden motivations behind what I say and do?

What am I ready to witness, integrate, and heal from the emotional consequences of my relationships, past and present?

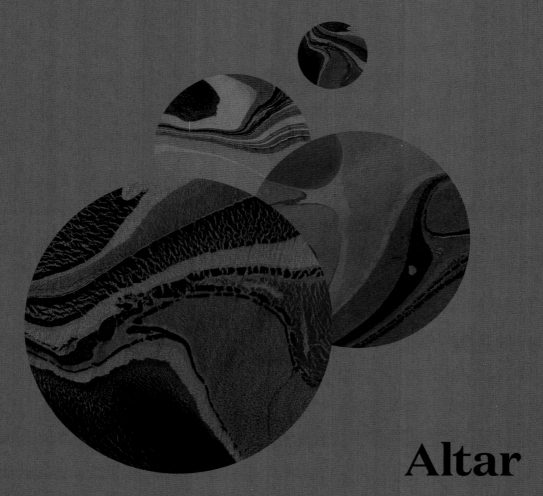

Altar

As discussed in part one, the purpose of creating an altar is to first prepare and then enjoy having a special space devoted to the themes and principles you're developing with each sign. The general qualities of Scorpio are listed below. I recommend you gather at least three items, but quantity isn't as crucial as choosing items of resonance for you. For example, this season, maybe you feel excited to build an altar to your ancestral lineage. Your entire altar space could be full of only items with references to family such as photos, old letters, folk costumes, and heirloom pieces that matter to you. Take the suggestions that feel aligned and don't worry about the rest. As you read through the chapter, more ideas may come to you for your altar that aren't listed here.

Go for it!

COLORS
black, purple, red

CRYSTALS
bloodstone, hematite,
iron, onyx, red jasper

GARDEN
apple, blessed thistle,
damiana, pomegranate,
pumpkin, witch hazel

SPICES AND FLAVORS
anything with spiky
leaves or a strong
spicy taste that causes
a physical reaction

**GODS AND
GODDESSES**
Ceridwen, Demeter,
Ereshkigal, Hekate,
Inanna, Kali, Lilith,
the Morrigan,
Persephone, Pluto

TAROT CARDS
Death, the Tower,
Judgment, 5 of Cups,
6 of Cups, 7 of Cups

ITEMS
art, books, ceramics,
fabrics, food, incense,
magazine cutouts,
photographs, quotes
on paper, or anything
else that inspires you

RELATED THEMES
ancestors, autumn,
death, decay, eagles,
eroticism, the
phoenix, regeneration,
scorpions, sexual
healing, shiny and
dark objects, snakes,
Tuesday, witches

SEASON

Middle of Autumn

The shifts that Libra initiated take hold in Scorpio. Here we are midway between the autumn equinox and the winter solstice. This point on the wheel of the year is variously known across cultures and beliefs by many names, among them Samhain, Día de los Muertos, Halloween, Calan Gaeaf, Kalan Gwav, and the Witches' New Year.

Many traditions hold that at this time the veil between our world and the Otherworld is thinnest. By "Otherworld," I refer to the spirit realm, or the realm that is mostly unseen by us humans in the material world. In my own personal cosmology, the spirits of all sentient and non-sentient beings—for example, our ancestors, angels, astral guides, planetary guides, and galactic guides—all reside in the Otherworld.

You don't have to share my cosmology to live Scorpio, but you might enjoy experimenting with the idea that this is a time of year when you're supported in honoring your ancestors. Healing through remembrance, games, offerings, intuited messages, and deep dreaming are all celebrated activities in Scorpio season. In some of the following sections, I will prompt you to call in any support from the spirit realm that feels resonant for you. You can ignore this prompt if it's not in alignment with your cosmology, but I encourage you to play around with it.

In the physical world, we experience a clear turn of the wheel. In the northern hemisphere, we're registering more darkness, natural death, and a time for more internal focus and rest. In the southern hemisphere, there is the polar phenomenon with the rebirth into warmer weather and lusher gardens. Either way, this window is a profound portal for recognizing the cycle of life and death.

In her incredible book *Women Who Run with the Wolves*, Dr. Clarissa Pinkola Estés encourages a regular meditative practice with the Life-Death-Life nature of all existence. She asks profound questions that can guide your time this season: "What must I give more death to today, in order to generate more life? What do I know should die, but am hesitant to allow to do so? What must die in me in order for me to love? What not-beauty do I fear? Of what use is the not-beautiful to me today? What should die today? What should live? What life am I afraid to give birth to? If not now, when?"

Take some time to journal about how this time of year typically feels for you. What patterns of experience, relational dynamics, or life questions tend to repeat for you in the season? The ways you personally connect to this time of year will inform how you experience Scorpio.

. . . .

MODALITY AND ELEMENT
Fixed Water

Like the other fixed signs (Taurus, Leo, and Aquarius), Scorpio roots down into the essential qualities inside ourselves that we're learning with the arc of the season. If the question is, what does autumn do? Then the Scorpio within is the part that facilitates what autumn requires.

Like the other Water signs (Cancer and Pisces), Scorpio cares for the emotional realm, the more primordial and mysterious aspects of our human experience, the deep wisdom of our ancestral lineage, the power of our intuition.

In nature, fixed Water can be ice and snow. Deep, slowly moving underground waterways in caverns and canyons. Bogs and marshes. Mud and flooded land. By analogy, we can imagine Scorpio's deep reservoirs of feeling and how it is not easily moved except by great force and effort.

Because of its fixity, Scorpio is more natural at holding boundaries than Cancer or Pisces. Scorpio knows how to say Yes and No to most people without feeling guilty or apologizing. However, your Scorpio will be intensely affected by the few people's opinions they deeply care about. Scorpio is also prone to absorbing other people's energy and the vibes in environments and benefits from learning how to ground out what isn't theirs to carry.

In human form, fixed Water is the surgeon successfully isolating a tumor. It's the detective brilliantly tracking clues. It's the comedian slinging targeted zingers. Each is resolutely fixed in purpose. You trust in your intuition to guide your direction as you traverse the unknown. You are determined and fully committed to get what you want. You know you're good—maybe the best—at what you do.

> You trust in your intuition to guide.

Fixed Water encourages you to identify the root cause of pain, insecurity, fear, a secret, or a shadowy behavior, and then extract that root cause and make it known, even if it's uncomfortable. And then, says Scorpio, you must enjoy your victory.

Fixed Water is a part of you that is very strategic. Coldly cunning. Icily shrewd. It's a part of you that isn't designed to please everyone. Not everyone likes the confidence of the surgeon who is always right. The detective reveals hard facts that someone designed to stay secret. Some people leave the room if the comedian's jokes cross their line.

When you engage your Scorpio in service to deep truths, it may bring up information not everyone is ready to see. Take some time to reflect on what comes up for you from your life as you read this. Have there been times when you had to sit in the discomfort of another's displeasure when you felt you needed to be raw with honesty? How did that feel? How did you care for yourself?

The Scorpion, Eagle, or Phoenix ♏

Scorpio has more symbols than any other sign. The ancient Babylonians called it "the creature with a burning sting," after the Scorpion. In Greek mythology, the great huntsman Orion boasted to the goddess Artemis that he could kill any animal on the planet. So Artemis sent a Scorpion to prove him wrong. When Zeus discovered the battle, he sent both Orion and the Scorpion to the sky as constellations as a warning to mortals not to be so proud.

We learn a lot about the Scorpio essence from the biological properties of a scorpion. Scorpions have a hard exoskeleton and find their way around by using receptors and hairs that pick up on vibrations and scents in the environment. They are thus incredibly sensitive, perceptive, and intuitive. Scorpions tends to stay low to the ground and hidden but will sting you if you get too close. If cornered, the scorpion will sting itself rather than risk getting hurt by another.

Scorpions are very ancient, very tough creatures. They can take on incredibly high temperatures, withstanding extremes in climate. Likewise, the Scorpio within can be hardy, enduring, persistent, and exceedingly strong through hard times. We admire the Scorpion just as we admire the Scorpio, but we're also afraid of both. This dichotomy is part of what attracts me to the archetype.

The Eagle is another apt symbol for Scorpio because of the bird's keen sight, patience, and skilled ability to penetrate when ready to hunt. Some eagles have visual acuity that is three to three-and-a-half times more powerful than humans. The Scorpio is the part of us with serious depth perception and sharp sight. The Scorpio is sharp-eyed, possessing shrewd intelligence.

Just as scorpions like the seclusion of shadow, so eagles build their nests up high in tall trees and on cliffs. Either way, these habits align with the Scorpio's desire for distance. Scorpio needs space. Scorpio craves alone time. In private, Scorpio recovers and regains strength before dealing with the world again.

My personal favorite symbol for Scorpio is the Phoenix, the fire bird who cyclically regenerates, lighting itself on fire, only to be born again from the ashes. The Phoenix was often associated with Sun gods, including Christ, because the Sun (Son) is reborn again and again.

Like the Phoenix, the Scorpio within us is that part of the self that knows that sometimes we must destroy before we can create. We have to let go of certain fears, masks, strivings, obsessions, and other ego-based clinging that keep us from evolving to the next level. The Scorpio is the part of the self that we can lean on through major change, transitions, and shifting identities.

The Scorpio inside of you is very, very brave, as it can be so hard to let go and trust in renewal that is as yet unseen and unknown. Just because the Scorpio story is about transformation, that doesn't mean transforming is easy for Scorpio. Remember that this is a *fixed* sign. It takes a major force to shift the Scorpio into change.

· ·

POLARITY

The Scorpio-Taurus Axis

All Water signs are opposite Earth signs, and all polar signs have the same modality. So fixed Water is opposite fixed Earth: Taurus.

Taurus is the middle of spring. It is about slow, sensual experiencing of the earth's abundance and the delights of being alive. It is juicy fruits. It is the mother's milk. It is the viscosity of honey and the ooze of the yolk. Taurus is our investment in what is beautiful, what is pleasurable, and what feels good.

The Scorpio-Taurus polarity tells a story about the spectrum between roots and fruits, and how our life-force energy moves within that spectrum.

- Scorpio is a graveyard; Taurus is a garden.

- Scorpio is about the ancestors you honor; Taurus is about the children (biological or creative) you bear.
- Scorpio is what you give up to share (Water: merged investments); Taurus is what you gather for yourself (Earth: personal assets).

At either end of this spectrum, we find Persephone. She is daughter of the Great Mother Demeter, who is the goddess of agriculture and all things Taurus. According to one telling of Persephone's story, she was abducted by Hades (or Pluto), ruler of Scorpio, and made to be his bride and the Queen of the Underworld. Eventually, due to her mother's pleading, a deal was struck to allow Persephone to go home half of the year, which is when we have spring and summer in the northern hemisphere, and return below for fall and winter. Because of Demeter's grief, no crops grow while Persephone is with the dead.

Thus, the Taurus-Scorpio spectrum has to do with deep acceptance of the Life-Death-Life cycle. We cannot have Taurus (the life of spring) without Scorpio (the death of autumn). And of course, since we are all nature, this is both a truth that manifests literally (cleaning out closets in Taurus season, clearing the garden in Scorpio season) and also one that describes an internal process of self-healing by going deep into our past and our unconscious realm to clear space for new emotional growth.

· ·

RULING PLANETS

Mars and Pluto ♂ ♇

Mars is the traditional ruler of Scorpio and Aries. Mars is the part of you that goes after what you want. Mars is your energetic force, your assertiveness, your passion. Through Aries, Mars moves quickly and ardently. Through Scorpio, Mars runs strategically and precisely.

The glyph for Scorpio has the same pointed tail as the glyph for Mars. For both, the thrust of that point relates to the thrust of our life-force energy. Mars gives Scorpio its pointed, unapologetic drive.

Mars is the God of War, and it's a part of you that likes to win, doing whatever it takes to secure its position of power. Mars as we feel it through Scorpio is like the war general who can calculate the opponent's weakness and strategize accordingly.

Mars also imparts bravery on Scorpio. Mars puts the "brutally" in the phrase "brutally honest." The Mars part of you knows it's actually not your job to protect people from the hot sensation of truth.

Tapping into this part of yourself this season has to do with trusting that you're brave enough to handle how other people respond to your honesty. In expanding your capacity to be direct, you're also expanding your capacity to sit with what that directness brings up for others, even if it's uncomfortable. This is incredibly helpful in your relationships because you can't establish loving boundaries when you aren't able to be direct.

After its discovery in 1930, Pluto became the modern ruler of Scorpio, an apt association for this frozen planet that stayed hidden from view for so long. (Though Pluto is no longer considered a true planet by the scientific community, for astrological purposes, it remains one.) I use both planets in my practice for Scorpio. Pluto is a planet that teaches you about your power hidden within that has explosive possibilities for creation and destruction, transformation and renewal.

Pluto has a reputation for being hard because it can feel like it's trying to take away things you are clinging to: ideas about yourself, masks you wear, identities you've come to rely on for your sense of self, memories you repress, and secrets you believe are unspeakable. When the Plutonic in life comes knocking, we're being pressed into releasing these things. In the churning, Pluto requires some kind of surrender, similar to the acceptance of the death process, a recurring theme of Scorpio.

What I've found from working with the planet's principles and stories is that Pluto only wants to help us clear out ways of being and modes of performance that aren't actually our truth. We take on these guises, habits, relationships, careers, and stylizations in ways and for reasons that are often unconscious to us. We may not be sure they represent the "real" us because it's the nature of the hidden to not be seen! So being asked to submit and surrender is often destabilizing and difficult.

On the side of working with Pluto, we are more humbled, but also way more empowered, because we know we can live through things that we had previously thought we couldn't. Let Pluto help you shed the things that no longer serve you.

. . . .

SKILLFUL SCORPIO
Unlock

Scorpio wants you to know: the most loving thing you can do is compassionately attune to the aspects of life that aren't considered beautiful, agreeable, respectable, or happy.

Scorpio wants you to look at all of life. Scorpio wants you to be brave enough to stand what you see—even the difficult parts. Scorpio wants you to trust that you can handle and move through whatever comes up.

In the old fairy tale "Bluebeard," a young woman is courted by a mysterious and charming blue-bearded widower who has six previous wives. Though she feels uneasy, he offers wealth and security, so she marries him and has access to everything in his huge palace—except one room. When he leaves town, she is overcome with both curiosity and dread and opens the forbidden door, only to find a blood-soaked room and the corpses of the other six wives. In a frenzy of fear, she drops the key into the sticky blood. She tries to clean it, but by magic she is unable to remove the stain from the key. When Bluebeard returns home, he sees the blood on the key and threatens to kill her. Luckily, she had called her siblings once she realized she was unsafe, and right before Bluebeard can strike her down, her brothers push him off the balcony of the palace to his doom.

The invitation of the tale is to see Bluebeard as an internalized inner voice that intimidates you into avoiding what is unpleasant or invalidates your intuition that something is off. That Bluebeard energy in your life exists within you and outside you, whenever you'd rather numb yourself to the truth so that you don't have to deal with it.

The key in the story represents the fact that you have access to your own knowing. Scorpio is an extremely intuitive part of who you are. Scorpio just knows: don't even think of lying to the Scorpio in yourself or the Scorpio in other people. Skillful Scorpio involves cultivating the courage to be the key holder of your own life, where no room is off limits, no corridor too spooky or gruesome to behold.

The key to this courage comes from self-trust. And self-trust is a practice of showing yourself that you can stand what you see in any closet. If something feels off, look into it.

This is a good place to note that intuition is not the same as fear. Intuition comes in calmly and firmly. It's a knowing. Fear is charged, anxious, blaming, freaking out. The more I practice listening to my inner voice, the more I know the difference.

Skillful Scorpio is also the part of you that can love another person's many-roomed palace: someone who doesn't ask another person to withhold the gruesome, someone who doesn't freak out at a secret, someone who gets that we all have shadowy parts of us that sometimes react from fear, jealousy, obsession, or quirky desire.

Skillful Scorpio would rather be with what is than be with a fantasy of what you want it to be.

· ·

PRACTICE

Vulture Magic

Vulture magic is my framework for inviting in more abundance by letting things go. Vultures are quite Scorpionic. They feast on the rotting and the dying. By eating what decays, they not only sustain themselves but they also clean the environment by supporting a healthy ecosystem. In this way, vulture magic welcomes the emergence of exciting new ways of being through death practice. Let's get into it.

Regularly noticing what is dying in your life isn't always comfortable. It often shows up as a feeling of frustration, a persistent sense of gnarly resentment, or a stagnation in your creative life. These symptoms point to a No emerging from deep inside. Scorpio teaches that there is death in not asserting your No. The No is telling you something is over, something has lost its vitality, something is rotting in your life. To disregard your No is to disengage from your pulsing, vibrating life force.

Abundance begins with No. Walking away from what isn't alive to us anymore—maybe a relationship, job, place, way of talking to ourselves, habit, worldview—impregnates our life with the energy of vitality. With every No, you grow more self-trust. With every No, expansion follows. With every No, there's clarity. Vulture magic is about regularly making a practice of noticing what is dying in your life—your No—and feeling into what wants to emerge—your Yes.

For this practice, sit with a pen and your journal or a piece of paper. Take a few deep breaths to connect with yourself. Try the grounding practice on page 57. Call on your wise inner voice to speak to you.

Make two columns: "What Is Dying" and "What Is Emerging."

Now it's time to name what is dying. What patterns, relationships, ways of being, modes of performance, habits, egoic attachments are ready to be released? Some of these have been ready a long time; some may surprise you when they show up to be seen. Write it all down without judgment or a need to analyze or edit yourself. Just witness what shows up. Let your future self deal with the list later.

Once you feel complete, write down what is emerging. What new ways of being are calling to you? What parts of your self are trying to find your attention? This is a list for how you want to feel in your body. Remember that this is just for you. Have the audacity to go big. Flaunt your dreams to yourself without shame, apology, or explanation. Write freely.

Here's what Scorpio wants you to know: You don't need anyone's permission to make vulture magic. It is through practice that we cultivate the audacity to self-permission.

· ·

TAROT CARD
Death

The card in the tarot that we associate with Scorpio is card thirteen, Death.

Thirteen, often considered an unlucky number, is the number of mystery. The ultimate mystery? Death itself, of course. We can never fully know or comprehend death; we can only humbly ask for more learning.

The Death card might seem scary at first, but it's actually a reflection of a pretty basic part of life: the fact that all things end. The card speaks to the whole cycle of Life-Death-Life, of which the actual death of someone or something is just one phase.

In the *Smith-Rider-Waite* rendering, Death is a horseman, which underlines the journeying nature of moving through loss. On the ground, the King lies dead, the crown fallen from his head. Three figures respond to Death's presence: the child who wonders at it, the youth who avoids facing it, and the spiritual leader who tries to talk to and about it. The message is that no one can avoid this passage, even the most rich and powerful.

Death is a shedding, a composting of some kind, but it is also a seeding. It is both sunset and sunrise, as conveyed in the card, where the sun shimmers in the background either way. Death is happening all of the time. We are constantly letting things go. Every birth is also a death, the parent never again to be the person they were before. Every move is a death, saying goodbye to the old home. A marriage is the death of the life one had before that commitment. The nature of life is also the nature of Death. It's important to reckon with this.

Death is an initiation. *Initiation* comes from the Latin root *initium*, meaning "a beginning." For every initiation there is a shift from "the normal" into the liminal, in-between space before we come to a new normal. Life-Death-Life again. Some deaths feel soft, easeful, natural. Some feel exciting and full of hope. Some deaths are horrific.

Grief is a natural component to endings. Just as we spiral back to Scorpio season every year and relive the same experience of mid-autumn, so too do we spiral through the grief process. The Death card wants you to know that grief takes its own time. Grief is mysterious. Grief shows up again and again, the same but different, as a pattern of return. Since astrology is the

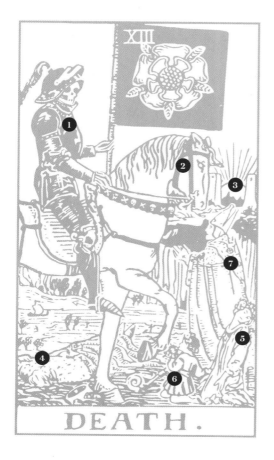

study of cycles, learning astrology can help you to contemplate all cycles you experience, including grief.

The Scorpionic parts of ourselves are attracted to Death. My Scorpio daughter began asking about death at age four! It's the part of us that is both terrified and exhilarated when we enjoy horror movies, roller coasters, and thrill seeking—any time we tap boldly at the doorway between worlds.

A Tarot Spread with Death

See the chapter *How to Navigate This Book* if you're new to the tarot and seek support for pulling cards and interpreting them.

This spread would be especially supportive if you are trying to clarify any resistance you feel toward change and grief.

Take Death out of your deck. (If you have more than one deck, you can pull the card from another deck so that Death has a chance to "participate" in the deck from which you will draw.)

Feel into the visual inspiration of the card.

Take a few deep breaths on purpose and arrive to the reading. Connect into your intuition. Ask Death-Scorpio energy to help you with this reading. Shuffle according to your unique, never-wrong style. Center and focus your question thus:

For my highest and best, at the highest levels of love and compassion for me and all sentient beings, what is the loving invitation to connect with Death?

Pull seven cards according to your own unique process of knowing with the following prompts, and then sit with the cards and journal about them.

1
-
THE
RIDER
-
Message
from Death

2
-
THE
HORSE
-
Message for
the journey

3
-
THE SUN
-
Message
for Life-
Death-Life

5
-
THE
YOUTH
-
Message
for denial

4
-
THE KING
-
Message for
my ego

6
-
THE
CHILD
-
Message
of wonder

7
-
THE
PRIEST
-
Message for
understanding

RITUAL FOR THE NEW MOON
Greet the Crone

Scorpio wants you to be brave enough to change, to destroy in order to create, to let go in order to renew. Change doesn't have to be huge. Even the subtlest shifts will offer incredible results over time. If you are not inclined to change, but you want to try, know that you can call in only that amount of change that will be most appropriate at this time.

Your guide for this ritual is your Crone self, who you may remember from the Cancer ritual on pages 146–49. The Crone teaches you how to be the older self who no longer gives a shit what anyone thinks, is totally liberated to cackle, lets her hair go gray and her boobs sag, and still feels totally fierce. The Crone has seen it all and speaks the truth, and she lives in you if you want to hang out with her. Dolly Parton gives us some Crone wisdom with the words, "If anyone tells you that your hair is too big, get rid of them. You don't need that kind of negativity in your life."

This experience needs to be about having fun and growing your Crone cackle. Your inner Crone self wants you to do this work to show yourself how tough you are, not to self-flagellate. Release the prim and the polite; they're an affront to the visceral.

This ritual is divided into three parts, as I have found that lunar ritual is especially potent in Scorpio season, and I want you to give yourself a long experience with this. You will honor:

- the Dark Moon (within seventy-two hours before the actual New Moon)
- the day of the New Moon
- the waxing crescent (two to three days after the actual New Moon)

The Dark Moon

Over the course of the three days before the actual New Moon in Scorpio, you are invited to clear things from your life. The more you clear, the more you birth. Below is a list of suggested forms of clearing. It is important to do everything mindfully with the intention of getting things out of your space. This is your version of molting, of shedding skin. Do one, do all of these; it's up to you. If any of this feels hard or difficult, remember that you don't have to do this alone. Magic cannot be micromanaged by the ego brain. If it resonates with you, ask any unseen guides from the spirit realm to carry this load away for you. Cackle as you release!

- Sweep and wipe down your whole house, especially the doorways, finishing with lemon-scented air freshener or leaving a lemon candle burning for a while.
- Go through closets and drawers to get rid of unloved, unnecessary items, especially ones you haven't already donated because they were gifts, or expensive, or whatever the reason you've leaned on in the past.
- Cry for the weary, cry for your weariness.
- Identify poisonous behavior, thoughts, and patterns and create your own ritual to clear these out.
- Throw away alcohol if your relationship to certain bottles is poisonous. Watch it go down the drain: "Byeeeee!"
- Spend time donating and giving back to your community. Volunteer at the community center; make donations to BIPOC organizations, those that support trans youth, bail-out funds, or whatever cause is on your heart; feed people who need food.
- Freewrite by candlelight in your journal everything that comes to mind and heart that you want to get out.
- Go for a long walk with a dear friend and get things off your chest.
- Clear your email inbox by deleting, responding, and unsubscribing.

The New Moon

On the day of the New Moon in Scorpio, make intentional space for dropping into the void. In the dark vacuum, what do you hear? The goal is to make time for doing basically nothing, trusting that rest will bring wisdom. A full day of rest is not possible for most people, so try to carve out something, even fifteen minutes, that you normally don't give yourself. Schedule it on your calendar in advance if you can!

Suggested ways to honor the void:

- Meditate in silence
- Nap
- Walk in silence after dark
- Eat a meal in total quiet

- Drink mugwort tea (not if you're pregnant or breastfeeding) before bed and invite in dreams from the void
- Enjoy the nothingness of simply being

The Waxing Crescent

About three days after the New Moon, we begin to catch a glimpse of the waxing crescent—that first sliver of bright moon peeking out. In many traditions, this is the true beginning of the new cycle. This is when you can begin to slither into a new skin. A great way of connecting to that self is through *scrying*, an old, powerful form of divination that involves looking into water—a well, a river, or a bowl of water—and visualizing images of what you ask to see. It can feel silly the first couple of times, but with practice, you might be blown away by what you see. It can be very empowering to support yourself this way.

Before beginning this ritual, gather:

- Your object for scrying: I find scrying into the bath to be amazing, but you can always use a bowl or chalice
- A dark room, at night if possible
- Candles, as many as you want, and a way to light them
- Any other items that will facilitate the magical and mysterious qualities of this ritual and help you get into the mood
- Your journal and a pen (optional)

The Ritual

1. Set up your ritual container, light your candle(s), and come to a grounded, meditative state (see page 57).

2.   You will want to bring yourself to a near trance state of deep meditation. You must get out of the analytical part of the brain for this. Trust completely in this process. Remember: if you have been clearing and resting these last few days, you are now highly receptive!

3.   When you feel deeply calm and trancelike, turn to your reflection in the water. Adjust your focus and let the outline of your body go soft. Call on the guidance of whatever resonates as unseen support from the spirit realm.

4.   Ask to see a vision of the self you are ready to receive. The one who has been waiting for you. The one who has been longing for you to love them back. This is not the self you wish yourself to be, but rather, the one you already are if you welcome back who you've left behind. The one you thought wasn't allowed. The one you shoved away for being unlovable.

5.   Notice this self. What does it feel like to be reunited? Allow yourself some time to receive from the water. Scorpio is deep water; let messages come up from the deep to greet you with truths you've long forgotten. If you feel like crying into the water or talking to the water, this is highly supporting. If you feel like laughing—cackling!—go for it.

6.   When you feel complete, ask your guides, ask yourself: *Is there anything else I need to know?*

7.   If you can take notes, you might want to jot down some thoughts in case they vanish later. That said, know that your body will remember what you learned even if your mind forgets.

8.   Conclude and open the ritual container (see page 66).

Happy New Moon in Scorpio!

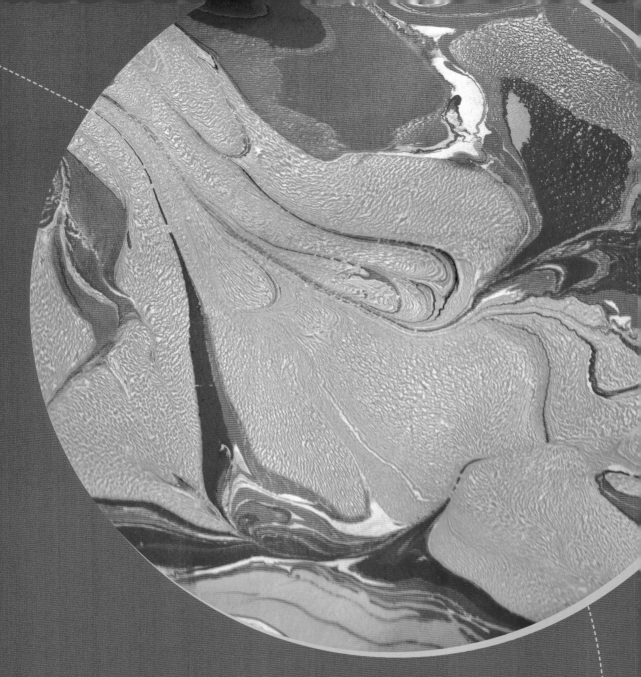

Sagittarius

NOVEMBER 21–DECEMBER 21

 SAGITTARIUS

 FIRE

△ MUTABLE

♃ JUPITER

Sagittarius

Questions to Live Into

How would I live today differently if I fully trusted that everything that happens is the universe trying to guide me and that I am deeply supported by forces seen and unseen?

Where does exuberance live in me and what if I participated in all experiences from that place?

How is the challenge of the present moment helping me grow skills to creatively participate in the unfolding of my life's adventure?

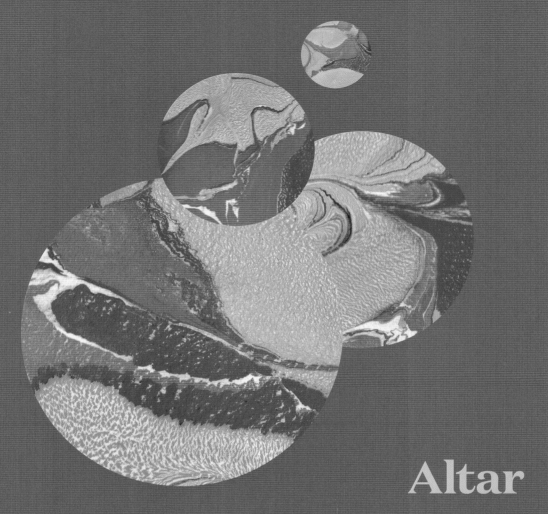

Altar

As discussed in part one, the purpose of creating an altar is to first prepare and then enjoy having a special space devoted to the themes and principles you're developing with each sign. The general qualities of Sagittarius are listed below. I recommend you gather at least three items, but quantity isn't as crucial as choosing items of resonance for you. For example, this season, maybe you prefer to build an altar based on firelight. Your entire altar space could be full to the brim with as many candles as possible. Take the suggestions that feel aligned and don't worry about the rest. As you read through the chapter, more ideas may come to you for your altar that aren't listed here.

Go for it!

COLORS
blue, red

CRYSTALS
blue lace agate, blue tourmaline, lapis lazuli, sapphire, tin, turquoise

GARDEN
calendula, chestnut, dandelion, mulberry, sage, willow

SPICES AND FLAVORS
balsam, cinnamon, clove, juniper berries, nutmeg, peppercorn, sage

GODS AND GODDESSES
Amun-Ra, Ceridwen, Dagda, Jupiter, Marduk, Zeus

TAROT CARDS
Temperance, Wheel of Fortune, 8 of Wands, 9 of Wands, 10 of Wands

ITEMS
art, books, ceramics, fabrics, food, incense, magazine cutouts, photographs, quotes on paper, or anything else that inspires you

RELATED THEMES
abundance, benevolence, bow and arrow, buoyancy, cauldrons, consumption, dogs, enthusiasm, expansion, fine whiskey, fire, good fortune, horses, joviality, life principles, luck, quilts, storytelling, tall tales, thunder, Thursday, upward momentum, wealth, wild soul nature, wise grandfathers

SEASON

End of Autumn

Sagittarius relates to the time of year when the nights are long. We burn candles and gather around the hearth to call in warmth and connection. We make meaning through storytelling, remembering, and song. We cook food and drink wine with gratitude in our hearts.

The preceding sixty days of Libra and Scorpio bring up a lot of discomfort and intensity as they work their important shedding magic. By mid-November, we're a bit laid bare. This is when Sagittarius comes in to help you remember what lifts your heart. You look for patterns to understand your stories. You put your trust in renewal.

Sagittarius is the sign of the Archer (see page 233). Its symbol is the upward-facing arrow. In the darkest time of the year, as the winter solstice approaches, we point up to the sky. We yearn to feel that our stories are worthy of those ancient constellations. We paint ourselves in the stars. We become the great stories.

Sagittarius is the part of you that you trust to move in the dark of the dark. At this time of year, we consume what brings us hope and optimism: song, wine, stories, cookies, parties, gifts, meats, and lots of candles. Sagittarius is rosy cheeks, twinkling eyes, broad bellies, and big laughs. Sag is your inner Santa Claus.

It is also a portal for your big questions: *Why am I here? What lifts my spirit? What do I want to call in, to hope for, to magnetize? What's so exciting to me that I'm willing to put my conviction behind it and sing its praises?*

The way you feel about this time of the year might tell you a lot about how you feel about Sagittarius.

MODALITY AND ELEMENT
Mutable Fire

Like the other mutable signs (Gemini, Virgo, and Pisces), Sagittarius closes the season and helps you integrate everything you were learning with the two preceding signs. It's a big job because autumn brings so much change. Sag has all the confidence for the task.

Like the other Fire signs (Aries and Leo), Sag cares about being creative, zesty, inspired, ecstatic, and adventurous.

I see mutable Fire as a torch. While Aries gets your Fire going like the spark of a match and Leo helps you tend the flame of your bonfire, Sagittarius wants to take your Fire on the road. You follow where it takes you.

In human form, mutable Fire is the inspirational speaker channeling guidance with passionate conviction. It's the ski bum who loves swapping stories at the end of the day as much as all the adventures on the slopes. It's anyone called to look up at the night sky to delight in the wonder of it all. You are the traveling bard of your life, says Sag, so sing your song wherever you go, allowing the expansive and wondrous crescendo of songs to lift your torch spirit. When you feel your spirit stirring beyond the bounds and confines of logic, let your expression connect to something beyond yourself. Home can be anywhere when you live inside your song.

Mutable Fire is charismatic. We're magnetized to its optimism and spiritedness. It encourages you to notice what animates your spirit: "Yeah, this really lights me up!" Then, you can let the torch of that excitement light your inner flame. Ride the joy of that flame as it lifts and takes you. It's a "Hell yeah!" energy. It's what "Woo-hoo!" feels like in the body. You don't need an audience for it, but it's sure fun to share your torch with those around you. After all, think about how Fire works. You lose none of your Fire when you share it.

Close your eyes and imagine a torch in the dark; it's the only light you can see. See it flicking, churning, shifting as it sparkles and draws you toward it. You have to find out what it wants to show you. You trust that there's magic in the journey. Along the way, others might join as you follow and get to know the torch. And in the experiencing, you understand that it's the joy of being with the torch wherever you go that matters much, much more than any destination.

The Archer

The center of our galaxy is located in the constellation of Sagittarius. It's the point around which all one hundred billion or so stars of the Milky Way, including our own, orbits. At that center lies a supermassive black hole, four million times more massive than our sun. We cannot see it directly; it is invisible, as no light can escape a black hole. But we know it's there because we can observe how it affects everything around it.

What a strange and wonderful cosmic rhyme it is that this invisible, animating force lies in Sagittarius. The sign that trusts that everything is connected. That all stories resolve. That all events orbit around a central theme, whether we can see it in the moment or not.

Sagittarius is Latin for "the archer." The constellation of Sagittarius is often depicted as having the rough appearance of an Archer, their bow nocked with an arrow, ready to let loose. There is tremendous optimism in the gesture of pointing our arrow toward the stars. The will to try to understand our place in the cosmos is an inherently optimistic position.

Like the galactic center, which draws us in with its gravity, so too do the stories we tell have their own magnetic pull, drawing us closer together and offering us a peek into the mysteries of the universe. The Archer aspires to understand the stars by becoming them, by burning brightly and exuberantly with the fire of the great heroes and heroines in the oldest stories. Sagittarius is an energy that yearns to retell the stories of our own lives and turn them into legends.

The Archer is often depicted as a centaur: half-human, half-horse. One part of the Sag in you is looking forward, aiming upward, craving an exhilarating experience, while the other part of you is firmly in the body, in touch with your wilder, more primal, instinctual nature. We aim the arrow toward earthly experiences that activate the stars in our eyes—adventures, risks, pathways into the unknown. Hiking the ground of a forest trail may be what most connects you to the heavens above.

The Archer doesn't always express itself through physical activity. For many, the zesty sprawl of the fiery spirit comes through in one's philosophical, religious, or spiritual pursuits. The arrow we point seeks teachers, mentors, and other guides to shape our belief system and path. There's a constant thirst to the Archer, always nocking a new arrow after integrating each teaching.

Whether you are a student of national parks, quantum physics, or the Bible, the Archer in you is looking for the next expansive experience to broaden your view and open your perspective. This book in your hands is a Sagittarian arrow. Astrology most certainly is a vast world for exploration and for feeling the interconnectedness of timelines and dimensions. Whenever something excites you so much that it takes you to another teacher for deeper learning, that is you being the Archer in your life, choosing your next adventure.

There is a Zen teaching that tells us not to confuse the finger pointing at the Moon for the Moon. The idea is that the teachings, strategies, frameworks, and rituals we may learn from teachers are like fingers pointing at the Moon. They are wonderful tools because they help us move closer to the illumination of wisdom and the aliveness of spirit we're seeking. But the wisdom and aliveness we seek is always already inside of us, not in external authorities. On your Sagittarian path, it's important to remember that the arrows you aim are always bringing you back to your own light.

POLARITY

The Sagittarius-Gemini Axis

All Fire signs are opposite Air signs, and all polar signs have the same modality. So mutable Fire is opposite mutable Air: Gemini.

- Sagittarius wants to inspire your spirit; Gemini wants to stimulate your mind.
- Sagittarius is the whole scope of something, its container; Gemini is each individual idea within the container.
- Sagittarius is the seminary, the astronomical observatory, the mountain trail; Gemini is the coffee shop, the coworking space, your TikTok feed.

Gemini is the buzzing of bees and the flapping of butterfly wings in late spring when insects pollinate nonlinearly. Gemini is interested in finding data: words, ideas, facts, formulas. For Gemini, data is nonhierarchical. It's not about truth or higher meaning. It's all nectar! It either tastes interesting or it doesn't, and then, on to the next fun thing.

The Sag in you is often looking to the horizon line, a place you can never, by definition, reach. The joy is in looking back and seeing how far you've come, and finding new adventure in the next leg of the journey. Gemini, on the other hand, isn't interested in going that far because a horizon is an abstract concept to help us understand our life philosophy. Gemini doesn't want philosophy to interfere or make you choose which of its multi-hyphenated identities has the most of your conviction.

Sagittarius is supported by Gemini when the part of us madly in love with our own version of truth becomes so certain of it that we veer into creating tall tales for a better story or ignore details that challenge our biases. The invitation of this polarity is to let Gemini temper our Sagittarian convictions. Gemini calls us down from the top of the mountain. Gemini brings us back to the village to have conversations with lots of people, get bits of different evidence to steer new thought around an issue, bring Air objectivity to the Fire of our passionate beliefs.

Gemini is not impressed with dogma and certainty. Gemini will hang out with "the other side" of any topic because Gemini isn't into sides. Gemini is the Ferris Bueller of the signs; it flirts with everything, which is a sweet gift to your Sag self.

Together, Gemini and Sagittarius endlessly expand into possibilities. Both help us activate the part of you that is forever the student of life. Any time you enthusiastically set about deeper learning, and whenever you share what you have learned with others, you are activating this axis within yourself.

RULING PLANET
Jupiter   ♃

Sagittarius's ruling planet, Jupiter, is the largest in the solar system. Jupiter, who also rules Pisces, is the one who teaches you about expanding, reaching, stretching, and growing.

The Jupiter in you has a very magnetic quality because people are inherently attracted to the spirit of enthusiasm. Jupiter rules good luck and good fortune in astrology, whether that's in money, opportunities, or relationships. Jupiter is your abundance. Jupiter is your privilege, and—I mean this in a neutral way—when we have a lot of something, we can give it away.

In Vedic astrology, Jupiter is the guru. We equate *guru* with the term *teacher* because Jupiter is the planet of learning and wisdom. The quintessential Jupiterian question for me is, *What have I been learning?* If you know what you've been learning, then you know what skills and tools you've been developing. And if you know your tools and skills, then you understand and appreciate what makes you unique when opportunities show up that require precisely the skills and tools you have.

This is the philosophy that every experience you have brings you exactly where you are supposed to be, even if you can't see how the pieces fit together until later. If you see all that unfolds for you as opportunities to experience the fullness of life, then it becomes easier to trust in what you're going through

> People are inherently attracted to the spirit of enthusiasm.

at any given time. In this way, Jupiter loves storytelling and meaning making. Through stories, you stitch together a larger meaning of your life. In storytelling, you magnetize wealth and abundance with words.

I want you to pay attention to how Jupiter lives in, through, and around you. And as you become conscious of Jupiter in your life, it will grow. The most powerful gift that Jupiter offers the Sagittarian in you is the trust that you are more loved and supported by seen and unseen forces than you can possibly fathom. Jupiter is alive in the qualities that come naturally to you. How are you ridiculously abundant? How are you absurdly gifted?

Maybe your Jupiter is not a part of you that you identify as a gift because your early teachers or caregivers thought you were "too much": too chatty, too pretty, too smart, too rule-breaking, too honest, too magnetic, too sexual, too rich, too happy, too good at things. If no one ever pointed out your Jupiterian qualities, that's okay. It's up to you to know your Jupiter, and then grow it and spread it around.

Jupiter says: You are a fountain that will never run out. Give away what runs over and share it with others. Let people experience your gifts. Pour them out with the abundant spirit of the you that trusts your gifts will never run out. Can you imagine a world where we all did this?

SKILLFUL SAGITTARIUS

Expand

Sagittarius wants you to know: the most loving thing you can do is to trust in the unknown, uncertain, and unplanned. You're not being irresponsible. In fact, it's this Sagittarian expansiveness that has helped us survive as a species!

Sagittarius has to do with the part of us that seeks to bridge the gap between the reality we're experiencing (the deep, dark, cold night before the winter solstice) and the one we're called toward (longer days, warmer temperatures). To our hunter-gatherer ancestors, building a fire served both to bring light to darkness and keep us alive with its warmth and transformative capacity to cook food.

Who doesn't love sitting by a fire—or even a single candle—and staring into it until vision goes soft? To me, this feels like the essence of Sagittarius because firelight is so intrinsic to the end of the calendar year. Gazing at firelight induces a shimmery, altered form of reality because everything drops away as you look into it, especially if it's a campfire in the wilderness and total night surrounds you.

Firelight creates a stroboscopic effect where darkness and light alternate rapidly back and forth. From such a state of consciousness, you produce low alpha- and theta-wave brain states that calm you and help you relax enough to channel your own wise guidance. You become the shaman, the seer, the prophet, the witch, the oracle, the sorcerer. The one who has the ability to access spirits within and without and to engage with them in some way that will be helpful to your community.

To be the seer is to know when and how to turn on your inherent porosity. Yes, we are porous beings! We feel the energy in the room, in another person, in a song, in a pair of shoes. This is a porosity that we can train to expand well beyond what the logical brain is taught to believe is possible.

Inherent to the shamanic worldview is the animist perspective that all physical beings possess a spirit or animating essence. When you view everything as alive and animated, then the foundation of all life has to do with cultivating a mutually beneficial relationship to the sentient beings that are both visible and not visible all around us. That interaction governs all culture; everything becomes co-creation.

Animism was intrinsic to our shared hunter-gatherer ancestors. To experiment and engage with animism today, especially if you've been cut off from this tradition, is to re-enchant your life as you begin to see yourself and everything around you as co-participants in the dance of life energy.

Skillful Sag is the part of you that you call upon to survive in the dark. It's the part of you that builds a fire in the dark so you can animate your life with new ways of seeing the world. You burn through any fear about starting anew. You gaze into the fires and channel the song that wants to run through you, the one that must be sung. You connect to the part of you that knows your stories are made from the constellations, everything is connected through story, and you are not alone.

And because you can't possibly know what comes next in the story, you accept all that you see as grist for creativity, for song-making, for more passionate living. I invite you to follow this simple mantra: *Since I cannot possibly know what's next in my story, I will dance with the unknown support finding its way to me.*

. . . .

PRACTICE

Trust in the Maybe

Sagittarius has a unique ability to free-fall into the unknown, trusting that it'll land wherever it needs to. To many, this trust can feel brash and irresponsible. You know you feel this way if you tend to judge or resent those who seem able to take risks and land on their feet. You might think something like, *Who do they think they are that they get to do that, have that, or be that?* Or maybe what you hear inside is something like, *They get that because they're just lucky.* The implication is, of course, that you aren't.

This month, I ask you to entertain the possibility that you are strongly Sagittarian, but you have learned to shut it down or contain it because you received messages that you are too much, or too lucky, or too wild for this world. Maybe both cases are true. Either way, let's help your Sag remember its home in you.

There's a magical phrasing that helps to channel Sagittarian trust when you're feeling doubt. It's simply: "Maybe _____. Or maybe _____."

After the first "maybe," name what you're afraid of or the uncomfortable feeling you're having. Respond with, "or maybe," and then name some other possibility that would feel much more expansive, healing, fun, hopeful, or empowering. The idea is to allow the opportunity for you to learn from whatever happens, trusting that you can't ever know exactly where the story will go next.

- "Maybe I'll get hurt if I go ice-skating. Or maybe falling and getting a huge bruise on my hip will be part of what makes the experience even more silly and fun."
- "Maybe they don't understand me. Or maybe I'm learning to release myself from the need to explain myself."
- "Maybe if I start my dream business, it will fail. Or maybe I can trust in myself to show up and listen to the process as I go."
- "Maybe she's annoyed at me. Or maybe I'm learning to let people have their own experience of me."
- "Maybe people don't like my post. Or maybe the algorithm swallowed it and it's just that no one saw it."

Start by invoking this practice every single time you feel doubt. As a doubt appears in your mind, offer a counter possibility with a second maybe. This exercise is inspired by the experience of helping my daughter move through Exposure and Response Prevention (ERP) therapy for her OCD. Her therapist told me to tell her "maybe, maybe not" any time she came to me for assurance that I had certainty about something that scared her. So if she asked me, "Are you sure this pork cooked all the way?" I answered, "Maybe, maybe not." This response released me from the panic of needing to provide absolute certainty to my child, and released her from the truth that she can't control everything that scares her. It became a radically healing practice in our house that I began using for my own uncertainties and then sharing with my clients as a magical spell.

Part of this practice is trusting that there's a larger intelligence at play in yourself, in others, and in the universe that you cannot possibly get your head around, much less control. The audacity to give yourself permission to trust in this intelligence can feel radically refreshing and rewiring. Go ahead and enjoy it!

Temperance

The card in the tarot that we associate with Sagittarius is card fourteen, Temperance.

The word *temperance* comes from Latin terms meaning "to moderate," "to show restraint," and "to refrain." Most imagery we see for this card depicts a process called *tempering* (a slow path of integration that leads to the perfect middle state). But wait . . . there's nothing moderate about Sagittarius, so how does this work?

In the traditional *Smith-Rider-Waite* version of the card, we see a non-gender-specific winged angel pour liquid between two cups at an angle that's not physically possible. The figure has one foot in water (the subconscious realm) and one foot on the ground (the material realm). These are all cues to the viewer that we are in a liminal space.

Temperance describes those periods of life when we are asked to moderate, restrain, and refrain from an overidentification with a purely material, instrumental, mechanical, or dualistic way of seeing the world. Instead, Temperance is an invitation into hybridity; it is not either-or, it is both-and. Matter (the square on the figure's chest) combines with spirit (the upward-facing triangle inside the square). Sag trusts that everything works together, and everything will be okay.

This card is an initiation into radical trust that you can hand over what you need and want to something otherworldly. It's not a concept that is easy or safe for a lot of people, especially if you grew up internalizing that you have to do it all by yourself. Perhaps what you are moderating with Temperance is the need to cling to a certain way of being or to have control over all aspects of a situation.

Just as Sagittarius brings buoyancy, hope, and festivity after Scorpio's death traditions, Temperance is the card that follows Death in the major arcana of the tarot. To me, this speaks to the arc of autumn's medicine.

We need this. After a lot of shifting, letting go, and death processes, Temperance, like Sag, comes in as a soothing balm that offers trust in the unknown and the illogical.

We can experience Death in any season of the year, of course. Temperance is the vibration of hope that we have seen and unseen support through transitional times. Yes, we can integrate and shift with change.

A Tarot Spread with Temperance

See the chapter *How to Navigate This Book* if you're new to the tarot and seek support for pulling cards and interpreting them.

Take Temperance out of your deck. (If you have more than one deck, you can pull the card from another deck so that Temperance has a chance to "participate" in the deck from which you will draw.)

Feel into the visual inspiration of the card.

Take a few deep breaths on purpose and arrive to the reading. Connect into your intuition. Ask Temperance-Sagittarius energy to help you with this reading. Shuffle according to your unique, never-wrong style. Center and focus your question thus:

With the most expansive levels of compassion for me and all sentient beings, what is the loving invitation to connect with Temperance?

Pull seven cards according to your own unique process of knowing with the following prompts, and then sit with the cards and journal about them.

2

-

THE CROWN

-

Message from my higher path

1

-

THE WINGS

-

Message from my buoyant spirit

3

-

THE IRISES

-

Message for hope

5

-

THE FLUID

-

Self-healing in this present moment

4

-

THE CUPS

-

How to access my many resources

6

-

THE FEET

-

How to trust in the unknown

7

-

SPIRIT

-

What else do I need to know?

Live the Questions Now

Sagittarius is intrinsically about the animating spirit within that carries us, despite the uncertainty and trepidation of the dark and the coming winter. In *Letters to a Young Poet*, Rainer Maria Rilke encourages the recipient of his wisdom to be patient with the unknown, with those questions that feel urgently unexplained and unresolved. Rilke reminds us that we often wouldn't even know what to do with the answers if we could get them now. He admonishes to "live the questions now," trusting that the future self will eventually come into the answers when we're ready for them. Rilke's words are an offering to us in times when we have sincere questions for our lives, and we're sitting in the uncertainty of not having the answers.

Rilke was a Sag Sun and Mercury. You can hear the Sagittarian "Don't worry; everything's going to be okay" in this passage. I invite you to remember that the constellation Sagittarius is in the same part of the sky as the galactic center, the site of a supermassive black hole. Sagittarius is an invitation to aim your arrow toward the questions that have no answers: *Why am I here? What is my purpose? What happens after death? What is God? Why do some people have lives with more pain than others? Will everything work out if I try?*

The skillful Sag move is to keep asking while you try on different answers. See how it feels to let in a teacher's answers or a wisdom tradition's explanation. Does it help you with the uncertainty? Maybe, maybe not. And this is not a problem. Rilke reminds us that "the point is, to live everything. Live the questions now." Living astrology is living the questions. Living astrology is to trust in not having all the answers.

This ritual is designed to deepen your knowing connection to Rilke's invitations to help you live Sagittarius more skillfully.

Before beginning this ritual, gather:

- Your journal and pen
- Candles, as many as you want, and a way to light them
- An after-dusk window of about thirty to sixty minutes to yourself
- Any other décor that reminds you of Sagittarius (see page 231)

The Ritual

1. Sit at your Sagittarius altar when ready. Set up your ritual container, light your candle(s), and come to a grounded, meditative state (see page 57).

2. Ask your intuition the following questions and then listen and write down your answers. Your intuition will never make you feel bad or bring you shame. If you hear anything like that, then breathe deeply, stare softly into the fire, and ask yourself to quiet the front brain and access your deeper self.
   - *What is unsolved in my heart?*
   - *What are the questions that I want answers to now?*

3. As you focus on these next questions, notice how it feels in the body to be with uncertainty, which may feel like a charge or a sense of clenching. If this comes up, ask:
   - *How does it serve me to have this uncertainty? Does it serve a role?*
   - *How am I currently coping with my questions? What behaviors or patterns do I engage in in order to survive with these questions?*

4. Visualize these last two questions as "locked rooms and like books that are now written in a very foreign tongue."

    - *What if I accept that I cannot know the answers because I am not ready?*
    - *What are the underlying desires in my questions? What am I hoping for? What am I longing for? Why? What do I imagine these desires will bring me?*

5. How does this feel? Feel into the energy of the longing in the questions. Notice how the longing is here now, in the present moment. Can you distill this longing into a simple word or phrase to describe, in its essence, what you long for in your questions? "I see now that what I long for in my questions that have no answers is _____." Write this down. This is your sacred longing. It's extremely useful to have this clarity.

6. Ask yourself, *In what ways can I now see that I already have the essence of what I'm longing for? What is the evidence in my life that I am living in my questions?* To live the questions now means to live charged with that essence.

7. Now swell your heart with your longing, your hope, and your highest levels of trust that as you "live your questions," you reach for them, and they light your body with purposeful excitement.

8. Say to yourself, *All possibilities exist. All possibilities exist. All possibilities exist.*

9. Now ask yourself what you can do across the lunar cycle in a daily way to connect to the energy in the longing of your questions and act in the world from that place. Are you willing to say Yes and No throughout the day in ways that honor your longing? Even if you're scared or even if you have self-doubt, say to yourself: *I am willing to trust that I have the courage to live the questions now. I am willing to live my longing.*

10. Take a few long, deep breaths now, centering back to yourself. How do you feel? What is coming up for you? Notice your mental, emotional, spiritual, and physical information. This is also important. Take your time. When you begin to feel like the ritual is finishing, breathe into a sense of completeness and gratitude. Thank any inner or spirit guidance you received here.

11. Conclude and open the ritual container (see page 66).

Happy New Moon in Sagittarius!

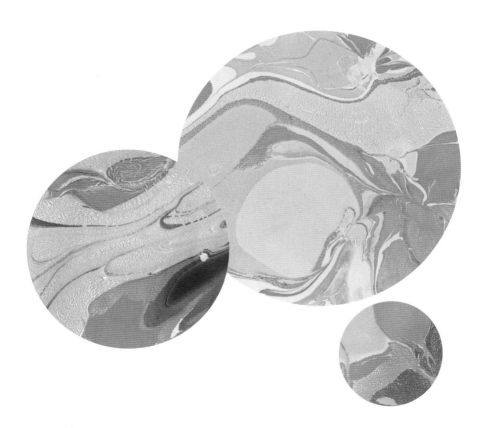

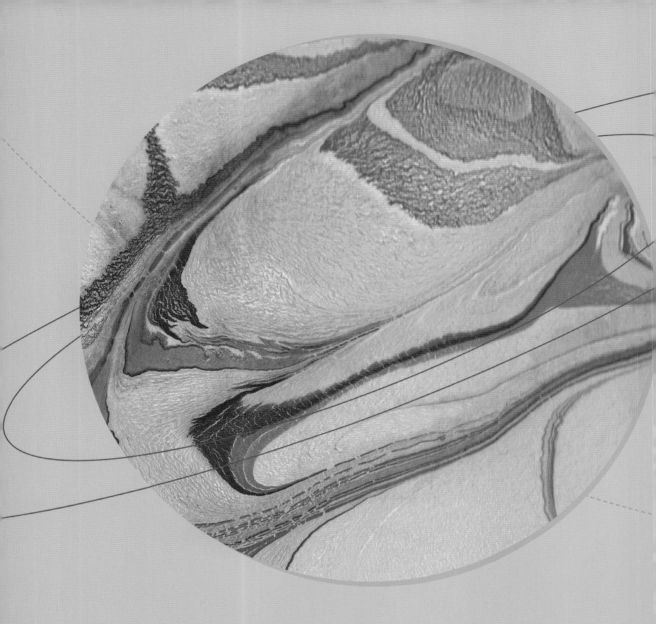

Capricorn

DECEMBER 21–JANUARY 20

☷ CAPRICORN

▽ EARTH

△ CARDINAL

♄ SATURN

Questions to Live Into

What root resources of inner strength do I know I can rely on when the world feels hard, cold, or brutal, and how can I access these more consciously in my daily life?

What do I need to do today to create evidence that I have the courage to follow through on the commitments that matter to me?

How can I turn more of myself toward what I want to show up for?

Altar

As discussed in part one, the purpose of creating an altar is to first prepare and then enjoy having a special space devoted to the themes and principles you're developing with each sign. The general qualities of Capricorn are listed below. I recommend you gather at least three items, but quantity isn't as crucial as choosing items of resonance for you. For example, this season, maybe you prefer to build an altar based on the theme of bones. Take the suggestions that feel aligned and don't worry about the rest. As you read through the chapter, more ideas may come to you for your altar that aren't listed here.

Go for it!

COLORS
brown, dark green,
gray, maroon

CRYSTALS
lapis lazuli, lead, onyx,
ruby, turquoise

GARDEN
belladonna, blessed
thistle, cypress,
hemlock, mullein,
vervain, yarrow

SPICES AND FLAVORS
cumin, rosemary

GODS AND GODDESSES
Baba Yaga, Bacchus,
Kronos, Pan, Saturn

TAROT CARDS
the Devil, the World,
2 of Pentacles,
3 of Pentacles,
4 of Pentacles

ITEMS
art, books, ceramics,
fabrics, food, incense,
magazine cutouts,
photographs, quotes
on paper, or anything
else that inspires you

RELATED THEMES
authority, bones,
boss, brittleness,
building, clocks, cold,
constraints, Crone
energy, Daddy, domi-
natrix, endurance, the
father, focus, goals,
goat, legacies, limits,
making things that last,
mountain, pathmaking,
patriotism, patriarchy,
root resources, rules
and breaking them,
Saturday, the sickle,
time, to-do lists, winter

SEASON

Beginning of Winter

Capricorn is the first sign of the winter season. The day the Sun moves into Capricorn is the same day as the winter solstice in the northern hemisphere—the shortest day and longest night of the year. This is a profound shift toward the coming light of the Sun.

You have been here, in the dark of dark, at the very brink of desolation and loss and despair. You know the place. It's where you fall on your knees. It's where you're held when you don't know how to keep going. But there, with the utter solemnity of your last exhausted tears, you find something stirring you back up again, something like what Paul Valéry describes:

> *Le vent se lève. Il faut tenter de vivre.*
> The wind rises. We must try to live.

It is only in the darkest night that you know—I mean *know*—what light is. The winter solstice is this literal turning point.

As we shift into winter, we rededicate to life and our place in it. Capricorn, Aquarius, and Pisces are transpersonal, collective energies, meaning that they are about more than the ego. The commitment to living past autumn means doing what needs to be done for the greater good. These signs and their energies end our zodiacal year. In them, we rededicate ourselves to what we want to see for our world, and the earth becomes pregnant once again with the seeds of our hope for renewal.

We must try to live.

One of the ways nature responds to harsher times is by hardening. Hardening is the process by which plants prepare and relocate nutrients to storage organs in order to acclimate to winter. This means they don't flower or grow; rather, they are still, hibernating and only doing what's necessary.

In the winter, we go inward, working hard to achieve and fulfill the goals and ambitions we've developed since spring. We discover what we have inside to nourish us through that endurance. We learn about what sustains us through discomfort and fear and hunger. When we harden, we adapt in order to survive.

It is true that we often don't learn how truly strong we are until we are forced to. Passing through literal and metaphorical winters brings you more intimacy with your inner power. Capricorn initiates this conversation with yourself, inviting you into winter and a new year.

. . . .

MODALITY AND ELEMENT
Cardinal Earth

Like the other cardinal signs (Aries, Cancer, and Libra), Capricorn initiates a new season. It is the energy to turn the wheel out of autumn and into winter.

Like the other Earth signs (Taurus and Virgo), Capricorn cares about being practical, reliable, and grounded in the way you go about things.

To initiate Earth is to build something. It is the persistent laying of structural foundations and then the slow process of finishing out. It is the work of scaffolding as well as the proof of that scaffolding. In nature, cardinal Earth is the Great Basin bristlecone pine tree, which can live to be five thousand years old! The species' long life can be attributed to the harsh conditions it lives in; it grows slowly and creates incredibly dense wood resistant to insects, fungi, rot, and erosion.

In human form, cardinal Earth is an Olympian, conserving energy efficiently for years and years after countless hours of training, with eyes on each smaller goal leading to the big goals down the road. It is an entrepreneur—someone who turns their visions into reality by starting a business and seeing it through each phase of growth and change. It is anyone who stops talking about the thing and starts doing the thing—the part of you that fucking shows up.

I am a Capricorn Moon. Once I discovered this, I turned up my Capricorn skill, becoming a marathon runner. I make a schedule and build out a program. In races, there is nothing that can throw my pace because I know how to hold it until the end. I am made for distance. As

> Your Capricorn only turns on full power when the path feels right.

soon as I started my astrology practice, I could feel how huge my vision was and I could see the scaffolding helping me get started, one move at a time, building out the dream. I created a home for people to find my very Piscean work. I want my community to feel and trust a solid structure since the topics are so intangible, mystical, and vast. I never knew I had this in me, but your Capricorn only turns on full power when the path feels right.

Cardinal Earth encourages you to notice what inspiration feels both worthy of your focus and actually accomplishable. Capricorn wants to take the inspiration of Sagittarius and put it to work. Capricorn is time oriented. You must identify the relationship between the amount of work to be done to complete something and the amount of time available for the execution. Once this is determined, you set containers of time and energy to show up to the work until it's done.

Our culture both praises and makes fun of Capricorn's brilliance. We want the feeling of accomplishment without the endurance of showing up for it. We shame ourselves for not having more discipline like Capricorn, and then we shame those we perceive as boringly hyper-disciplined and over-Capricorn. The issue here is that we have fairly fucked up values around success and accomplishment. When your Capricorn truly believes in the project, you will show up. And it will not be boring.

Capricorn is a world builder. It's an extremely magical part of you! But in order to structure things that will endure, the Capricorn in you must create limits around your energy and attention so that your concentration can be as enduring as what you want to build. This means that your Capricorn can be perceived as cold and aloof while you do your thing, but this brittleness is impersonal. It's not your job to help people feel comfortable with your hard angles. Don't relax your focus to put someone at ease who feels ashamed that they haven't accessed the same persistence. Your Capricorn is here for a reason. Let your tenacity be an inspiration!

. . . .

SYMBOL

The Sea Goat or Mountain Goat

In the sky, Capricorn is a triangular constellation, which is often illustrated as a Sea Goat—a creature with the head and front legs of a goat and the tail of a fish. One potential origin of Capricorn's connection to the Sea Goat comes from Pricus, proud father of the sea-goat race. Pricus had many happy sea-goat children. But over time, they began to spend more and more time on the shore of the land. As they did, they began to evolve to look like goats with four legs. This was painful to Pricus, who didn't want to be left alone in the great sea. And so, he reversed time and brought the children back to when they enjoyed being sea goats and hadn't yet tasted the feeling of sand in their hooves.

This time, he warned his children about the perils of land and even forbade them to go ashore. But his plan did not succeed. Eventually, they found their way to back to the land and again evolved into goats. Pricus tried turning back time again and again, and each time he would lose his children to their desire to roam the earth. Eventually, Pricus came to a crisis point, realizing he had to surrender his desire to control his children. He let go and encouraged them to seek their own destiny. He accepted his fate. In his loneliness, he beseeched the gods to allow him to die. Instead, he became a constellation in the sky, forever looking down on his children.

There is something of the isolation and melancholy in this story that speaks to the Capricorn in me. And I appreciate the lesson around control; expectation is the partner of disappointment, so I've heard. The Capricorn in each of us must ask: *Why am I being so rigid about this? Who said it has to be like that?* Our rigidity or stubbornness around certain things often points to a fear of losing control.

There's also something about the sea goat that reminds me of evolution. We all began in the sea. Over time, water beings became land beings. There's a great meme with an illustration of the first water-to-land animal and it reads something like, "Because this guy decided to move onto land, I have to go to work and pay taxes." So hilarious, and also there's a Capricornian melancholy there, longing for the imagined ease of water. Some animals did return: seals, whales, dolphins, and penguins are a few that come to mind! Their ancestors said "Oops, never mind" to the land grind! We can laugh and even envy their return. What if the Capricorn Sea Goat in each of us holds the energetics of making it here with our land-world responsibilities while also supporting us with the water-world gifts of flow and flexibility?

Capricorn is also connected the symbol of the Mountain Goat. The mountain goat is a sure-footed climber. Goats can climb and climb on up any rocky mountain face. What can happen to the Capricorn in us is that we become so concentrated on enduring that we move into a neck-up state of being. We can deny bodily signals like hunger, thirst, and exhaustion in order to meet the goal. We lose touch with where we are in space and time because of that intense concentration. At some points down the line, the Capricorn in us stops and looks around. There can be this moment of, *What am I doing? How did I even get here? I don't even like this path.*

What Capricorn most wants is to feel authentically committed to a path. And the good news is that the Capricorn part of us has every tool we need to start an entirely new path. To begin again is not a problem; Capricorn is meant for the long haul and can honestly do anything. The question to ask yourself this month is: *Am I on the path I'm meant to be on?* You are the only one—not your mom, not your wife, not your boss, not your guru—who can tell you what your path is.

POLARITY
The Capricorn-Cancer Axis

All Earth signs are opposite Water signs, and all polar signs have the same modality. So cardinal Earth is opposite cardinal Water: Cancer.

With Capricorn-Cancer, we're looking at a polarity that feels like summer versus winter and contemplating how they make each other possible.

- Capricorn is an energy that calls for dispassionate, impersonal focus; Cancer is deeply personal, sensitive, and feeling.
- Capricorn can wall up your heart when it's needed; Cancer is your open, bleeding heart.
- Capricorn loves by building the structure to make dreams happen; Cancer loves by energetically attuning to those dreams.

To be in your Cancer is to receive all experience from a receptive space of sensitivity. Your psychic feelers go out into the world to see how you can give more care to it as well as to accept care in return. Information rolls in as if by the tides and your body responds based on what you feel. Tides roll in and you're in a mood. Tides roll out and the mood has passed.

Cancer wants to know how to bring a situation, person, or project to your symbolic breast and give the unique and vital nourishment you're specifically made to offer. In that embrace, you attune to what you're nourishing. This is Cancer's superpower.

Capricorn can fear that Cancer's gifts are a waste of time, but this comes from our cultural conditioning about what productivity looks like. We tend to compartmentalize the two signs so that we don't have to be both at the same time. It takes practice to trust that you can let the Cancerian tides roll in and still be able to maintain Capricorn's focus. Cancer helps your Capricorn to return to yourself and remember that nothing is truly impersonal.

As a culture, we are in deep reprogramming with Cancer and Capricorn, and this is why the axis often feels harder to express skillfully. I spend a lot more time here with clients and students than some of the other polarities for this reason. The polarity craves sustained reparenting to support you in growing your wise inner parent.

On the Cancer end, you're learning how to be the most nurturing anchor your inner children could ever ask for, the fierce provider who will never abandon you. On the Capricorn end, you're learning how to be the author of your own life, the boss who gives you permission to be the only one to decide to what and whom you commit your sacred time and discipline.

. . . .

RULING PLANET

Saturn ♄

Saturn is the traditional planet that gives both Capricorn and Aquarius their ways of being. Saturn is the planet that is furthest away while still being visible to the naked eye, and thus the mythology around the planet's principles underlines the idea of Saturn as the final teacher, the limit, that which we reckon with before we can reach self-actualization.

Saturn rules borders, walls, and limits; it is the principle of constriction and rules all things that have to do with reality here on the ground. Saturn is the part of you that puts a container around your time and your energy output in order to get something done. You could have the greatest idea in the world, but unless you carve out a container to do something with it, it just exists in the conceptual realm of the mind. Saturn says you can't relax until you finish the task at hand. Thus we associate Saturn with our discipline and the focus we need to concretize something on the earthly plane.

Saturn also rules your bones: the skeleton of the body, including the teeth. It holds you together. It is what will be left of your material existence when the rest is gone. Saturn is that indestructible part of you here on earth.

Saturn offers the Capricorn in you the way to become your own authority—and it's always a choice. You accept Saturn or you don't. It's a choice to put in the time. It's a choice to endure the lessons. It's a choice to earn things for yourself. It's a choice to stop turning to others to write your script. In the process, you become your own symbolic father: the author, authority, and provider of your own life. When we ask, "Who's in charge?" Saturn wants to know the answer is you.

Saturn is self-responsibility. Sometimes, Saturn can feel very serious, stern, and grim. Saturn can feel like self-criticism. Saturn anticipates difficulty. Saturn sometimes isolates. We all know this Saturnian voice. But I like to imagine Saturn as this wise elder inside. I see Saturn sitting across the table from me to hear about my dreams. When this Saturn asks, "What is your plan for this idea?" it's not to belittle me, ignite fear, or bring me into doubt. It's because without a sincere plan for execution, I won't get to experience my visions. And this is what Saturn wants for all of us: manifestation.

As intimidating as it may be, Saturn also holds you. If you've ever felt adrift, if you know addiction, if you are mired in excuses, if you've resisted your own empowerment, if you seek comfort in dysfunction because it's all you know, Saturn can be your best friend. Saturn pulls you together so you can live through the winter. Saturn will save your life!

Your discipline gives your life alignment, and your alignment buttresses your sense of self-esteem, and your self-esteem feeds your wisdom and authority. May Saturn support the Capricorn part of you in making discipline a devotion rooted in your loving commitment to being here.

. . . .

SKILLFUL CAPRICORN
Commit

Capricorn wants you to know: the most loving thing you can do is to be a deeply committed person.

Everyone will experience Capricorn in different ways. Some will give those commitments to their work. Some will want to give them to their hobbies, their relationships, or their home. For some, Capricornian commitment will apply to nearly everything about them.

In pop astrology, Capricorn is often called ambitious, but this often doesn't resonate with those born with their Sun in Capricorn. I wonder if we could expand our definition of ambition. What if ambition isn't tied to external concepts, such as fame or success, but rather to a sincere and ardent desire to participate in your life, and then actually doing it? What if ambition describes someone who seems "in" their channel and able to stay with the flow as long as necessary?

Perhaps we've been projecting our own shame onto the word *ambition*, wanting it to be a negative thing so we don't have to feel so bad about ourselves. If so, then how would it feel to neutralize ambition and release it from expectations of results, outcomes, or achievements? Then when we say, "She's really ambitious," what we mean is that she's focused on her committed desire.

This quote from *A Wizard of Earthsea* by Ursula K. Le Guin is the most Capricorn piece of writing I've ever found:

> You thought, as a boy, that a mage is one who can do anything.
> So I thought, once. So did we all. And the truth is that as a man's
> real power grows and his knowledge widens, ever the way he can
> follow grows narrower: until at last he chooses nothing, but does
> only and wholly what he must do.

Skillful Capricorn is when you wholly do what you must do. The path grows narrower because your inner Goat decides which paths *not* to take. The root of the word *decide* (the Latin *caedere*) means "to cut." Deciding means limiting your available options—and this takes courage. It takes courage to destroy possibilities.

But when you want to devote yourself to something or someone, and you know in your whole body that it's the choice for you, it doesn't have to feel brave. It feels like you had no other choice because you're on your path. And you're the one who decides these things, says the Capricorn part of you.

Many of my clients have shared with me a fear that they'll make a mistake and pick the wrong path. It freezes them, shackling their Goat to the bottom of the mountain. Here's what I have in response to this fear: the magical thing about Capricorn is that it's your toolkit for walking the path for you *in that moment*, not for picking one and never changing your mind. Your Capricorn is allowed to change paths and has all the tools you could ever need to do so.

PRACTICE

Meet the Inner Critic

Capricorn is one of the signs where I spend the most time with clients. I attract those who seek healing journeys, and I personally have done a lot of healing with Capricorn since my Moon is in Capricorn. I've found that the practice that most serves Capricorn is a daily check-in with the inner critic. As with all the practices in this book, your whole world can change with this one.

The inner critic is that voice in your head that says you're not good enough, that thinks mean things about your work or how you look, that deploys its favorite word—should—which constricts you with the fear that you're really an imposter, refusing compliments or opportunities to celebrate your achievements and isolating you from others. Sound familiar? I have never met someone who doesn't have an inner critic. It's a part of you that thinks it's being helpful, but it's not.

The first thing to know about the inner critic is that even though it's a part of you that you hear and feel, it's not the whole of who you are. It may not even be you at all. Initiating the practice of relating to your inner critic means sitting with the voice when you hear it and giving yourself an opportunity to get curious. For example, you hear: "I can't wear that because I'm fat." "Why would anyone want to hear my ideas?" "My work is shit." (Fill in with yours.)

First, say hi. "Hi, Inner Critic! I see you're here again." (Yes, you can make this silly. In fact, a spirit of humor will relax you.)

Next, clarify something very important. Ask yourself, *Is this voice mine or someone else's?* Sometimes just being able to notice when you've let the inner critic hijack your thoughts is the most difficult part. Asking this question can begin to neutralize things straight away. Then your inner dialogue can go one of two ways:

1. *Yes, I see that this voice is not even mine.* More often than not, the voice you're hearing is from an early caregiver or other person from your childhood. Whatever the case, if this happens, tell this voice, *Thank you for trying to help*, and say goodbye.

    Then, visualize sending it back to wherever it came from. You don't need to know who it belongs to as long as you get that it isn't you. I want to underline how important it is to get that voice consciously out of your space. Let your whole self witness you rejecting it. In this instance, you really do not owe that voice any respect.

2. *Well, actually, that voice is mine.* If the voice feels like it's yours, then ask it to show you how old you were when this voice started trying to help you. You might be surprised by the answer, or you might not be surprised in the slightest. Notice what this version of you looks like, especially their vibe: upbeat, cold, scared? Either way, say hi. Introduce yourself as the wise adult version of you. Then sincerely and lovingly ask your younger self what it's trying to do for you. What you hear might be heart melting.

    The goal here is to notice the worldview of your younger self who is trying to help you survive, convinced that criticizing you will help. Though that might have been the case back then, you are in a different place now. Let this part of you relax. Let your younger self rest. Start by assuring your younger self that you are a wise adult now, and while you appreciate their efforts, you don't need them right now.

Say goodbye by warmly offering them watercolors or slime to give them something to do until the next time you hang out together. Encourage them to go have fun.

Then touch base with the self that is your wise inner parent. How old are you? Notice and acknowledge your age in years. Connect to the highest levels of self-compassion you can imagine and flood yourself with all of it. Say to yourself, *You're doing a great job learning to be the parent your inner children need.*

TAROT CARD

The Devil

The card in the tarot that we associate with Capricorn is card fifteen, the Devil.

Of all of the tarot, it is the Devil that most craves a reputation overhaul. Personally, I find this card to be deeply encouraging and exciting.

In the *Smith-Rider-Waite* depiction of the Devil, we see the Capricornian Goat morphed into a hybrid goat-man with bat wings. That image has had associations with Christian depictions of Satan since at least the medieval period, as well as occultist Éliphas Lévi's drawing of Baphomet from the mid-nineteenth century. The Devil also has an upside-down pentagram on his forehead, symbolic of dark magic. The figure crouches atop a tiny plinth, with a naked man and woman tied to him with shackles around their necks. They have tails and small horns, suggesting they are becoming less human by association.

Traditionally, this card has to do with our demons: addictions, greed, excesses, "sins," self-sabotage, or self-destructiveness. In this framing, pulling the card feels like getting shamed, with the deck (and anyone else present) as your shaming witness. From my point of view, the Devil is about shame. But it's not here to shame you; instead, it works to help you notice the shame you're tethered to. Shame grows in silence and isolation. And if you're not talking about it or looking at it, shame quietly infuses your thoughts, actions, reactions, and dreams with a toxic poison that tells you something is wrong with you. That you're bad. That you're unworthy.

Before and beyond Christian categories of sin, we know the goat-man hybrid from the Greek figure Pan, a nature god who helps us remember our relationship to our inherent wildness. Pan was often represented with a massive phallus, symbolic of the creativity and fertility of the parts of us that can never be tamed or domesticated. Many tarot images of the Devil card nod to the playfulness of Pan, rather than the Devil of Christian morality. Pan wants to help us love being alive in these bodies rather than shame them.

Notice how the shackles on the two humans in the image are loose enough to remove if they choose to. The Devil reaches out and asks, "Why don't you dance with life like the nymphs and satyrs who danced with the wine god Bacchus? Why don't you approach everything with the pulsing creativity symbolized by the giant phallus of Pan?" As the Devil takes your hand, the invitation is to go within and query your own knowing: *Where does shame live in me that I resist fucking life with all my ferocious potency?*

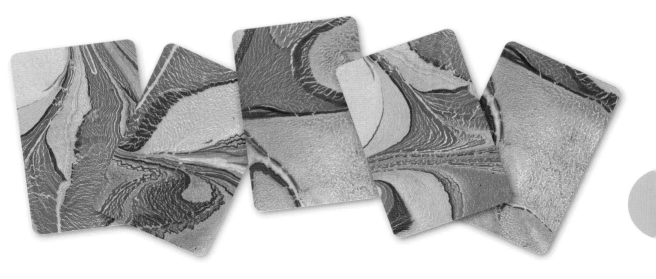

Yes, carnality is a huge piece of the Devil. We are unlearning that conditioning that our bodies are sinful. We are reprogramming the belief that desire is depraved. We are re-wiring the codes that taught us that pleasure is bad. Which is to say: we are unshaming. Capricorn learns from the Devil because our Capricorn discipline dries out when we're working from a shame place of "never enough." Skillful Capricorn is—is there a more appropriate word?—horny!

Capricorn via the Devil sounds like a broad, earthy laugh at anything and everything that life brings up. A sense of humor is really everything. Fully embody all that you are and aren't with utter self-acceptance and self-awareness, and gamely respond to the world from an unashamed position. If you are wondering what it would be like to live without shame, then I hope you find working with Capricorn and the Devil deeply healing and nourishing. Living Capricorn means appreciating that this walk takes time, and you have the endurance for it.

A Tarot Spread with the Devil

See the chapter *How to Navigate This Book* if you're new to the tarot and seek support for pulling cards and interpreting them.

Take the Devil out of your deck. (If you have more than one deck, you can pull the card from another deck so that the Devil has a chance to "participate" in the deck from which you will draw.)

Feel into the visual inspiration of the card.

Take a few deep breaths on purpose and arrive to the reading.

Connect into your intuition. Ask Devil-Capricorn energy to help you with this reading. Shuffle according to your unique, never-wrong style. Center and focus your question thus:

With the most expansive levels of compassion for me and all sentient beings, what is the loving invitation to connect with the Devil?

Pull seven cards according to your own unique process of knowing with the following prompts, and then sit with the cards and journal about them.

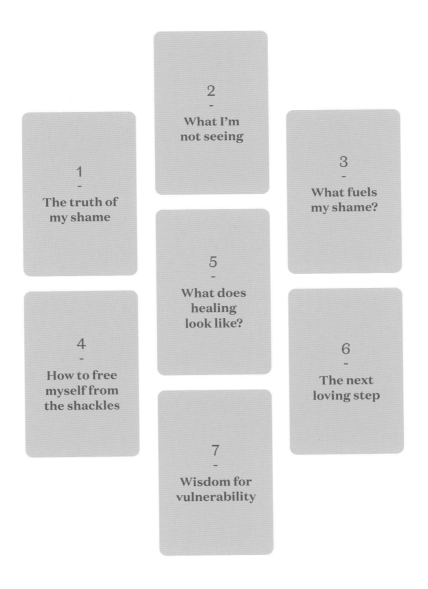

RITUAL FOR THE NEW MOON

Inner Resources

Capricorn initiates winter. It's fair to ask: *What is winter? What does winter do?*

Like the plants that respond to harsher times (winter) by hardening and relying on their storage organs (see page 252), so we can find a process to acclimate to winter. This requires understanding your resources and where your strength comes from. It is about literal resources, like feeding your body with warm, nutritious, supportive meals. It is about supporting your inner resources, like taking care of your mental health. It is also about the outer resources of our connections to family, friends, ancestors, and the land itself.

It is good to know these things. But we often don't learn how truly strong we are until we are forced to. Passing through literal and metaphorical winters brings us into more intimacy with our inner power and also strengthens it, so that when winter comes, we are ready.

What I've come to see is that the fuel of our inner storage organs comes from the strength of the Fire we trust from the Sagittarius inside of us. All Earth signs follow Fire signs, and this is meaningful. The Earth signs ground, stabilize, and build a home for what lights up your spirit. If you haven't read the Sag chapter yet, that's perfectly okay; you will have time to go around the circle again and integrate your knowledge. But if you received some valuable support in the Sag chapter about your mutable Fire, bring what you learned to this ritual with Capricorn.

Before beginning this ritual, gather:

- Candles, as many as you want, and a way to light them
- Your journal and pen
- Tarot deck

The Ritual

1. Sit at your Capricorn altar when ready. Set up your ritual container, light your candle(s), and come to a grounded, meditative state (see page 57).

2. Draw in your journal a rendering of a great tree: a tree you love or maybe an imaginary tree that feels inspiring to you. If you don't want to draw, then visualize yourself as this great tree. Draw or see the branches with needles or leaves, maybe there are birds or animals in the branches. Draw or see the broad trunk. Draw or see the ground and then the vast realm of roots under the ground.

3. Feel into or draw this tree in the summer.

4. Now feel or draw into this tree in the winter. Notice how very different the tree looks and feels in the winter. How the whole ecosystem is different. How the energy is slower.

5. Draw or visualize all of the energy of the tree pooling into the root system of the tree. What does it look like above ground to have a vibrant well of life energy stored away below?

6. Sit back within yourself and feel into *your* storage organs (the deep wells of life force you draw upon). Think of times in your life that have been hard, periods we might call "winters," perhaps when you were moving through grief, loss, burden, and disappointment. Ask:
   - *How do I acclimate when the world feels colder and harsher?*
   - *How do I resource my storage organs when things aren't comfortable or easy?*
   - *What boundaries help me endure what is difficult? What is not helpful for my energy when I'm going through a rough patch?*

7. Know these. Name these. Write them down.

8. Now feel into the life-force energy of the tree again, seeing
   it move upward and out in the summer, and move down and
   under in the winter. This is a Fire part of you that comes
   through as your passion, your excitement, your exuberance,
   your hope, and the song of your heart. Ask yourself the
   following questions, listening and writing down answers as you
   sense them:
   - *If my Fire is a color, what color is it? What's its
     temperature? Does it make a sound vibration?*
   - *What people, activities, and environments encourage my
     Fire to feel more alive?*
   - *What people, activities, and environments dampen my Fire
     or discourage its aliveness?*
   - *What boundaries do I crave to support me in feeling
     connected to my Fire?*
   - *What daily structures do I crave to support me in finding
     time to connect to my Fire?*
   - *What deadlines do I crave to support me in spending time
     finishing projects where my Fire comes through?*

9. Now you have some information for the lunar cycle and some
   guidelines to give your Capricorn self to support your Fire.

10. If you'd like to pull some cards to support you in intention
    setting, please do this now. Some suggestions include:

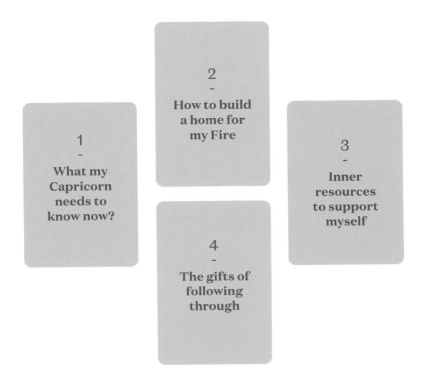

11. What feels true here? Write these down. Weave any yummy insight from the tarot pull into your lunar intention. Feel free to continue meditation or journaling as long as you'd like, as long as the container remains closed to outside distraction.

12. Conclude and open the ritual container (see page 66).

Happy New Moon in Capricorn!

Aquarius

JANUARY 20–FEBRUARY 19

〜〜 AQUARIUS

△ AIR

⊡ FIXED

♄ ♅ SATURN AND URANUS

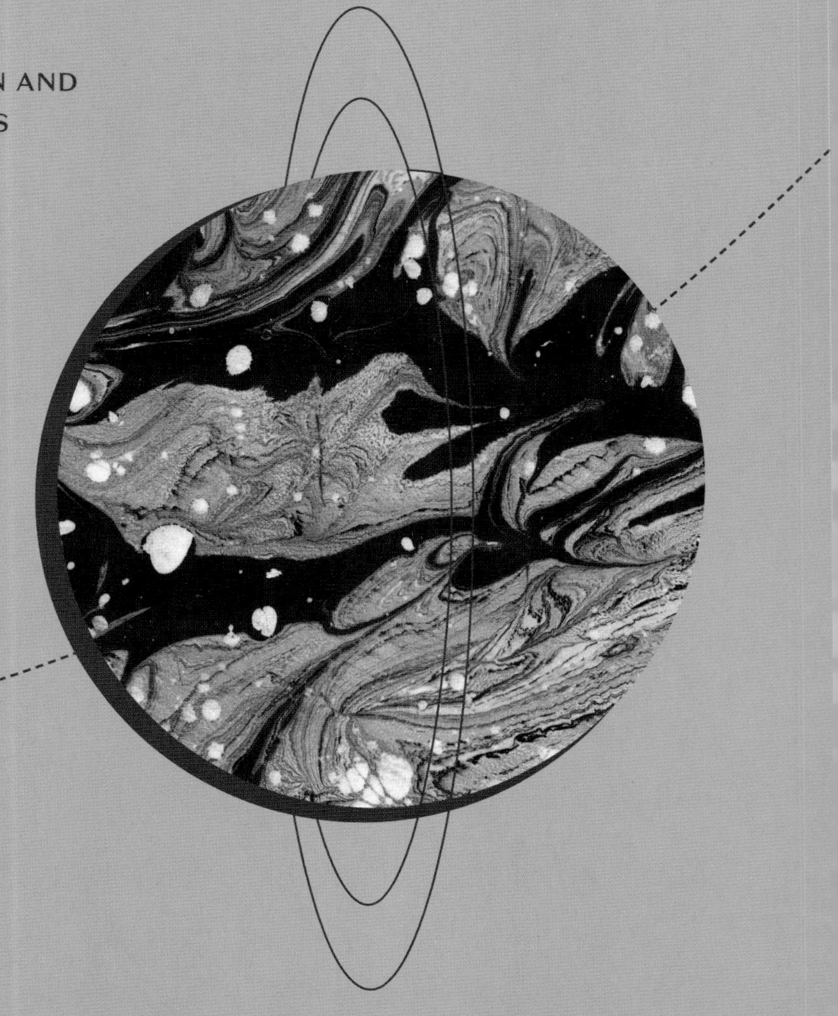

Aquarius

Questions to Live Into

What rebellions are worth fighting in order to stay true to my ideals?

If I looked at my life as if I was a total outsider to it, how would I describe my principles based on my work in the world, media choices, social networks, hobbies, and spending habits?

What if I trusted that the greatest gift I can give others is my weird, eccentric, un-boxable self?

Altar

As discussed in part one, the purpose of creating an altar is to first prepare and then enjoy having a special space devoted to the themes and principles you're developing with each sign. The general qualities of Aquarius are listed below. I recommend you gather at least three items, but quantity isn't as crucial as choosing items of resonance for you. For example, this season, maybe you want your altar to honor those who've used their voices to champion progressive social change. Your altar could have photos, quotes, and other symbols that inspire you to envision new futures. Take the suggestions that feel aligned and don't worry about the rest. As you read through the chapter, more ideas may come to you for your altar that aren't listed here.

Go for it!

COLORS
purple, sky blue, violet

CRYSTALS
amber, aquamarine, garnet, lapis lazuli, malachite

GARDEN
lavender, vervain, witch hazel

SPICES AND FLAVORS
cardamom, fennel, ginger, piri piri, saffron, turmeric

GODS AND GODDESSES
Bacchus, Ganymede, Kronos, Pan, Saturn, Uranus

TAROT CARDS
the Fool, the Star, the World, 5 of Swords, 6 of Swords, 7 of Swords

ITEMS
art, books, ceramics, fabrics, food, incense, magazine cutouts, photographs, quotes on paper, or anything else that inspires you

RELATED THEMES
aliens, astronomy, avatars, collective consciousness, collectivity, conceptual architecture, conspiracy theories, coworking spaces, hilly and uneven places, human rights movements, intuition, inventions, meetups, mineral quarries, paradigm shifts, poetry readings, quirks, Quora, rallies, rebellions, Reddit, Saturday, science, science fiction, seminar rooms, sit-ins, Twitter, UFOs, wells

SEASON
Middle of Winter

Aquarius carries the essence of all that winter is. This is a time of deep cold, when humans would sometimes work in isolation from one another and other times gather to envision and share goals for the coming season. Aquarius holds this dichotomy in its nature. It's a way of being that we associate with collectivity, but it's also a part of us that needs a lot of alone time.

Aquarius season coincides with the midpoint between the winter solstice (initiated with Capricorn) and the spring equinox (initiated with Aries). In Irish tradition, this point is known as Imbolc, celebrated on February 1. *Imbolc* is said to come from the Irish *i mbolg*, meaning "in the belly." The earth is pregnant, though it's still the thick of winter. And what happens in nature is happening within you.

I like to think of Aquarius season in terms of the quickening of the earth. Something is reviving, turning on, going faster, fluttering, and waking up beneath the quiet surface. What do you want the year to bring?

What ideals do you have within you that want to be shared? What is worth working hard to see happen?

Aquarius relates to emergence then. Like quickening, emergence has to do with the energy of coming forth from concealment. It suggests that something is arising. Aquarius wants to become approachable to what is emerging and arising in yourself and in your world. Aquarius wants to make room for the vision to drop at a moment's notice.

It is traditional at Imbolc to do some housecleaning. Don't think of this as dreary work or just another chore to tick off your list. This is the soul's preparatory devotion. When we physically sweep out our clutter, dust off the past, and release the old and stale, we are embodying that clean slate for our inner selves. We do this in order to tend to what is longing to emerge.

What needs to be cleared out to make space to envision your own quickening?

. . . .

MODALITY AND ELEMENT

Fixed Air

Like Taurus, Leo, and Scorpio, Aquarius is a fixed sign. Each of these is the part of you that is rooted. In your fixed parts, you have a Yes or a No without waffling.

Like Gemini and Libra, Aquarius is an Air sign. Through the Air signs, you learn, communicate, relate, think, and share space with others.

I see fixed Air as a spaceship, seeing us earthlings from above and deciding to come down and pretend to be humans so they can help us connect more lovingly with the planet and with each other. In the human realm, fixed Air is the inventor who brings us a tool we didn't know we wanted and now can't imagine living without. It's the conceptual artist whose work speaks to the zeitgeist in ways we hadn't named before they showed us. It's the activist who starts a movement.

Fixed Air encourages you to notice what's missing or what's under-represented in the world and then create a role for yourself to contribute to change. It has a very transpersonal viewpoint. The motivation is to apply the principles you long to establish in the world to a cause or framework that will work better for everyone. Collectivity is important to the Aquarian in you.

When your Aquarius names what feels important to name, it isn't attention seeking or button pushing. It is simply what you must do. You tap into your fixed Air when you don't really care how people might judge you for going to the rally, sharing thoughts on an issue at the dinner table, or disagreeing with someone's read on a film.

The straight talk of Aquarius doesn't come from ego. For the other signs within us that worry about not being perceived as difficult, the Aquarian ability to not give a shit is a gift. It's liberating to speak your ideals freely for folks to take or leave as they will.

Interpersonally, your Aquarius can be that friend to someone who has personal drama. You can offer advice without getting emotionally tangled up in the energetics. Aquarius is able to hold their own Air and not get mixed up in Air that's not theirs.

. . . .

SYMBOL

The Water Bearer ♒

Sometimes people are surprised to find out that Aquarius is an Air sign because they had presumed it was a Water sign. There is good reason for this presumption: the word *Aquarius* comes from Latin, meaning "water carrier" or "water bearer," as Aquarius is sometimes known.

The constellation of Aquarius is located in an area of the sky often called The Sea. There you can find a nexus of constellations related to water, such as Cetus (the Whale), Pisces (the Fish), and Eridanus (the River). The stars of Aquarius's configuration look like a vessel with a stream of water pouring out that flows toward Pisces, the Water sign that follows. Sometimes Aquarius is illustrated with a human figure holding the upturned vessel.

The Water Bearer, in many ways, is the "baptizer" of humanity. Aquarius has this capacity to bathe us, nourish us, and bless us with the ideas and tools we need to progress into the next age. The Water Bearer serves the collective. The waves that pour out of the Water Bearer's vessel do not represent literal water so much as the knowledge and insight that Aquarius shares with the rest of humanity in the form of science, technology, art, social policy, and mathematics. You can think of it as the human vessel for cosmic consciousness, crystallizing intelligence from a spiritual dimension. As Aquarius, you give your unique genius and capacity for discipline over to these larger transpersonal ideals.

Aquarius isn't a part of you that has a lot of interest in personal hobbies, free time, or friendships that don't support your service. You have other signs in you for these. Aquarius is a part of you that's here to work. And I mean this is in the most celebratory way possible. It's important for you to serve your Aquarius. Your cosmic consciousness has a unique frequency that supports us all.

Aquarius is unimpressed with individualism—with rugged heroes whose swagger and independence steal the show. At the same time, there's a war within our Aquarius, because even as we dislike individualism, it's easy to adopt that attitude when you feel like an outsider. Or at least, it's easy for our culture to mistake the isolated work of Aquarius for that of the lone hero.

The world shames the Aquarius for being different. Only certain types of swagger are considered safe to those who are invested in conserving old paradigms. Knowing this is important for claiming your Aquarius. You will want to decide how invested you are in maintaining norms to avoid being seen as deviant or disruptive. Holding back your Aquarius has serious consequences on all facets of life.

Thus, a part of working with Aquarius is noticing your relative openness and willingness to speak from a sincere place on topics that relate to your principles. If you notice that you want to speak your truth but hold back, then this is your data collection practice right now. Speaking truth can also refer to how you express yourself through style and (body) art. It's the books you showcase on your shelves. It's the movies and shows and gatherings you give your time.

What I have found is that access to your intuition gets jammed when a block exists. This month, begin building a home inside yourself where it's safe to emerge as your whole self. In what ways can you let your inner Aquarius nudge you to be a little more public?

· ·

POLARITY

The Aquarius-Leo Axis

All Air signs are opposite Fire signs, and all polar signs have the same modality. So fixed Air is opposite fixed Fire: Leo.

- Aquarius is just one star in a galaxy of countless star systems; Leo is the focal point, the brightest star right in the center.
- Aquarius connects; Leo radiates.
- Aquarius is the bear hibernating in the depth of winter; Leo is the seal basking on the beach in the bright glow of the summer sun.

Leo is a bonfire, drawing people around with its warmth. Ruled by the Sun, Leo has a centripetal quality of being the center. Leo gives its heat from an abundant home of vitality. Leo plays. Leo creates. Leo loves. In medical astrology, Leo rules the heart. Leo encourages Aquarius to evolve by helping you stay heart-led, compassionate, and playful even while you reform the world with your big ideas. Leo says to the Aquarius in you, "Listen to your heart. What does it want?"

Have you ever built a moat around your heart in order to keep out feelings or not have to deal with a situation? Who hasn't? The Aquarius in you can be aloof and unfeeling. It might feel judgmental and impatient with those who don't agree with you or see your brilliance. You might find personal drama distasteful and annoying—and make it obvious you feel that way. Leo looks Aquarius in the eye and reminds you that you live in a human body that has passionate responses to what life brings up—just like everyone else. You are allowed to be a person with passions!

As fixed signs, both Leo and Aquarius tend to be obstinate and stubborn in their point of view and share an aura of self-containment. The Leo-Aquarius polarity tells a story about the spectrum between centralization and decentralization. Aquarius helps Leo break away from the burden of being special. Leo's gift is to help you tap into your unique special frequency, but this part of you can also be consumed with a desire to have your specialness constantly affirmed. Aquarius says to the Leo in you, "Yeah, but everyone is special."

Aquarius is not impressed with hero mythology. Instead, it is invested in the idea of bringing people together to collectively express their gifts and talents and change the world in the process. But Aquarius needs Leo's proud heroes because a collectivity of superheroes is only going to be as powerful as each individual knows themselves to be.

This is a polarity that wants you to have the audacity to permit yourself to be exceptional, and then submit those gifts in service to the world through interconnectivity.

. . . .

RULING PLANETS
Saturn and Uranus

Since ancient times, Saturn has been the ruler of Aquarius and Capricorn. So, who is Saturn? Saturn is the one who sobers you up. The teacher you have no choice but to work with. The one who brings you back to the reality of what's here. The one who shows you the steps to a goal. The one who guides your discipline.

The Saturnian nature of your Aquarian is here to work. But you have to understand and be deeply impressed with the principles of that work. Through Aquarius, Saturn expresses strong preferences and opinions. Saturn doesn't give its discipline to bosses, vocations, companies, or groups that aren't worthy of its devotion.

Uranus has become the modern ruler of Aquarius because the planet's qualities match naturally with so many of Aquarius's expressions. I honor both planets in my practice with Aquarius.

Uranus is, quite simply, the Great Awakener. Uranus represents your capacity for breaking out of boxes. Like the Aquarius in you, Uranus must be free. Uranus must feel liberated to resist stagnation and all chains of oppression and control.

Uranus is radical. It wants to stay open and receptive to even the most unforeseen changes, the most unexpected shifts, and the most shocking pace. This requires incredible trust that the truth will set you free.

I like to think about Uranus as the queer planet. I'm using a broad definition of *queer* here, one that celebrates choices and principles outside of any dominant framework. It aligns with options that include the nonbinary, nonlinear, and decolonial.

Uranus offers the Aquarian in you the chance to embrace the creative potential of disruption. *Disruption* is a word that sounds scary, but it's actually a natural stage to pass through. Have you ever had a toxic habit or relationship get disrupted? Disruption can literally save your life. Any time truth is spoken, it's disrupting and destabilizing to those who aren't up for it. Uranus invites the Aquarian part of you to destroy temples to gods that don't really matter to you. Take down the altars to a dead past and prepare for the future, for the beginning of a new cycle. The Aquarius in you is up for it.

Together Saturn and Uranus want you to understand: you have an assignment. You were beamed here with instructions. You are not on this planet to reply to emails promptly! We earthlings are clearly struggling to live together. Your spirit chose to be embodied on this timeline so you're here to help us. Take responsibility for the unique frequency you've been given to emit.

What this means is that you are not here to be like other people. Please hear this. Other people have their own instructions, and their instructions are none of your business. You are not here to please or satisfy someone else's strivings, and likewise no one on this planet came here to satisfy your strivings. That's your job.

Saturn and Uranus take your hand, look you in the eye, and ask: What if you're here to disrupt all expectations placed on you? What if your disruption is crucial to this planet?

SKILLFUL AQUARIUS
Diverge

Aquarius wants you to know: the most loving thing you can do is to be an alien from the future. Aquarius is a gift of sight, insight, and visioning. It is an energy and a tool that—when we open up to it—facilitates downloads, knowledge, and understandings that seem to come from beyond ourselves. And because you see so much, you know how it could be if certain changes were made.

Aquarius is an attunement to institutions, ways of being, and paradigms that cease to adequately function—which is to say, it is attuned to malfunction. Aquarius-dominant folks are often accused of being contrarian just to be "difficult." Does this resonate?

What you are sensing is the future. And you see that to be approachable to this incoming future, we need to shift things now to support the emergence. This is extremely valuable to the collective. The resistance people feel to hearing the future includes a range of possibilities such as apathy about quality control, fear of change, and basic unwillingness to put in the work. Aquarius doesn't understand or have patience for these responses.

As cosmic Air, Aquarius relates to the starry night sky and realms of outer space. Since Aquarius energy is tied to being paradigm-shifting and highly intuitive about collective consciousness, there can be a sense that the Aquarius parts of yourself are a little "out there" compared to whatever the "normal" is in your mind. Aquarius has an energy of being out-of-the-box, extraordinary, and at the edges. And yes, this is destabilizing for those who are fine with how things are or have been. Those are not the people for your Aquarius.

The degree to which you're comfortable being seen as difficult or divergent relates directly to the degree to which you give your Aquarius permission to be a brilliant genius. Skillful Aquarius cares more about the importance of truth than whether or not other people find it agreeable. This is why you must find work that matters; in doing so, what other people think becomes none of your business.

Also note that I said "comfortable *being seen as* difficult or divergent" not "*being* difficult or divergent." Skillful Aquarius protects space from other people's perceptions and does not let those perceptions affect what they know needs to be done. Skillful Aquarius knows that your refusal to be standardized isn't personal, even if some may find it a personal attack. There's a reason people have a reaction to what they don't want to be true, and their reactivity is really not about you.

If you felt different or singled out from established norms in your childhood, there can be a deep sense of severed belonging for your inner child. The wound of it comes from a person's or group's lack of attunement to your unique gifts. It's painful when a caregiver, sibling, or admired teacher doesn't "get" you, no matter what you do. This is part of why there seems to be a large number of Aquarius-dominant folks who find their own chosen family among friends. They magnetize each other and redefine normal together. As a group, they create safe spaces to just be who they are and celebrate one another.

Skillful Aquarius models holding to a larger truth that feels worthy of your devotion. It means letting other people have their own experience of you. You can't possibly comprehend the effect you have on anyone. Trust that if you are honoring principles that feel good and just for all, then even someone's judgment of you is an experience that serves an intelligence beyond you.

PRACTICE

Tarot Question of the Day

The practice of living Aquarius is the practice of taking responsibility for the energy you bring to the collective. I want you to get connected to your unique frequency—because it matters. Your frequency is the vibrational imprint of your spirit.

I like to think of the human self and the spirit self. The human self has pain, biases, convictions, triggers, limiting self-beliefs, and judgments of others. Your spirit has a longer, more expansive view and is made solely for love. Your spirit's frequency is not biological, in that it's not given to you by the sperm and egg of your incarnation. Your spirit self is the gift of your light. It is not fully containable to the body because it spills out into your energy field and is felt where your body isn't, like in your writing, your voice messages, and the evidence of your contributions to the spaces you inhabit. Your frequency is your unique way of being from the spirit self: here for love in ways very specific to you, not to your conditioning. Being a Water Bearer means acting in the world as a spirit in a body.

It's difficult to be intimate with your personal frequency if you aren't spending time alone. Because we are porous and because we are all connected, we are constantly absorbing other people's ideas, wants, goals, opinions, needs, and viewpoints. While this is a wonderful, exciting, and engaging experience, it can be tiring and even confusing, as you can lose clear sight of yourself. Spiritual loneliness is an undesired consequence of not spending time with your spirit.

So to get clarity about your own wonderful weirdness and important divergence, I invite you to gift yourself plenty of nourishing solitude to cultivate special interests, go down curious rabbit holes, and let strange food land on your tongue. Your wanderings will nourish us all.

Consciously choosing to be alone is a practice for nurturing your channel, or the communication line you have with your spirit self. In a fractal conception, you attract the communities that reflect your conscious goals as well as your unconscious motivations and needs. What you put out into the world has rippling effects on everything. The more you care for yourself as a vessel (the Water Bearer), the more you support collective consciousness.

> Your spirit self is the gift of your light.

To anchor into the rhythm of this, try this tarot practice every day of Aquarius season. Please review the introduction section on starting a tarot practice on pages 58–62 if you are new to the tarot.

1. Find a time and space where you can be fully alone. It helps you build a habit if you do this at the same time every day if possible. Bring your tarot deck, journal, and a pen.

2. Settle into yourself and come into a grounded place (see page 57).

3. Connect to your deck and shuffle it according to your unique, never-wrong style.

4. Before pulling your card, ask a question. Don't be afraid to get specific. Here are some ideas for questions you can ask your deck, and I encourage you to come up with your own as well:
    - *What is Aquarius wanting me to see today?*
    - *What might presently block me from sharing my Aquarius with the world?*
    - *What is a loving invitation for my Aquarius self?*
    - *What does my cosmic family want me to see about my creative intelligence?*
    - *Where should I look for Aquarius today?*
    - *What are my hopes and dreams teaching about my role in the world?*
    - *How might a queer perspective help me open a new way of thinking about old problems today?*

5. Pull a card.

6. Allow your intuition to lead you to an internal knowing about how the card wants to guide you. Feel free to check guidebooks but don't let them override your own gut feeling. See tips on pages 61–62 for interpretation. Remember: the cards are your friends. They are not here to shame you or judge you or make you afraid.

7. Close the pull with a thank you to your deck.

8. Track the cards you pull in your journal. Each day write down the date, the question you asked the deck, the card you pulled, and any first feelings and ideas about the guidance. You might enjoy keeping the card in an open place like at your altar, desk, or bedside table. Then just let what happens in your day teach you more about how the card is showing up for you. Let yourself be surprised. Let the cards have a sense of humor. Let them not mean what you worried they meant. Keeping the interpretation open will keep the practice delightful and warm.

TAROT CARD

The Star

The card in the tarot that we associate with Aquarius is card seventeen, the Star.

In the *Smith-Rider-Waite* version, a naked woman is depicted as kneeling before a body of water. She has one foot on land, referring to one's embodied presence and practical life, and one foot impossibly on water, referring to one's intuition and connectedness to the nonrational and unseen.

The figure holds two vessels, one in each hand. With her right hand, she pours liquid back into the water. This speaks to one's relationship with Source: divine energy, mystery, spirit, the life force that ties all beings together across all timelines. The ripples of the water remind us of the untraceable effects of our relationship to the whole.

With her other hand she pours water into the earth. This relates to the ways in which our actions, words, and most especially the energy we bring to any environment have an actual effect on the earthly plane. The five rivulets that run off from the vessel's flow mirror the five senses of one's embodied experience.

Above the figure, there is not one star but eight. The largest star might refer to your life force, that part of you that has and will evolve across countless timelines, while the other seven signify the seven chakras or the seven traditional celestial bodies. You are always watched over and guided. You are always connected and held. The universe is into you!

In the major arcana storyline, the Star follows an intense sequence of cards. Life can bring rough periods, but the Star reemerges as a welcome reminder of hope. You lean on the Star in order to tap into that hope, along with the divine guidance, healing tools, and inner resources you most need to keep going.

In the *Thoth* deck, the woman pictured is the star goddess Nuith. She is the channel for cosmic consciousness and celestial wisdom. What spirals out of the chalices in each of her hands is not water but vortices of electric energy to inspire and nourish the planet.

This is Aquarius. What you're going for when you are in this card is trust in your capacity to receive and be a channel for cosmic consciousness and grace. In deep winter, it is time to connect with your hopes and dreams for your work and how it can benefit the world.

You can ask yourself:

- *How do I open and trust myself as a medium for a healing revolution?*
- *What limits do I put on my access to grace?*
- *What would it feel like to expand my connection to cosmic consciousness?*

A simple thing you can do to connect with the Star inside yourself is to go outside at night and stare at the stars. Notice that you are connected. You are not separate from the heavens. You are literally made of stardust! Ask the sky which star watches over you, and talk to your cosmic family.

A Tarot Spread with the Star

See the chapter *How to Navigate This Book* if you're new to the tarot and seek support for pulling cards and interpreting them.

Take the Star out of your deck. (If you have more than one deck, you can pull the card from another deck so that the Star has a chance to "participate" in the deck from which you will draw.)

Feel into the visual inspiration of the card.

Take a few deep breaths on purpose and arrive to the reading. Connect into your intuition. Ask Star-Aquarius energy to help you with this reading. Shuffle according to your unique, never-wrong style. Center and focus your question thus:

With the most expansive levels of compassion for me and all sentient beings, what is the loving invitation to connect with the Star?

Pull seven cards according to your own unique process of knowing with the following prompts, and then sit with the cards and journal about them.

2
-
THE IBIS
-
For magical words to share

1
-
THE BIG STAR
-
To channel cosmic consciousness

3
-
THE SEVEN SMALL STARS
-
To clear and heal my chakras

5
-
THE VESSEL IN HER RIGHT HAND
-
To channel my intuition

4
-
THE VESSEL IN HER LEFT HAND
-
To serve with grace on the earthly plane

6
-
THE FIVE RIVULETS
-
To embody the expansiveness of the cosmos

7
-
THE BODY OF WATER
-
From the well of my imagination

Make the Future

At the New Moon in Aquarius, you have a powerful window to create a quiet container for reconnecting with your hopes and dreams for humanity. Skillful Aquarius takes big, lofty ideals and truths from the cosmic sky above and sets them down to find a home in your heart. As Aquarius Sun Oprah Winfrey teaches, "The key to realizing a dream is to focus not on success but on significance—and then even the small steps and little victories along your path will take on greater meaning." What grows from these star seeds becomes your guide to a life of significance, connection, and significance.

Skillful Aquarius constellates people together around shared hopes and dreams. I love that the root words of *constellation* (the Latin *con* and *stella*) mean "together with the stars" or "a collection of stars." To constellate, then, is to bring stars together. Every human being is a unique star, and what constellates us to our networks of friends and colleagues are the hopes and dreams for the world that we share.

Wondrous things happen when we get specific with those hopes and dreams. We magnetize those who want to participate with us on what we most hope and dream. We bring people to us who care about our ideals, priorities, and values for this world, and who want to do things with us to expand them and make them more palpable. This is how we build new worlds and materialize new timelines. When you are aligned with your world visions, anything is possible.

Before beginning this ritual, gather:

- Candles, as many as you want, and a way to light them
- Your journal and a pen
- Mason jar or vase
- One or two sheets of paper
- Tarot deck (optional)

The Ritual

1. Sit at your Aquarius altar when ready. Set up your ritual container, light your candle(s), and come to a grounded, meditative state (see page 57).

2. Ask yourself: *What kind of world makes it possible for us to wildly love living here?* Visualize a desirable future, maybe twenty years out. You are visualizing a future you want to make. Invite in as much detail as possible. Notice technologies and societal concerns. Do not set limits on what is possible. Do not stop dreaming because you don't believe it's possible. Just go to the edges and beyond.

3. See yourself. *What kind of world makes it possible for you to wildly love living here?*

4. See other people, including and especially people who have different positionalities than you. *What kind of world makes it possible for all people to wildly love living here?*

5. Create a written list of what you want to belong here. For everything you don't want (systemic oppression, urgency with time, food scarcity), reframe it as something you do want. Personally, I am interested in building a future that is designed for maximum softness for all. What about you? To help you, you might feel into your will at the solar plexus (just below the diaphragm and above the belly button in the body), and then say, "What I *really* want is a world where
    *   _____ is/are protected.
    *   _____ is valued.
    *   _____ is celebrated.
    *   _____ is normalized.
    *   Everyone has access to _____.
    *   And so on. Feel free to create more of these.

6. When you feel complete with the list, put your paper in the jar or vase you gathered. This is your Water Bearer's vessel. With both hands on it, feel the full force of your hope for this future run through your whole body and then surge through your hands with the full force of your loving attention.

7. Now ask yourself and your guidance to show or tell you what you need to know today to show up for this future right now. You do not need to know how to get the whole collective from here to there. All you're doing is showing up for your part in the larger disciplined vision.

8. Optional tarot card pull: If you want to, pull one card to help you understand your vision of the future. Pull a clarifying card if you're not sure how to read it. Then pull three cards to go underneath the first: a card for how to show up to the vision today, a card to remind you of any blocks or resistances to showing up, and a card for remembering you don't have to do it all.

9. When you feel complete, feel into an intention for this month that feels most nourishing and appropriate to whatever came up across the ritual and write it down.

10. Conclude and open the ritual container (see page 66).

Happy New Moon in Aquarius!

Pisces

FEBRUARY 19–MARCH 20

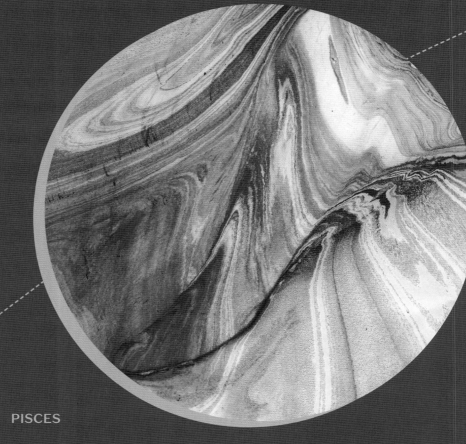

⟨ PISCES

▽ WATER

☊ MUTABLE

♃ ♆ JUPITER AND NEPTUNE

Questions to Live Into

What if I trust that I cannot possibly
know what happens next, so I might as
well surrender to the flow of experience?

What compassion would I give myself
and others if I believed that we are
all doing the very best we can, given
our current capacity, tools, and
circumstances?

How can I allow in more love,
imagination, and wonder today?

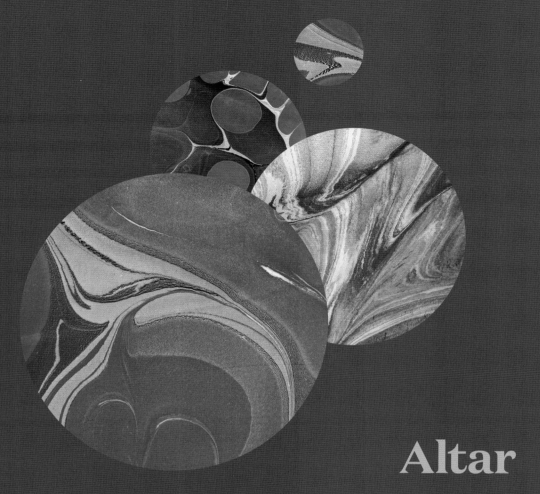

Altar

As discussed in part one, the purpose of creating an altar is to first prepare and then enjoy having a special space devoted to the themes and principles you're developing with each sign. The general qualities of Pisces are listed below. I recommend you gather at least three items, but quantity isn't as crucial as choosing items of resonance for you. For example, this season, maybe you prefer to build an altar to your imagination. Your entire altar space could be full to the brim with drawings, quotes, pictures of movie characters, and objects that represent this expansive realm of possibilities. Take the suggestions that feel aligned and don't worry about the rest. As you read through the chapter, more ideas may come to you for your altar that aren't listed here.

Go for it!

COLORS
blue, purple, sea green

CRYSTALS
amethyst, aquamarine, fluorite, jade, labradorite, moonstone, sapphire, turquoise

GARDEN
evening primrose, ferns, iris, kelp, moss, plants that grow near water, poppy, water lily

SPICES AND FLAVORS
clove, saffron, sea salt, sea spice

GODS AND GODDESSES
Aegir, Aphrodite, Diana, Dionysus, Jesus Christ, Jupiter, Neptune, Poseidon, Venus, Vishnu

TAROT CARDS
the Moon, Cups court cards, 8 of Cups, 9 of Cups, 10 of Cups

ITEMS
art, books, ceramics, fabrics, food, incense, magazine cutouts, photographs, quotes on paper, or anything else that inspires you

RELATED THEMES
altered states, clairvoyance, compassion, connecting to Spirit, deltas, the dissolution of separateness, dreaming, enlightenment, forgiveness, grace, illusion, imagination, lagoons, love, meditation, mermaids, music, mysticism, poetry, sea-based items (coral, driftwood, pearl, sand, shells, anything else that reminds you of water), Thursdays, treasure at the bottom of the sea, water creatures (dolphin, fish, jellyfish, seal), watercolor

SEASON
End of Winter

Pisces represents the end of winter, the period of time when the weather swings between last gasps of serious cold and sneak peeks of the spring to come.

The winter signs of Capricorn, Aquarius, and Pisces invite us into our most mature and wise ways of being. We need these parts of self in order to survive and endure, to envision the future, and make peace with the past. While Capricorn and Aquarius are energies that still strive to work, work, work, Pisces lets go.

Pisces is the twelfth and final sign. In many ways, Pisces is the part of you that has lived all the signs. As the zodiacal calendar closes, Pisces looks both wistfully back on what was and energetically forward to the new dream.

Of what does Pisces dream? As I like to say: Pisces dreams of Aries. In one hand, Pisces holds all the melancholy of the past and, in the other hand, Pisces identifies and uplifts the ideal that will be born in spring. Thus, Pisces is like a bridge between one way of being and another. It's a great time of year for reflection, dreaming, wondering, making art, brainstorming, ending things, clearing space, and forgiveness.

How do you connect with this time of year? What comes to mind when you think of late February and the first half of March? What makes late winter beautiful? What is the essential dignity of this time of year? I love this word *dignity* when applied to signs. How do the qualities of this time of year live in your personality, your being, your psyche? How are you a late winter person?

Just as all your seasonal feelings reveal your relationship to that season's sign, how you feel about late winter will help you open a door to your relationship to Pisces.

> It's a part of you that can feel and then envision how to help a person.

Born March 4 at the thirteenth degree of Pisces, I am utterly, madly, ecstatically in love with this sign. Pisces is one of the most difficult to sum up in language. It describes a part of each of us that's more mysterious and otherworldly. When astrology found its way to me, it was deeply healing to learn about Pisces because it reflected back to me so much about my human experience that I had felt but not known how to describe.

It is my hope that this chapter supports you in enlivening your personal connection to the Pisces within you and around you.

MODALITY AND ELEMENT
Mutable Water

Pisces is the last of the mutable signs after Gemini, Virgo, and Sagittarius. Pisces closes the season and helps you integrate everything you were learning across winter and the whole of the prior year.

Like the other Water signs (Cancer and Scorpio), Pisces cares for the emotional realm, the more primordial and mysterious aspects of our human experience, the deep wisdom of our ancestral lineage, and the power of our intuition.

Mutable Water is the most chameleonlike part of you. Water is the most adaptable of the elements, and mutability is the most flexible of the modalities. In nature, Pisces is a jellyfish moving gracefully with current.

In human form, mutable Water is a dancer who becomes one with the medium. An orator capable of channeling precisely the feeling they want to convey to rouse their audience. The barista who can tell right when you walk in how to raise your vibration with their body language. Each of these skills has to do with attunement, opening yourself to the energetics of deep listening. Why? In order to understand. Pisces *understands*.

Mutable Water encourages you to attune to whatever you feel like: a person, your imagination, music, a vision you want for your life. In the space of that listening, you align yourself in order to understand the spirit of the thing. It's that sense of "Ah yes, this is what this person is about," or "This is what this book is about." It's a feeling that becomes a knowing. Then you can ask, *How do I want to respond? What would be the most appropriate response to what I am sensing, based on my current capacity to go there?*

Mutable Water is a part of you that can completely identity with and even become that which is in front of you. It's the part of you people seek out when they want you to see their suffering, relate to the sweetly human strivings behind their behavior, or ask for your forgiveness. It's a part of you that can feel and then envision how to help a person, community, or cause.

The Pisces in you can become the frequency of personality required of nearly any job, task, or skill. You can become the you who is a kindergarten teacher. You can morph into the you who is a human rights activist. You can shape-shift into being the you who is married to this person right in front of you.

Pisces is extremely magical this way. This is also a wildly confusing and draining ability if you haven't been encouraged to say No to what's not really meant for you. Pisces so deeply feels the sadness in others that you might become someone you are not in order to make someone else happy. Pisces is so skilled at meeting the needs of others that becoming what other people want can be how the Pisces in you secures love and validation.

SYMBOL

The Fish

The constellation Pisces shows two lines emerging from a single point, like a V, with two oval formations seemingly leaping from both ends. The ancient Babylonians saw it as a pair of Fish joined by a cord. The name *Pisces* is a Latin plural form of "fish."

I see the two Fish of Pisces like salmon moving in different directions of the river. There is the pull toward the delta, toward the vastness of the ocean—which is to say, the pull toward losing oneself in the oneness of all things. And then there is the drive to return upriver to spawn new life, to regenerate, to carry on. In a similar way, Pisces is both fascinated by and longing for thirteen—the number of mystery—and also called to return back to one—the number for the sign that follows Pisces and begins the cycle anew: Aries.

In this way, Pisces is the part of you deeply connected to collective feeling, the communal unconscious, to mysticism, to the mysteries of multidimensional knowing. But in order to carry on, you must know the dream you're living for. And it's the force of your love for the dream that carries you upstream. If you haven't figured out the dream you're living for, then you might let yourself get pulled out to sea.

Pisces is unbounded imagination, playful flexibility, shifting and regenerating again and again between endings and beginnings. It is the desire to connect into the infinite to find a dream, and then the will to see that dream unfold in reality. Pisces is a deep well of empathy and the ability to channel feeling into song, poetry, dance, music, healing, and other forms of intuitive communication in service to the world.

Pisces is the youngest part of you and the oldest part of you. Pisces is the you that will always be a magical fairy child, elegant and alien to this world. At the same time, Pisces is the part of you that has always been the wisest old wizard at the wizard counsel. The eyes of the Pisces are lit by trust that others might call "naive," but they are also deep like ancient wells.

The greatest challenge to Pisces is the vast world of options that the ocean presents the Fish. You could go this way, or that way, or yet another way again. To choose can feel like death to Pisces because it means eliminating all other available options. This is the paradox for the Fish: craving the oneness of the Water medium that connects all life, and yet having to choose a particular, specific channel to move through that Water.

The joy of the vastness the Fish feels is the gift of Pisces. To the Pisces in you, all possibilities exist for whatever you have the audacity to dream. We are drawn to the Pisces in others because we sense the possibilities they have access to.

Even more, the wells of compassion we feel from Pisces create the most radical possibility of all: that we can forgive ourselves and others for the harm that we have consciously and unconsciously caused and known in this lifetime. You are that person, too, because you are also Pisces. It comes down to trust. The Pisces in us trusts that there are no limits.

POLARITY
The Pisces-Virgo Axis

All Water signs are opposite Earth signs, and all polar signs have the same modality. So mutable Water is opposite mutable Earth: Virgo.

Water is essentially formless; it knows no shape on its own. It takes the form of whatever container it has. Without form, Water spreads out until there's nowhere else for it to go. Virgo offers an earthen vessel for Pisces.

- Pisces is as vast as the ocean and sky; Virgo is right here and nowhere else.
- Pisces is free-flowing; Virgo is precise and specific.
- Pisces becomes one with the frequencies of sound bowls; Virgo becomes one with the whetstone that strikes the bowl.

Pisces and Virgo are a polarity that is service-oriented. The evidence of Virgo service is—naturally, as an Earth sign—visible and tangible. The evidence of Pisces service is more felt and intuited, often unappreciated until it's gone, when the Fish swims away to another channel.

Virgo helps Pisces focus. Virgo teaches Pisces that details really do matter. Tinkering until the work is just right is as much an act of spiritual devotion as channeling the abstract concept from the ether. Preparing for whatever could come up or "go wrong" is as much an act of love as trusting that things will work out no matter what happens.

The Pisces perspective is oceanic, and as such you can feel everything everywhere all at once. Whenever Pisces feels overwhelmed, like you're drowning, you can call upon Virgo to order your system for doing things. "One thing at a time," says Virgo. Break it into steps in a process, and then show up to the process. Eliminate what's unnecessary. Skim off the fat. Simplify. And in this way, the Pisces in you can ground into your love for the work at hand.

As a polarity, Pisces-Virgo teaches that you cannot hold the infinite in your hands without limiting it somehow. Limiting factors—such as boundaries, preferences, and standards—support your capacity to be creative. Virgo knows that all form has to have contour. We can shape these limits to line up with our values. We can also love and lean into the ones we call our limitations. If you could sing every note, then how would you know how to write a song that feels just right for your voice? How can you serve the world with your point of view unless you're willing to notice that life has given you the contours of some experiences and not others?

The Virgoan contours of your gifts create channels for your Piscean power to come through. Pisces-Virgo wants you to call your power back from whoever told you your limitations are problems. The ways in which you are specifically you—including so-called flaws—are deeply connected to your assignment for being here on this planet.

What if your grief is your gift? What if your disability is your gift? What if your sacred rage is your gift? How can you know unless you see these as the very contours of your power rather than barriers that obstruct your power?

RULING PLANETS

Jupiter and Neptune

Jupiter, representing your capacity for learning, grow-ing, expanding, and connecting, rules both Pisces and Sagittarius. In its Piscean guise, Jupiter is the part of you that wants to reach out and merge with, consume, and fuse with all things.

Like water spilling out across a surface, shifting and noodling into and under every crevice and around every corner, Jupiter gives Pisces your will to expand toward and attune to the whole of life, even the unseen, mysterious, and magical.

Jupiter is an inherently curious, optimistic, and enthusiastic teacher that bestows on Pisces its dreaming, hoping, and trusting nature. Jupiter has instructed the Pisces in you to believe in love and oneness with all things. Jupiter urges Pisces to see the beautiful in everyone and everything, which gives the Pisces in you a deep well of compassion.

Through Sagittarius, Jupiter seeks conviction in a belief system or philosophy. Through Pisces, Jupiter no longer cares about which religious doctrine or philosophical discipline is right or best. It only sees one Spirit, one Love, one web of all things. Through Water, Jupiter merges all into feeling.

Many modern astrologers recognize Neptune as Pisces's ruler. I use both in my practice. Neptune represents our capacity to dream, to connect to the collective unconscious, to "lift off" from the earthly plane into what feels like a higher vibration. Neptune—as Lord of the Seas—lives the world through water: intuition, dreaminess, illusion, delusion, fantasy, possibility, intuitive connectivity, and alternate states of being.

Neptune can bring you to the heights of multidimensional consciousness. This is heady stuff! Through these higher realms, Neptune helps you transcend your past pain, find grace, cultivate forgiveness, and reach for the most glorious dreams of your imagination. But because we're talking about such a high, transpersonal vibration, the Neptune in you can struggle to stay grounded, deny reality, mire you in a dense fog of confusion, or push toward escapism.

Jupiter and Neptune are here to teach you not to hold back your gifts to make other people comfortable. Your privilege, your abundance, your overflow—these are yours to share! Do not hide or hoard your gifts because the world has taught you that you're too much. Jupiter and Neptune counsel that scarcity is an illusion that separates us. Surrender to trust. You don't have to withhold.

I really want you to hear me: you are a love fountain of great and sublime power, and you're meant to spill it out all around you. Your gifts cannot help but move through you. They simply cannot help it.

SKILLFUL PISCES

Dream

Pisces wants you to know: the most loving thing you can do is to be misunderstood, projected upon, and resented for living a life you're channeling from your dream field. In other words, it's okay to have a dream and fiercely live it, no matter what other people have to say about what is or isn't possible.

In order to access your dreams, you grow skill in attuning to your intuition, guidance, and knowing, and you learn to quiet the noise of overculture or folks who may love you but whose imagination is limited by scarcity.

Pisces wants you to swim in your own waters. Think of how it feels to be underwater, whether in the ocean, a pool, or even a bathtub. Submerged, you can't speak. You can't hear very well. Vision is distorted. Movement is slowed, meeting resistance. Here you float and just exist, appreciating your altered sense of perception as well as the solitude required to appreciate it.

To swim in your very own waters means to truly slow down, to talk less, to say no, to tune people out a little bit. To resist the cultural denigration of naps and daydreaming. Time that is categorized as unproductive by our capitalist society can in fact be exactly what you most need to return to your creative source.

The most "productive" thing you can do for your Pisces might be to consciously, purposefully zone out for a few hours. By this I mean playing and singing to old music you used to love to release the repressed nostalgia. I mean dream journaling to see what bubbles up in your subconscious. I mean staring at your reflection in the bath water until you hear your wise voice speak to you.

Let your mermaid tail lead. You know the way to your dreamworld. All possibilities exist for the Piscean once the dream has been identified and willed into reality! The surest way to access the heart of the dream is to tune out all the noise so you can hear it speak to you.

Sometimes, in these oceanic spaces, you recognize the past you've repressed or a truth you are ready to see. These potentially scary or painful realizations are often why we avoid alone time in the first place. Remember that Water represents the unconscious parts of us that bubble up in sleep, therapy, or meditation. When you zone out in the Piscean realm, you turn off the analytical brain that insists on being logical, linear, and practical all the time. But this is an absolutely *essential* part of living through this season.

Actively allowing yourself to sort through old memories so you can feel any unresolved feelings and then release them is part of the closure of Pisces, given that it's the last sign before the cycle begins again with Aries.

The end is the beginning, so Pisces teaches us, making this a time of year for culminations, letting go, and little deaths. And this is not a bad thing. Why? Because in the letting go, you permit the start of a new cycle, a fresh and exciting new beginning.

But before you can get there, take your time to soak in Pisces. Pisces understands that endings are part of life; it is the part of you that doesn't attach too dearly to outcomes because the ultimate outcome is death. The skillful Pisces in you is able to grieve endings and then bounce back because you took the time to integrate the lessons of the past before moving on.

PRACTICE

The Freedom to Be You

What the Pisces in you most wants is to be free to move like a dolphin: to elegantly glide, to exuberantly jump, and to gracefully change lanes as you feel called. This may sound lovely, but it's not easy when your Pisces feels what other people want from you, think of you, or dream for you in your own body.

Ideally, you can surround yourself with people who fully and joyously celebrate all the facets of you and let you be complex and complicated and changeable and true to your spirit. But alas, we can't rely on other people. I've found, as a very Pisces person, that it's got to be me who models who I am to other people and it's got to be me who knows who I am more than anyone else.

This practice is a daily meditation where you direct this desire for freedom to a different set of individuals each week of the four weeks of Pisces season:

- Week 1: to your loved ones (including animals and plants if you wish)
- Week 2: to beings you don't know
- Week 3: to those who bother you or have hurt you
- Week 4: to yourself, including your younger selves and older selves

It's a very Piscean thing to see all people, even your enemies, as worthy of love and the highest levels of compassion. Let's wish for all beings to receive the same unbounded freedom as we'd want for those we most love and adore. Feel free to change around the week order or change up the categories to your taste.

1. Follow the grounding steps on page 57.

2. See the person or being you are directing your attention to that day. Imagine them about five to ten feet away from you.

3. Fill yourself with the highest levels of love, compassion, and trust; maybe feel the energy of a dolphin soaring above the surface of the ocean in your heart.

4. Say to the person or being: *I fully accept you as you are. You don't have to shape-shift to please me. I honor your Yes and your No, even if I am disappointed. I respect your alone time and your solitude. I cherish your capacity to dream. I won't tell you it's all a waste of time. I will honor your boundaries. I will not ask you to lose yourself by taking care of me. I will allow you to be as big and bright and beautiful as a shining star. I accept that you are adaptable. I will let you change. I will not hold you to the same way of doing things. I know you will find your way. I wish you beauty. I wish you grace. I wish you ease. Thank you for letting me witness you.*

5. Notice any feelings or thoughts that come up for you. Say hello to them. Let them be there.

6. Ask your intuition if there's anything else for you to know or hear right now.

7. Close the meditation and thank yourself for showing up.

. . . .

TAROT CARD
The Moon

The card in the tarot that we associate with Pisces is card eighteen, the Moon.

This analogy underlines the deeply intuitive and mysterious qualities of Piscean energy.

In the *Smith-Rider-Waite* deck, artist Pamela "Pixie" Colman Smith depicts a large Moon that appears as both full and crescent at once, underlining the Moon's shifting nature. This card is first and foremost an invitation to own and love the parts of yourself that shift, roll, foam, swirl, burst, and crash like the waves and tides of the ocean that the Moon controls.

Pisces is the shape-shifter. Pisces must be free to try on guises, roles, ways of moving and speaking. Like a chameleon, Pisces wants to see what it would be like to merge into different skins.

At the bottom of the Moon card, we see a crustacean coming up out of the waters of the shoreline. Water is symbolic for our intuition, inner world, dreams, and feelings. The crustacean scuttering up the shore represents our dreams, aha moments, memories, intuitive feelings, spiritual guidance, and deepest knowings that can suddenly rise up and out of our unconscious realms. Moon time is akin then to the darkness of the inner life. It's hidden and mostly nonvisual and nonrational. This is why we associate dance, music, painting, dreams, and oracular visions with Pisces.

In the card, we also see a dog and a wolf howling to the Moon above. This pairing represents the duality between our domesticated personality and our primal nature. We are all deeply conditioned, programmed, and thus domesticated by our families, the institutions that educated us, the communities to which we assign our belongings, the rhetoric of the country we give our allegiance, and the all-pervasive media. The Moon card challenges you gently and lovingly to study your conditioning in the privacy of the dark. To help you, the card invites you to let your inner wolf guide you.

Pisces wants this too. Pisces is a mermaid diving! Pisces is a siren calling! Pisces is a jellyfish dancing! The reason Pisces can feel so much melancholy, the reason Pisces often wants to escape, is because, well, it's sad to be caged and domesticated. It sucks to be asked to forgo your primal nature. It's a bummer when people refuse to see the magic that is everywhere. It's disheartening to be asked to standardize.

But ultimately, the journey in the dark is truly, ultimately, *solo work*. The Moon card also depicts two towers in the distance, inviting the viewer to move toward and through these pillars, suggesting a passage, a journey, a process. Being "in the Moon"—which is to say, living your Pisces—is a passage to the self.

A Tarot Spread with the Moon

See the chapter *How to Navigate This Book* if you're new to the tarot and seek support for pulling cards and interpreting them.

Take the Moon out of your deck. (If you have more than one deck, you can pull the card from another deck so that the Moon has a chance to "participate" in the deck from which you will draw.)

Feel into the visual inspiration of the card.

Take a few deep breaths on purpose and arrive to the reading. Connect into your intuition. Ask Moon-Pisces energy to help you with this reading. Shuffle according to your unique, never-wrong style. Center and focus your question thus:

With the most expansive levels of compassion for me and all sentient beings, what is the loving invitation to connect with the Moon?

Pull seven cards according to your own unique process of knowing with the following prompts, and then sit with the cards and journal about them.

2
-
THE PATH
FORWARD
-
Guidance on
my journey

1
-
THE
MOON
-
A beacon in
the dark

3
-
THE
PILLARS
-
How to trust
the portal

5
-
THE WOLF
-
Message from
my wild self

4
-
THE DOG
-
Message
from my
domesticated
self

6
-
THE
CRUSTA-
CEAN
-
Message
from the deep

7
-
THE
WATER
-
My access
to mystery

RITUAL FOR THE NEW MOON

Nightswimming

In the Skillful Pisces section, I discuss the idea of "swimming in your own waters." In honor of the perfectly Piscean R.E.M. song "Nightswimming," I offer this suggested New Moon in Pisces ritual. You will be invited to let an image appear—to swim forth—as a tool to support you this lunar cycle.

Photography is inherently Piscean. I think of Roland Barthes's book *Camera Lucida*, where he explores how in every photograph we behold, we're looking at death, because the instant of the photo is dead and gone. Photographs carry a built-in melancholy whose beauty the Pisces appreciates. Photos are also screens for projection: we create stories of success and failure about our lives based on the evidence of the photograph. Photos are not reality: they are phantoms, illusions, and fantasies of experience. They are a dream of what once was.

The darkroom is a Piscean space. In the low light, hard edges soften and the rest of the world feels far away. You can lose track of time without signals from outdoor light or the movement of people doing things. In the fluids of photo trays, images emerge as if by magic. If you're unfamiliar with photography darkroom processes, you might enjoy looking this up before the ritual.

This ritual is designed to help you recover a memory, or a dream, or a fragment of a possibility from your past, present, or future. Let whatever emerges be supportive—not because it's "real" so much as because it's what wanted to be seen by you today.

Before beginning this ritual, gather:

- Candles, as many as you want, and a way to light them
- A few items that connect you to Pisces (see page 293)
- Your journal and a pen, or paper and watercolors
- "Nightswimming" by R.E.M.
- Tarot deck (optional)

The Ritual

1. Sit at your Pisces altar when ready. Set up your ritual container, light your candle(s), and come to a grounded, meditative state (see page 57).

2. When you're ready, state your intention to work the Pisces within. *I want to go nightswimming. I want to see in the dark. I want to know what I need to see.* Play "Nightswimming" wherever you stream music and just sit and listen. If insights come to you as you listen, write these down so you don't forget.

3. Now imagine you are in a photography darkroom. In your hands you hold a piece of white photo paper. Set your desire to see a picture you are ready to see. Ask to see something that will be a comfort to you at this time in your life, for whatever reason.

4. Allow yourself to see this paper swirling around in the photo fluids. With every cell of your body, ask to see what you need to see right now. Perhaps an image from the past, maybe from the present, possibly in your imagination. Maybe what you need to see is your dream, your purpose, your heart's desire. Let it appear. Whatever was the first image you saw is perfect. Maybe you see different images and not just one. This is all wonderful.

5. Now ask yourself, *What do I need to know about this picture? In my heart, what is the photo about? How does it make me feel? Is there healing here?* Ask more questions of yourself. Get curious about whatever you saw. Finish by asking, *What else do I need to know?* You may not hear language. You may just have feeling sensations in your body. This is normal.

6. Write down everything that came forward for you, including more thoughts, feelings, knowings, sensations, and questions. Draw if you'd rather capture the image with art.

7. If you work with the tarot, draw a few cards to help you understand what the image wanted to tell you. You can ask:
   - *What is the invitation of this image?*
   - *How will this invitation help me?*
   - *What else do I need to know?*

8. Journal more or meditate more until you feel completion.

9. At this point, feel into and call up in your body the will and desire to name an intention for the lunar cycle, maybe to keep listening to whatever visions and dreams want to talk to you right now.

10. Thank whatever forces have guided you with this ritual. Feel grateful for your willingness to explore the possibility that this might feel helpful to you. Feel proud of your bravery to venture into your own "quiet night."

11. Conclude and open the ritual container (see page 66).

Happy New Moon in Pisces!

Epilogue

If you resonated with the approach to astrology in this book, then I want you to know that this is only the beginning. This book is an invitation to participate with the Cosmic Body in the daily process of living as a human being right now. The way you want to love and live astrology can be very much like the way you love and live as a human. I invite you to listen to your own wild template and weave astrology into all the other things that make your life meaningful, beautiful, and satisfying.

In this way, the end of this book is the beginning of a new way of life. Closure is a part of any cycle. In closure, we hold both grief and wonder. I invite you to listen to both and let them guide you to the next appropriate pathway. You are not a beginner at living astrology anymore. What now?

Before I share some suggestions, I'd love to help you close out this phase with some guiding questions. May you be a compassionate witness to yourself as you investigate, continuing the practice of noticing what comes up with the question as more important than any answer. I recommend recording voice notes to yourself as you contemplate each, taking your time to receive answers, and letting your insights be nonlinear and weird. Ask yourself:

What have I been learning about how astrology
- *can help me experience new ways of being in my body and in relationships?*
- *wants me to transform old patterns into unforeseen pathways that feel more creative, empowering, and fun?*
- *enlivens my life with stories that feel more expansive, open, generous, and buoyant?*
- *supports me in growing self-trust and the role it plays in accessing my intuition?*
- *encourages me to stop speaking unkindly about myself?*
- *is a guide to living in wonder, trusting that it's inevitable?*
- *wants me to rewire my relationship to time?*
- *isn't something that happens to me but rather something that I live?*

You understand what this approach feels like in your body now. You are ready to explore bigger questions, such as those that have emerged for me since living this approach:

- *What if astrology is an outreach program from the cosmos to help us cute, sweet humans navigate being and belonging here?*
- *What if we've been given this language as an offering to help us witness ourselves and one another?*
- *What if, in witnessing ourselves and one another through astrology, some unforeseen beauty emerges within and through us that heals and transforms our experience, and, by extension, our worlds?*

In my experience as an astrology teacher, I am privileged to witness firsthand, again and again, how astrology heals and transforms us by serving as the language we use to witness one another. It's not the language itself that does it. It's the way the language holds us in the process of witnessing one another share our truths.

There is a deep grief in this world, and it is the grief of holding back the unique frequency of our truth. It is the grief of silencing. The grief of masking. The grief of having to caretake or manage other people's experience of us. Astrology creates the space for us to trust that it's possible to be seen in our vulnerability.

The root of the word *vulnerable* is the Latin *vulnus*, meaning "wound"; therefore, *vulnerability* refers to our capacity to be wounded. Being vulnerable is brave af because it means letting other people see both our wounds and our capacity to be wounded. When you speak the truth of the part of you that is each sign, that's fucking vulnerable! Your Aries path— the path of your rage, reactivity, and confidence. Your Capricorn path—the path of your inner critic, your brittleness, and commitment. Your Pisces path—the path of your naivete, melancholy, and the wealth of your dream field. And it is the same for all the signs. Speaking astrology means speaking vulnerably.

When I started teaching astrology, I set out to share how this language helps me hold myself more compassionately in my vulnerability, and I wondered if it might be supportive to others. I discovered that as my students shared their stories in community, as they opened up to the parts of themselves that are each sign, something marvelous happened: in witnessing one another in their truth, they fell in love with one another, which in turn cracked them more open to loving themselves. This aspect of astrology came as a surprise. I knew it could help us heal as individuals, but I didn't realize how potent it could be in community.

If this book has helped you to love yourself more through the practice of living astrology, then I encourage you to seek communities where astrology is presented not as a system of techniques as much as a medium for vulnerability speech. Whether it's one of my own spaces or another teacher's, I have found that community is essential to this path.

> I didn't realize how potent it could be in community.

If this book has catalyzed in you a deep desire to get into reading charts, how exciting! In my series of self-published workbooks known as *Living the Signs*, I help you anchor the approach you've been learning here into chart interpretation, sign by sign. As in this book, *Living the Signs* invites you to deeply connect to every sign, not just the ones where you have your Sun, Moon, or Rising. I also teach chart-reading courses that open periodically throughout the year.

In addition to my own offerings, I list astrologers whose teachings I admire in the Resources section that follows. I encourage you to spend time following a potential teacher in order to be clear that you are in alignment with their voice, presuppositions, and integrity. Remember: If it's not resonant, it's not fucking resonant!

Maybe you're realizing that you don't have to learn chart-reading techniques in order to have an embodied fluency with the language for your creative, mystical, intuitive life. Yes, that's true! I encourage you to see all of the technical parts of astrology as zones for philosophical or metaphysical contemplation rather than mechanical processes that you get right or wrong. Run the teachings through a strainer and take what feels powerful for you.

Wherever you go next, thank you for trusting me as your guide to living astrology. We can stay connected through my newsletter at www.brittenlarue.com, on Instagram @brittenlarue, and through my podcast *Moon to Moon*.

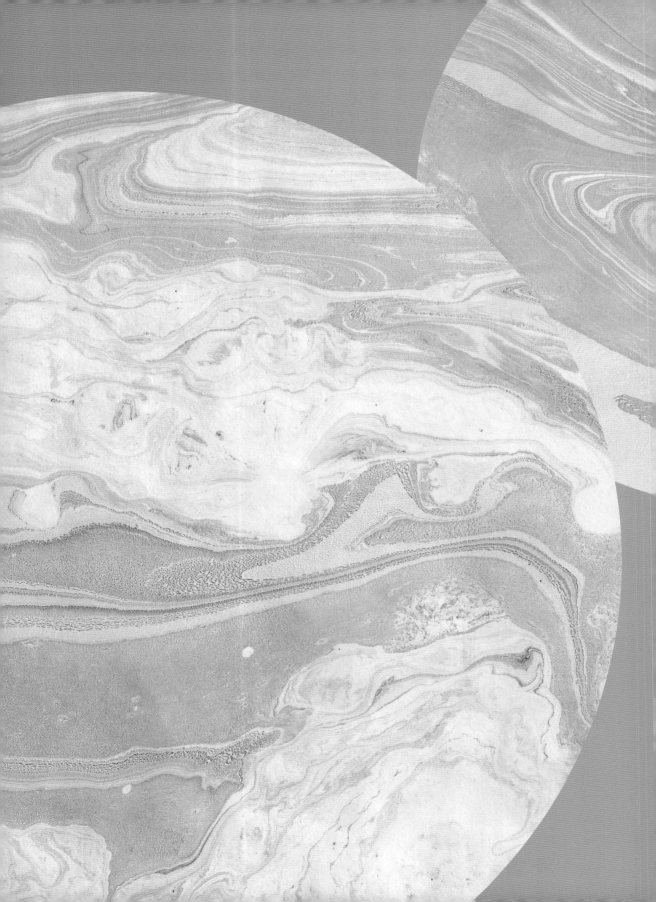

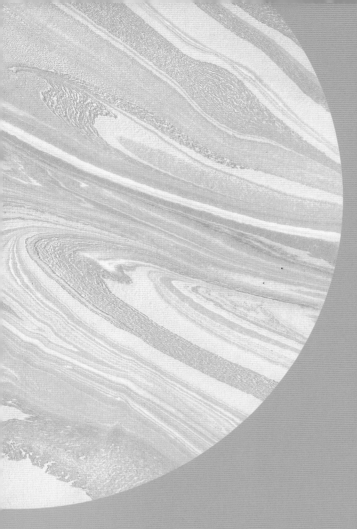

Acknowledgments

I would like to begin by acknowledging the relationality of all that I share in this book. I am wordlessly grateful in the face of the mysteries that brought me to the *Living Astrology* project. I am honored by and am humbled before all the beings, forces, and experiences that created this timeline. I thank the planets, spirit guides, and cosmic family that walked with me all these years, even and especially in the moments before I knew they'd been there all along.

First, thank you to my editor, Juree Sondker, for reaching out to me and Angela to work together after she found our *Living the Signs* workbook series. Thank you for seeing the possibility of this collaboration and trusting in us to make it happen. I am in awe of your skill for sniffing out talent. And thank you to my developmental editor, Audra Figgins, for supporting the spirit of the work with such a knack for structure and clarity. You're incredible at your work. Thank you to everyone at Gibbs Smith for investing in a publication about the transformative capacity of astrology!

Thank you to my collaborator and dear friend, Angela George, who has been aestheticizing my content since 2019 with her Venusian genius. You have been my cheerleader since the beginning and your designs helped scaffold a world for people to find my work. You are a treasure, and you create treasures.

Thank you to Dr. Janis Bergman-Carton, Dr. Adam Herring, Dr. Randall Griffin, and Dr. Charissa Terranova, the core scholars and mentors who shaped my personal voice in academia. I am forever grateful for our years together, where I fell in love with the magic of critical theory.

This book grows from the catalyzing written and recorded teachings of astrologers such as Caroline W. Casey, Demetra George, Chani Nicholas, Jeff Hinshaw, and Renee Sills. Special acknowledgment goes to my mentor, Adam Sommer, with whom I apprenticed for a year.

The intuitive, energetic, and somatic lenses of my approach to astrology evolved from coursework with Deborah Kremins, Achintya Devi, Luis Mojica, and my dear friend, Natasha Levinger.

I am also so grateful for the paid and free guidance of witches, healers, teachers, and tarot mavens such as Leah Garza, Amanda Yates Garcia, Sarah Faith Gottesdiener, Lindsay Mack, Lara Veleda Vesta, Angela Mary Magick, Layla Saad, Simone Seol, and Danica Boyce.

Heartfelt love to everyone I've met through Instagram, the first home for my astrological voice. It was through Instagram that I experimented with finding a community for the approach to astrology wanting to move through me, and I am in awe of the magical logic of the algorithms that bring us together.

Sending so much gratitude to my clients—past, present, and future. I am constantly delighted by the courage and bright spirit of the beings who arrive in my space. I am deeply privileged to hold space for you.

My students are also my teachers. I am blessed af to constellate the most wondrously curious, heart-led, clever, generous, and brave individuals to my circles. Thank you to every single one of you who has passed through my school portal, especially those who said yes to my old astrology class Charting Your Course and those in my current container Astrology as Praxis. Thank you to those who have walked with me through many years of growth and vulture magic in my work: Mariola Rosario, Rebecca Padgett, Jaclyn Skeans, Nicole France-Coe, Mary Schuch, Erin Kelley, Bridget Scanlon, Megan Frye, John Beynon, Kelsey Brooks, Amy Lauricello, and Mallory Dowd. Your voices are woven into this book.

I wrote *Living Astrology* while deep in a shared collaborative field with Jonathan Koe. Jonathan started as my client and student, then became an assistant, and is now my teaching partner. We're ancient friends who happen to have the same birthday—March 4! Jonathan is quite simply my favorite person to talk astrology with. Who knows how many hours we spend sharing ideas, insights, fears, questions, and revelations?! Thank you, Jonathan, for finding me so I could know this kind of friendship. Thank you for sharing your light so generously with me. There is no one else I'd rather whale myself with.

Thank you to my ecosystem of friends and family, past and present. It's important to name the foundational impact of knowing the expansive gifts of love and then the sudden deaths of my dad, my cousin Shannon, and my Gramma and Grampa. My work grows from the wells of grief and wonder that I've known from the lives of these four individuals.

Thank you to my big Sag brother, Bailey, and his family for the brightness and sincerity of your loving. Thank you to my super Aquarian brother, Rhett, for being the one who always knows what I'll love next, and for giving me my birth chart. And to my Cancer mom, who loves me with such ferocious commitment.

The first reader of this book was my twin flame, Matt Bull. Matt, my magus. The universe's most extravagant gift to me. Every page of this book shimmers with a memory of us talking through it. This book poured out from the libation of your attunement to my genius. It all had to go somewhere, my love.

And finally, to my daughters, Sylvia and Arden, the stars who chose my belly. The honor of all my honors. You have been so supportive, so patient, and so trusting of all that led to the unfolding of this book. I know to my bones how proud you are of me. It is done. It is done. It is done. Let's go to Disney World.

(Re)sources
Are Sacred

Everything listed here was supportive to me in the beginning stages of learning about various topics. My top choices in each category are boldfaced to help you get started, but feel free to follow the information wherever it leads you and make your own catalog of resources.

On Astrology

I recommend using an astrology app to determine the exact day the signs progress forward. I personally use TimePassages to track daily astrology.

BOOKS

Caroline W. Casey, *Visionary Activist Astrology*
Swami Kriyananda, *Your Sun Sign as a Spiritual Guide*
Demetra George and Douglas Bloch, *Astrology for Yourself*
Steven Forrest, *The Inner Sky*
Alice Sparkly Kat, *Postcolonial Astrology*

PODCASTS

Astrology of the Week Ahead with Chani Nicholas
Cosmic Cousins
Cosmic Guidance for All
Embodied Astrology
Ghost of a Podcast
Healing the Spirit
The Magic of the Spheres

INSTAGRAM CREATORS

@dark_moon_astrology
@nate_qi
@ddamascenaa
@alicesparklykat
@sabrinamonarch
@thestrology
@kelseyrosetort
@etshipley
@thedreammami
@suprasensoryshahir
@heidiroserobbins

Thinkers, Writers, and Teachers

ON MAGIC, REWILDING, WITCHCRAFT, AND THE TAROT

Danica Boyce
T. Susan Chang
Carolyn Elliott
Dr. Clarissa Pinkola Estés
Amanda Yates Garcia
Sarah Faith Gottesdiener
Mary K. Greer
Jessie Susannah Karnatz
Nicholas Kepley
Lindsay Mack
Maria Minnis
Rachel Pollack
Lane Smith
Rashunda Tramble
Benebell Wen

ON SOMATIC HEALING, TRAUMA, AND DECOLONIAL HEALING

Karine Bell

adrienne maree brown

Leah Garza

Robin Wall Kimmerer

Dr. Bessel van der Kolk

Ixchel Lunar

Resmaa Menakem

Dr. Rosales Meza

Jo Miller

Luis Mojica

Dr. Jennifer Mullan

Carmen Spagnola

Sophie Strand

ON ENERGY SOVEREIGNTY, PSYCHIC ABILITIES, AND INTUITION

Achintya Devi

Maryam Hasnaa

Deborah Kremins

Natasha Levinger

Rebecca Padgett

In addition to the resources above, I offer self-published workbooks for deeper learning with me. You can purchase these at my website or in boutiques across the United States and Australia:

Moon to Moon: A Journal for Working with the Lunar Cycle

Seeding the Year: Setting Intentions with the Symbolic Language of Astrology

Living the Signs: Aries

Living the Signs: Taurus

Living the Signs: Gemini

Living the Signs: Cancer

Living the Signs: Leo

Living the Signs: Virgo

Living the Signs: Libra

Living the Signs: Scorpio

Living the Signs: Sagittarius

Living the Signs: Capricorn

Living the Signs: Aquarius

Living the Signs: Pisces

Index

About the Author

Britten LaRue, MA, is a public astrologer, author, teacher, and intuitive guide. A self-described "recovering academic," she left behind a twenty-year career in art history to reinvent herself at mid-life. Britten is known and loved by her community for modeling what it looks like to live from one's dream field. Creator of Emergence Astrology, Britten's deepest calling is to be a midwife for those in the process of birthing their own inner knowing, healing from shame, and learning to trust themselves again with the reckless freedom they deserve. She's a Pisces Sun, Capricorn Moon, and Aries Rising. You can find Britten online at www.brittenlarue.com.